D0462497

SIGNS OF LIFE

By Mark Mosier,
Mobile Intensive Care Paramedic

Copyright © 2014 Mark Mosier MICP.

All rights reserved. No part of this book may be reproduced, stored, or transmitted by any means—whether auditory, graphic, mechanical, or electronic—without written permission of both publisher and author, except in the case of brief excerpts used in critical articles and reviews. Unauthorized reproduction of any part of this work is illegal and is punishable by law.

ISBN: 978-1-4834-1299-3 (sc)
ISBN: 978-1-4834-1300-6 (e)

Because of the dynamic nature of the Internet, any web addresses or links contained in this book may have changed since publication and may no longer be valid. The views expressed in this work are solely those of the author and do not necessarily reflect the views of the publisher, and the publisher hereby disclaims any responsibility for them.

Any people depicted in stock imagery provided by Thinkstock are models, and such images are being used for illustrative purposes only. Certain stock imagery © Thinkstock.

Lulu Publishing Services rev. date: 09/25/2014

SIGNS OF LIFE

PREFACE

There's an army of dedicated men and women on the front lines of our streets. They proudly belong to the EMS or Emergency Medical Services system. This is the system that provides an incredibly capable and competent response during a person's worst nightmare, an injury, an illness or just a helping hand in time of need. They face daily challenges and are often the difference between life and death, making order out of chaos.

It's difficult to put a price on bringing a child back from near death, stabilizing Grandpa after a massive heart attack, patching a victim from a bar fight only to have him, or her, try to beat the crap out of you in the back of the ambulance or, in the ultimate act of compassion, providing comfort to someone as they take their final breath.

Emergency medicine in the pre-hospital arena has evolved to a very high level over the last 30 years. Dramatic lifesaving scenes play out every single day throughout the country. You really are in very good hands when you find yourself in the back of an ambulance. You're in our office. This is where we work our best, flying around the back of the ambulance like gymnasts, starting IV's and performing procedures while moving in and out of traffic, not only with skill, but with the latest and greatest equipment, all for you.

No two calls are ever exactly the same: the sights, the sounds, the smells, the emotions, the outcomes. One thing is constant and that is the desire to try to achieve the best outcome for every patient. The profession will change you as a person. You will see parts of yourself that very few people get to experience: your strengths, your weaknesses, both physically and emotionally.

These journeys and experiences will challenge the most seasoned veterans. No matter how long you work the streets, you never know what that next call will bring. Why does one person live? Why does the other die? Is it fate, coincidence, bad luck or, "just their time?"

Every call is a chance to make a difference in someone's life.

Why would someone choose this profession? Sometimes the career chooses them. There were two guys on TV back in the '70s that kept us on the edge of our couches witnessing everything from seemingly impossible rescues to the kid with his head stuck in a fence. John Gage and Roy DeSoto, from the very successful weekly television show *Emergency,* were America's first heroes in EMS and in many ways helped to shape the industry to where it is today. I always wondered how they got all of those calls.

Settle in and get ready to ride along with the crew and be part of their experiences. These stories and characters are based on actual events and real people. For those that do this every day, you'll feel right at home and appreciate the challenges they're dealt. For those that have never experienced any part of EMS yet have that deep curiosity, it'll be hard not to develop a compassion for what we face and somehow make it work.

CHAPTER 1

GETTING STARTED

I can remember being fascinated with ambulances from an early age. I'd see them responding through the city, lights flashing and sirens blaring, all hours of the day and night. It was hard not to stare with curiosity and awe as they went speeding by.

What happened? Did someone die? Are they hurt badly? I had an inherently strong desire to be part of this mysterious and exciting system and one providing this response.

While growing up, I was the one that seemed to have the cool head during the emergency. When the neighbor kid fell off his bike splitting his head open with blood gushing down his face, it seemed natural to take control of the scene, apply direct pressure to the wound and then keep him calm while everyone else panicked. I was amazed how at ease I felt being in that role.

I tried several different jobs after high school and never seemed to find that "right one". It may have been fate that guided me to working for a large construction outfit and after a sequence of small accidents and mishaps, the company brought in a first aid/CPR instructor. The class felt natural and ignited me with an even stronger desire to learn.

At the end of the class, the instructor commented, "You seem to have quite the passion for this stuff."

"That's an understatement," I replied.

He then put my future in motion with a simple and innocent suggestion, "They always need people like you at Station 4. You could become a volunteer and further your emergency training and see if it's something you'd like to do as a career."

At 21 years of age, single and with no committed direction, my life was about to change. I was about to begin a spectacular journey. One that, in my wildest dreams, I never would have imagined.

I took him up on his advice and went to Station 4. It's a busy county run department with EMS and Fire response. It's staffed by both volunteer and paid crews. I would learn volunteer members are the unselfish backbone of EMS and Fire services across the country.

From the moment I walked through the front door, the allure was overwhelming and almost mesmerizing. I could see the shiny emergency vehicles parked in a large garage area next to the lobby, the ambulance, the fire engine. The ambulance looked so much bigger than it did flying by with illuminated lights and siren wailing.

I approached the lady behind the front counter. "Good morning, my name is Mark Mosier; I'm interested in becoming a volunteer and being part of your department."

She smiled back and said, "Very nice to meet you Mark, I'm Sandy Martin. We're always looking for good people that want to join our team. Welcome."

She turned and pressed two buttons on her phone and said, "Hi Joe, I have a gentleman here that would like to talk to you."

The name plate next to her phone is impressively engraved, *"Sandy Martin, Administrative Secretary."*

A moment later an office door down a small hall opens and out walks a man with a sharply pressed uniform and a stethoscope dangling from around his neck.

"This is Mark Mosier, he's interested in joining our team," Sandy said.

"Great," he said, "I'm Joey Capthorn, nice to meet you Mark; you can call me Joe."

We hit it off right away. I learned Joe has been a paramedic for seven years and is the Station 4 EMS training captain and in charge of EMS operations. This position not only ensures EMS operations run smoothly, but all personnel stay current with their on-going training.

Joe made a point of Sandy hearing his next statement, "If you need anything, Sandy is the go to person, she's the "glue" for this station."

Sandy grinned without looking up.

Next we began a tour of the station; first stop is the training room. There are rows of tables and it actually looks like a large classroom.

"This is where we conduct all of our training," Joe said.

"You'll get to know this room very well," he added.

The day room is a huge common area with several recliners arranged in a semi-circle and facing a large TV. There are two walls of shelves with EMS books and plaques across the wall with awards and recognition of various accomplishments of the members of Station 4.

Adjoining the day room is the kitchen. It's a spacious area with large counters. Down a short hall is the sleeping area with small individual rooms that become your "home away from home" while you are on duty.

Then the truck bays. This is where all the emergency vehicles or apparatus are parked. There are three large overhead bay doors. The ambulance is parked in front of the right door, the center bay is for the rescue unit which is currently out of the station and the fire engine is parked in front of the left bay door.

Joe took me over to the ambulance and introduced me to his partner, Brandon Dawson who's in the back of the ambulance cleaning and restocking the main kit.

"Brandon, this is Mark Mosier, he's thinking about working with us," Joe said.

"Excellent," Brandon said.

"I was exactly where you are about a year ago, it's a great path," he added.

"I really appreciate hearing that and good to meet you," I said.

Brandon looks to be mid 20's and is an Emergency Medical Technician or EMT. I learned he joined the department as a volunteer last year and recently finished his EMT training; he's now assigned to the medic unit or ambulance. Brandon's primary job is driving the ambulance and then fulfilling whatever role Joe assigns him on an emergency scene.

Joe then explained how Station 4 responds to 9-1-1 calls.

"When someone calls 9-1-1, the dispatcher enters the information into the computerized system. The closest station is dispatched. Here at Station 4 we will hear "tones" throughout the station to alert us we have a call. This will be followed by brief information about the nature of the emergency and the address. When our tones go off, the ambulance responds as the primary unit. The rescue squad is also dispatched to provide manpower and additional resources as needed. Our ambulance is called Medic 41 and the rescue squad is Rescue 41," he explained.

"Sometimes it takes more than Brandon and me to provide all the care that's needed," he said.

"So how do I fit in?" I asked.

"As a volunteer you can sign up for 12 or 24 hour shifts," he said.

"You can be a third person on the medic unit or the fourth person on the rescue unit," he added.

Suddenly the large middle bay door started rolling up and the rescue squad started backing in. It's a large heavy-duty crew cab truck with compartments along both sides. They had been to the hospital to retrieve medical equipment. Joe then introduced me to the rescue crew.

Steve Risley is the officer in charge on the rescue. He's an EMT and looks to be in his early 40's. I learned he's been with the department for eight years and was a military police officer prior to joining the department.

"So you want to hang out with us huh?" Steve said.

"Definitely, everything looks exactly like what I've been looking for," I said.

"Well, very good to meet you Mark, and let me know if I can help in any way," he said.

Eric Wright is also an EMT. He's the assigned driver on the rescue. He's in his early 20's and I learned he's been with the department for the past eight months as a volunteer. He's a part time college student and has "no idea" what he wants to do, so, until he figures it out he wants to continue college and working on the rescue.

"Nice to meet you Mark," Eric said.

"You too Eric, I'm pretty excited to be here," I said.

"This place has that effect," he said with a strong affirmative nod.

Samantha Grieves is the third member of the crew. She also looks to be in her early 20's and I learned she has been with the department as a volunteer for the past eighteen months and currently going through her EMT training. She wants to work for the department full time when an opening becomes available.

She walked up and said, "Hi there Mark, I'm Samantha, you can call me Sam."

"Hey, nice to meet you Sam," I said.

We then moved into the training room where I seemed to have question after question. Everyone is very personable with positive and extremely encouraging attitudes. It was an easy decision to move forward and after completing all the paperwork, I became an official rookie and newest member of Station 4.

"Joe then said, "Let's go over to the ambulance, there are some things we can go over and kind of get you started."

Brandon opened the back doors and I climbed in with Sam and Eric right behind me. There is so much equipment it is almost overwhelming. I couldn't help but notice how clean and organized everything was.

"This is our LifePak 12," Joe said as he pointed to an intimidating looking piece of equipment about the size of an overnight bag.

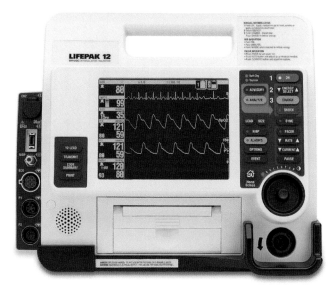

"We use this for any cardiac or heart related emergency. We can monitor someone's EKG or heart rhythm; shock them if they are in cardiac arrest. We can also run what's called a 12 Lead which shows the heart from different angles and we can see if they're having a heart attack in real time. It can also automatically measure blood pressures as well as measure oxygen levels in the blood," he explained.

"Wow, seems pretty complicated," I said.

Sam chuckled and said, "Roll up your sleeve; I need your arm, and a finger."

With the blood pressure cuff around my upper arm she pressed a button on the front of the monitor and it automatically pumped up the BP cuff and seconds later displayed a reading on the front of the LifePak screen, "128/84."

"Not too bad," she said.

"Now to measure the oxygen level in your blood or Sp02 level is the official name," she said.

She placed a thimble-looking clip on the end of my finger and the wire from it plugged into the front of the LifePak 12.

The reading on the front of the screen says 98%.

"Not bad," she said and then added, "We want that number to be over 94%. If we see it go below that we'll give the patient oxygen by mask."

Joe then said, "We also have a main kit which has our medications and other supplies, an airway kit, portable oxygen bottle and a portable suction unit."

"One thing about the airway kit," he said with a serious tone.

"There's a piece of equipment in there that's extremely important. It's called the BVM or bag valve mask. This is what we use in order to breathe for someone when they aren't breathing," he explained.

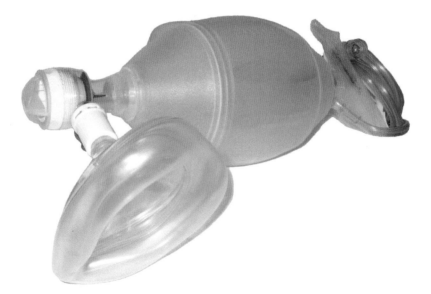

"That should be enough to get you started, at least you know what to grab if we ask for something," Joe said and then gave me a reassuring pat to the shoulder.

We then walked over to a row of lockers in the truck bay before stopping at an empty one, "We'll get your name on there and welcome aboard Mark," Joe said with a confident grin and solid handshake. Steve and Eric and Sam also shook my hand and it was great moment for me.

Suddenly the calm is shattered with tones reverberating through the station and a dispatcher announcing a call for assistance. Smiles changed to focused looks as everyone headed to the vehicles.

"Medic 41, Rescue 41, respond code three for a male subject choking…1250 Main Street, Gino's diner…time out 1145 hours."

Joe looked at me and said, "Ready for your first call?"

My heart started racing, hands were shaking, and I responded with a wide eyed look and an affirmative nod. Steve and Eric and Sam had all gotten into the rescue as their big bay door was going up.

"Climb in," Joe said and opened the side door to the ambulance.

I'm sitting in the jump seat behind the front cab area and watching our bay door roll up. Joe is seated in the passenger seat and securing his seat belt. As Brandon starts to move the ambulance forward, Joe is on the radio and acknowledging the dispatch.

From here I have a good view of everything. The siren is blaring as traffic is moving to the right, to the left, and some of them are just stopped. Brandon isn't fazed by any of it as he is cautiously navigating through it all.

The response takes four minutes. We pull up in front of the diner, there are several people standing out front nervously waving with concerned and panicked looks.

"Mark, bring the main kit," Joe said.

Brandon grabbed the LifePak 12 and small oxygen bottle and Joe has the airway kit.

Rescue 41 is arriving and parks behind the ambulance.

On entry into the diner, we notice a small crowd gathered around an elderly man lying on the floor. There are two women performing CPR on him. One is pushing on the man's chest and counting loudly; one-two-three-four-five-six...the other lady is kneeling next to the man's head and giving breaths.

Joe instructs Steve to take over compressions and Eric and Sam to take over on the breathing. Steve takes out scissors from a leather holster on his belt and cuts the man's shirt off, then places his hands in the center of the chest and began compressing with textbook perfect form.

I opened the airway kit and handed Sam the BVM. She then positions herself above the man's head and places the face mask over his mouth and nose. Eric is off to his side and squeezing the BVM. Between Steve's compressions and Eric and Sam's control of the airway, they look like a CPR instructional video.

"Thanks for helping. Can you tell me what happened?" Joe asked the two ladies.

"Well, he came in holding his chest and was really pale; he sat down and started making choking sounds. He quickly turned blue and slumped out of his chair to the floor," one explained emotionally.

The other one added, "We couldn't just let him lie there, he had no pulse, we started CPR right away."

Joe nodded with an empathetic appreciation. He looked up at Brandon and said, "Get the LifePak 12 hooked up and let's see what we have for a rhythm."

Brandon worked around Steve and applied large rectangular adhesive pads on the man's chest, one to the upper right chest and one below the left nipple line. These are called combo-pads that will allow the EKG rhythm to be displayed on the LifePak screen and then allow a shock to be delivered if needed. He then plugged the adapter wires from the combo-pads into the LifePak 12.

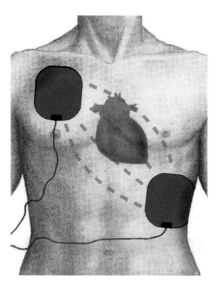

Joe asked Steve to stop compressions as he looked intently at the EKG screen and said, "V-fib, charge it to 200 watts, Brandon, and get ready to shock."

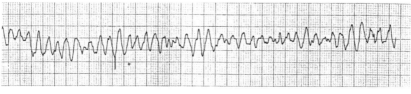

Ventricular Fibrillation or V-fib

The LifePak 12 made the same familiar whine it makes on TV or the movies as it was charging. Joe gave the "everyone clear" warning and pressed the button. The patient jumped at the shock which was followed by a collective gasp throughout the room. Joe immediately ordered Steve to continue compressions.

After the call, Joe explained to me that V-fib or ventricular fibrillation is a heart that is quivering; no pulse is being generated, cardiac arrest. This rhythm needs defibrillated with a shock from the LifePak 12. The charge or "shock" is measured in watt seconds or joules. This is enough energy to make the body jump and hopefully stop the fibrillating heart and allow it to restart on its own.

Less than a minute later, Steve looked up at Joe and said, "I think he may have a pulse back. He's starting to move with each compression."

It was now more obvious, the patient was moving his right arm as if he were trying to push Steve's hand off his chest. Joe ordered Steve to stop compressions and checked the man's left carotid pulse on the neck.

He confirmed the pulse was strong and regular then took out his pen and put a small 'X' over the carotid and did the same over the man's radial pulse at the left wrist.

I asked him later why he put the 'X' over the pulses.

He said, "Now I can find them quickly if I have any questions about their patency."

I will always remember this important tip!

Sam looked up Joe and said, "He's starting to breathe on his own."

"Okay Sam, switch him over to an oxygen mask," Joe said as he finished listening to the man's chest with his stethoscope.

"Roger on the mask," Sam replied.

I couldn't help but notice every eye in the place was fixed on what we were doing. One lady had tears in her eyes; some had their hands over their faces, others looked on with disbelief at the experience that was unfolding. When Joe affirmed the pulse had returned, a small round of applause was heard along with soft mumbling between them.

It was an indescribable feeling being involved in this experience even with my small role.

Steve looked at me and said, "Mark, let's get him moved onto the gurney."

I was part of the crew!

The transport to the hospital was like a synchronized ballet in the back of the ambulance. Joe, Eric and Sam were all busy, Joe was starting an IV, Sam was checking vital signs, and Eric was assessing for injuries and writing information down. I sat in the jump seat taking it all in with awe, feeling like this was exactly where I was supposed to be. Steve was following us with the rescue unit.

Joe leaned over and got close to the patient's ear and asked him if he could hear us. He then began explaining everything that was happening and told him not to worry, that he'd stay with him and make sure he wasn't alone. The guy didn't respond but somehow I think he heard everything Joe said.

When we arrived at the hospital, it seemed like the "red carpet" had been rolled out. The back doors to the ambulance opened and there stood two hospital security guards.

"Good job," one of them said to Joe.

Joe winked at him and said, "That's what we do."

Going into the E.D. or emergency department, we were met by a small army of nurses and the emergency physician and were directed into one of the large treatment rooms.

Joe started talking and the room fell silent. He described everything from when we arrived on scene to pulling up to the E.D.

The emergency physician is Dr. Stein. He thanked Joe and said, "We'll take care of him from here; great job guys."

This was something that obviously plays out every day in this emergency department and they were very good at it.

If I ever had thoughts of whether this was something I could do, they were answered in that one fateful morning. We got back to the station and Joe said he wanted to meet with everyone in the training room. After a few minutes everyone was assembled and Joe took to the front of the room.

"I want to thank everyone today for the great job and teamwork. Because of our efforts we gave this man a chance to go back to his family," he said.

I could not have felt more proud. Joe later told me not to expect this outcome on every response. He described this as the "perfect storm" type of call: immediate bystander CPR, quick EMS response and quick advanced life support intervention.

As we were wrapping up the critique, Sandy came into the training room.

She said, "The emergency department called and gave an update on your patient, Mr. Gustafson, he was awake and stabilized and being moved to the Coronary Care Unit (CCU) and his wife and son were at the hospital with him."

She then added, "The family wished to express their gratitude and tomorrow is his 70th birthday."

I thought to myself, "What a great gift, Happy Birthday Mr. Gustafson."

The first month had been a very good introduction to the world of EMS. I spent as much free time at the station as I could. My training was progressing and Joe had me heavily involved on calls from taking blood pressures to setting up equipment. I was quickly gaining confidence and becoming a stronger member of the crew with each and every run.

We carry a lot of equipment. Because of this, we conduct some type of training every shift and cover not only the use of the equipment, but scenarios where it would be used as well. Joe wanted all of us to understand every piece of equipment no matter what our certification level was. There was a confidence that when we showed up to help someone, we had no doubt we could make a difference.

What I also realized was we were just one important part of the system. Everyone had "their part" to do in order for the patient to have a favorable outcome. From the bystander who called 9-1-1 and provided basic care, the interventions from EMS, the continuation of care through the emergency department, the specialty care and then eventually reunited back to one's everyday life with their family and friends.

One afternoon all of that came together in the most unlikely of ways. Sam and Eric and I had just finished reviewing the ambulance's main kit when the station tones interrupted our little study session.

"Medic 41, Rescue 41, respond code three for an elderly female, unknown problem…88 Viola Place…time out 1545 hours."

We arrived at the address and noted two police cars parked in front of the house. There are two officers standing at front of the residence and a middle aged female with a concerned look about her standing next to them.

We walked up to them and an officer immediately began explaining the scenario.

"Hi guys, this is Mrs. Evelyn Phillips, she notified 9-1-1 after she was unable to reach her mother who lives here alone. She said it's unlike her and is worried she might have a medical problem," he said.

"Hello Mrs. Phillips, my name's Joe, I'm a paramedic, what kind of problems does your mother have?" He asked.

"She has high blood pressure and diabetes, we talk several times a day on the phone, I last heard from her at six this morning, she had a bad headache, I know something is wrong… her name is Betty, Betty Phillips," she said.

The officer then spoke up, "Her car is in the garage and the doors are locked, we're sure she's home and Mrs. Phillips has given us permission to force a door," he said.

Sam and Eric and Steve went around the back of the house when Sam came around the corner and said, "Hey guys, we got the back door open, she's on the floor in the kitchen."

We made our way in to the home and indeed Betty is on the floor in the kitchen. She's on her left side and we can see her occasionally raising her right arm, non-purposefully.

Joe knelt down next to her head and said, "Betty, can you hear me? Can you talk to us? My name is Joe, I'm a paramedic."

There is no response.

"Mark, see if you can get a blood pressure, Eric, get her on oxygen, Steve, let's get the LifePak 12 hooked up and Sam, check her sugar," Joe ordered.

As part of our pre-hospital care guidelines, blood sugar or glucose levels are checked on any patient with a decreased level of consciousness or altered mental status. They may have other reasons for being unconscious or disoriented, but the sugar levels are always checked.

The glucometer is used to measure those levels. It can display any amount between 20 and 500. Below 20 it reads "LO", above 500 it reads "HI". Normal ranges are from around 80-120. It's measured in milligrams per deciliter (mg/dl) but we just say the number.

Sam checked the blood sugar by a finger stick and said, "Joe, the sugar reads HI."

We know that her blood sugar level is over 500. This is very serious. This level can have adverse effects on the brain, heart, kidneys and could be the reason she's unresponsive.

Joe starts conducting a head to toe assessment and we all noticed Betty has no movement on her left side and the left side of her mouth has a notable droop to it.

"Heart rate 84, Sp02 96%," Steve called out. Joe nodded to him.

17

"I'm getting 216/124 for a pressure," I said. Joe nodded again and gave the direction to gently get Betty on the gurney and start heading for the ambulance. He then walked over to Betty's daughter.

"It looks she might have had a stroke, and her blood sugar and blood pressure are pretty high," Joe explained.

"We're going to take good care of her and we need to get her to the hospital," he added.

Her daughter started crying and put her hand over her mouth. She finally asked Joe, "Is she going to be okay?"

"She needs evaluated at the hospital and they will run some tests, we won't know anything definitive for a while," he said and then put his hand on her shoulder offering reassurance.

"I'll meet you guys up there, I need to call my sister and we'll both be there, please take care of her," she pleaded.

Joe nodded and after getting Betty placed on the gurney, we headed to the ambulance. During the transport Joe placed an IV in her right arm. Betty's eyes are open and I noticed she tries to talk but it is only mumbling. It's a frightening presentation.

I got down next to her ear and introduced myself. I then started talking to her and explaining what we were doing and that her daughter would meet her at the hospital and just really wanted her to know we were here for her. I could only imagine how terrified she must be feeling. As Joe had told me once, "What if this was you lying here, what would you want to hear from us?"

We arrived at the hospital and as we transferred care to the emergency department staff I noticed how gentle and deliberate they were with their movements around her. Several of the nurses would pat her hand reassuringly as they would perform a procedure or walk near her.

We later learned she had suffered a stroke. They got her blood sugar stabilized and she was admitted to the ICU. Her daughters had made it to the hospital and were with her in the ICU. The neurologists were optimistic because she regained some movement with her left hand several hours after being admitted. Betty was eventually discharged back home with no permanent deficits.

CHAPTER 2

TRAINING

After a few months, I had become a regular at Station 4. I couldn't get enough. When I was working at the construction site, I was placed in charge of safety because of my new "hobby."

During our breaks and at lunch, I would count pulses on some of the workers. They would ask me questions about medical problems and I had to laugh because they treated me like I was a doctor. Anytime someone had a cut or scrape, they immediately came to me for treatment.

It was Saturday, my day off from my real job and I was just finishing a 12 hour shift on the ambulance when Joe approached me and asked, "How are things going Mark?"

I smiled nervously and said, "Okay--great, actually."

He explained there was an opening in an upcoming EMT course next month and wanted to know if I was interested in taking it. The department would sponsor me and pick up the cost of the program. He then added he would be happy to recommend me if I was interested.

I couldn't say "yes" fast enough and told him I'd work very hard and do the best I could.

He said, "Perfect, I already signed you up...you start in two weeks."

This was a bombshell I wasn't expecting. Suddenly I was feeling apprehensive as I realized how complacent I had become with the assistant role I was in.

And apparently I was the last to be aware of this new direction because Sam magically appeared and said, "Hey congratulations on getting in to the EMT class."

"Yeah thanks," I said, "Any advice?"

"Study-study-study, then study some more," she said with a big grin.

"Oh, well that helps a lot, you're a ton of help," I said as she high fived me with a devilish smirk.

Our conversation was cut short by the tones. After hearing the dispatch, I decided to go on the call.

 "Medic 41, Rescue 41, respond code three for baby not breathing, CPR in progress, 4982 Orion Lane...time out 2016 hours.

I got into the ambulance and sat in the jump seat and suddenly was absolutely horrified--a baby? How could this happen? What happened? How would I perform? We've had responses for children but nothing close to this nature. During the response, Joe assigned roles for after we arrived.

"Brandon, I'm going to have you handling the LifePak 12," he ordered.

"Roger that," Brandon replied with a quick and confident response.

He then yelled back to me in the jump seat and said, "Mark I'm going to have you take over on CPR, you okay with that?"

I said, "Sure, no problem," and not sure how confident I sounded.

As we were pulling up to the residence, a little girl about 10 years old came running out of the house frantically waving to us. We grabbed our equipment and followed her through the front door where we met by a nearly hysterical mother holding a 14 month boy.

The boy is conscious, looking up at his mother and actually looks pretty good considering the initial dispatch information and anxiety level his mom is having.

"He stopped breathing," she said excitedly in between sobs.

"Okay, let's start from the beginning, what happened?" Joe asked.

"I was putting him to bed when his eyes rolled into the back of his head, he started shaking and turned blue, and I think he stopped breathing," she described in between heavy sobs.

Joe placed his hand on her shoulder with an empathetic smile said, "We understand. It's very scary to see. We're here and we'll take care of him. It'll be okay."

She closed her eyes and exhaled and said, "Thank you."

She then added, "He's been sick for the last two days with a cough, runny nose, and fever and we ran out of acetaminophen today. "

Steve and I brought the gurney over as Joe took the child from the mother and placed him in the center of it. Sam and Eric are on both sides of the gurney.

Joe then looked at Sam and said, "I need you to get a rectal temperature."

Sam nodded affirmatively and removed the one piece jumper sleeper outfit and in less than a minute she announced, "103.6," that was displaying from the electronic thermometer.

Joe administered a pediatric acetaminophen suppository rectally which would bring the fever under control and then we wheeled the gurney and child to the ambulance.

Brandon helped the mother into the passenger seat and made sure her seat belt was fastened. When family members ride with us, we rarely will have them in the back of the ambulance. If we are performing critical procedures, it makes it difficult with them so close.

By the time we reached the hospital, the child was smiling at the silly faces Joe was making and so were Eric and Sam and me.

Joe took me aside after the call and asked if I had any questions.

I said, "Now I'm not so sure about that EMT course...it was pretty scary dealing with the child."

Joe smiled and said, "Don't get too worried about the EMT course. It doesn't teach you how to run these calls. It gives you the knowledge to understand them, but nothing can replace experience."

He then explained how febrile seizures work and said, "They're usually brought on by sudden or on-going high fevers in infants and small children."

He importantly added that you're not dealing with just the child.

"Don't forget you also have the parents who can be scared out of their minds," he said with a serious look. I knew this would be another valuable lesson.

The next question he asked was just what I needed to hear.

"If you're on another call like this one, do you think you'd have a better understanding of what's going on and what needs to be done?"

With a renewed confidence I said, "Oh yeah, definitely."

The EMT course started on a Monday night. It would be every Monday, Wednesday and Saturday for the next eight weeks. There were sixteen of us in the program. I was the only one from Station 4, the rest of the students were from neighboring departments.

I thought maybe I was in the wrong class for the first few nights. We started off learning more about cells and body parts than I ever could have imagined. The medical terminology seemed like another language with way too many letters. After the first week, I really wondered if I was going to learn everything I was supposed to. My mind was on overload.

We had just finished the Wednesday night class when I was getting ready to leave the station as the tones went off. It sounded like extra help would be needed so I joined the crew.

"Medic 41, Rescue 41, respond code three for a motor vehicle collision, SR 3 and Cole Road, possible DOA…time out 2145 hours."

As we went en route we heard a second dispatch coming over the radio adding a neighboring department to respond as mutual aid for fire response. Our response would take about nine minutes.

Time seems distorted during the response as I found myself trying to mentally prepare for what might be one of the most traumatic scenes I have been to, am I ready for this?

We arrived to what looked like a small plane crash, vehicles damaged beyond recognition. There are several police cars on scene with their overhead lights creating a surreal setting. This was a head-on collision with both cars in excess of 50 mph.

One of the police officers met us upon exiting the ambulance and told Joe the two occupants in the small compact were DOA (Dead on Arrival) and the lone occupant from the other vehicle was ejected and lying in a ditch over a small embankment approximately twenty-five feet from the impact site.

Another officer is talking with two young females that were witnesses to the collision and first on scene. One of them is sobbing and the other is trembling, staring blankly in a state of shock.

Joe yelled over to the rescue unit, "Eric, Sam, check the patients in the small car and confirm they're DOA."

Brandon and I are following Joe as we are preparing to check out the ejected driver. Steve has the side compartment on the ambulance open and grabbing a long spine board.

There's a heavy gasoline odor permeating the air. The mutual aid response is Engine 61 from District 6. They are on scene and have two charged hose lines deployed with focused attention in protecting the scene in case a fire erupts.

Eric and Sam are both visibly shaken after returning from the confirmation of the DOA's. Sam would later describe both occupants as a young couple in their 20's.

The male driver had massive open head and chest trauma and was heavily entrapped in the driver's compartment. The female passenger was ghostly pale with less obvious trauma; hers were probably massive internal injuries.

Joe told us, "They likely both died instantly, no time to even react."

Whether this was true or not, it somehow made us feel better than wondering if they suffered.

As we approach the embankment, our ejected patient is unresponsive, lying face down and making loud grunting, moaning type sounds that are very graphic along with some obvious horrific injuries. His right leg is grotesquely fractured at mid-thigh and angled backwards near his back.

This is the most severely injured person I have ever been around. I am staring at him and can't help but wonder if he is aware of how critical he is or if he's in any pain. Suddenly, I hear my name being called out and recognize it is Joe's voice, "Mark, are you okay?"

"Yeah, yeah I'm fine, what do you need me to do?" I asked.

"I want you to take C spine control," he said.

"Roger that," I said.

This means which I would be in charge of keeping the patient's head and neck still while the rest of the crew gets him secured to the long spine board and not allowing any movement in case there's a cervical spine injury.

Steve is right behind us with a long spine board; Sam and Eric behind him. Brandon stayed at the top of the embankment awaiting orders from Joe.

Joe called out to the patient, "Buddy, can you hear me? Hello," and got no response. He checked for a radial pulse at the right wrist and couldn't feel one.

Not feeling a radial pulse is an ominous finding. The top number of the blood pressure needs to be above the 80 to 90 range to generate a radial pulse. In its absence, we know the blood pressure is less than 80 and his condition is critical, he is in shock. This is a true and valuable, "trick of the trade."

Joe looked at Steve and said, "Let's get him secured to the board and get out of here, Sam, make sure his airway stays open."

"Roger that," was Steve's reply and Sam nodded affirmatively.

Joe yelled up to Brandon, "Get the back of the rig ready, I need it set up for securing this airway." Brandon gave thumbs up and was gone in a flash.

Eric had to re-align the right leg to its correct anatomical position and it made terrible sounds as he moved it in place. These are sounds that replay in my head and I will never forget.

We were then able to secure him to the long spine board and made it out of the ditch despite the difficult terrain and poor scene lighting and into the ambulance with a six minute scene time.

Brandon finished preparing the back of the ambulance. He had IV's and airway equipment set up. The transport to the trauma center would take eight minutes.

Eric and I cut all the clothing away exposing the severity of the injuries. From the top down there wasn't much that didn't have something wrong. Blood is coming from both ears and nostrils, the jaw is fractured and deformed, and teeth are missing. The left eye is swollen shut. There's a large scalping laceration to the frontal skull at the hairline. There's heavy bruising with full thickness abrasions over the chest and abdomen, the right mid-shaft femur fracture has an inch of bone protruding; the skin is pale, cool and clammy and his breathing is erratic.

Suddenly, I am focused on a ring on his left hand, it's a wedding band. This is someone's husband, maybe someone's dad; there was no other way to think of it.

Joe applied a rubber tourniquet above the elbow on the right arm and after a few "taps" to a vein he inserted the large IV catheter. The IV bag hooked into the IV is called normal saline. This is fluid that is infused to temporarily replace some of the fluids that have been lost.

Joe then looked at Eric and Sam and me and said, "Let's get this airway secured."

Getting the airway secured would be a very invasive procedure, one that would require everyone to be in the right place at the right time in order for it to be successful. The procedure is called RSI or Rapid Sequence Intubation.

This is an elective procedure that puts a person into a deep sleep and then paralyzes the gag reflex to allow a breathing tube to be inserted into the trachea which not only protects the lungs from aspiration but allows greater control of the oxygenation process. It is a procedure reserved for only the sickest patients.

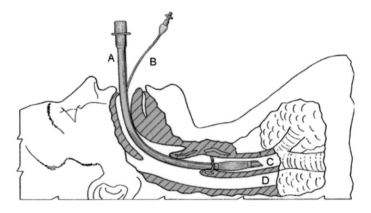

This is a more in depth view of the intubation procedure. 'A' is the end of the endotracheal tube that is attached to the bag valve. 'B' is where the syringe is attached and air injected in order to inflate the small balloon cuff just inside the trachea and sealing it off. 'C' is the trachea and lungs are below that. 'D' is the esophagus, the food pipe. We need to be careful not to insert the tube in this opening as there will be no oxygenation taking place and we will hear "gurgling" or "bubbling" coming from the stomach when we place the stethoscope over that area.

We review this procedure and our respective roles frequently during our training sessions. This will be my first experience seeing it actually used. My role will be a support position and help as Joe directs me.

Joe will first administer a powerful drug called etomidate. This induces the patient into a deep anesthesia or sleep. Next the muscle paralyzing drug succinylcholine which we call "sux" is administered and this paralyzes the patient for up to eight minutes.

Joe will then use a laryngoscope with a long stainless steel blade with a bright light on the end of it that he will insert down the throat looking for the epiglottis.

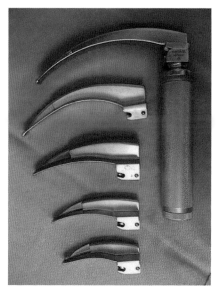

Laryngoscope handle and blades

Below this is the vocal cords and opening to the trachea and lungs. He'll then insert an endotracheal tube, or "breathing tube" into the tracheal opening.

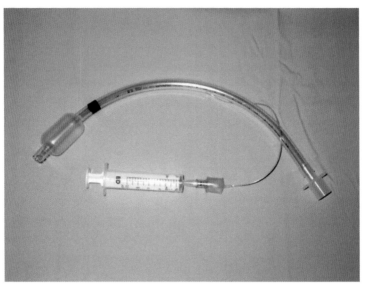

Endotracheal Tube

He'll have to accomplish this in under thirty seconds once the drugs take effect. This is considered the "gold standard" for securing an airway.

Joe sat in the jump seat at the head of patient. Eric sat next to him on the floor with the portable suction unit and Sam was ready to assist with the BVM. I got the patient hooked up to the LifePak 12.

Joe pushed the etomidate into the IV line which induced the patient in to the anesthetized state and I noticed the breathing quickly went very shallow. Next the sux was administered and he became flaccid and stopped breathing.

Joe held the laryngoscope in his left hand and gently opened the mouth to slide the long curved blade down the throat in search of the epiglottis. At the same time he asked me to start calling out numbers: heart rate and oxygen levels.

My first report was, "Heart rate 136, Sp02 96%."

We want the Sp02 to be above 94%...ideally 98% or 99% was great. As a patient starts running out of available oxygen in the tissues, we would see the Sp02 drop. If it got too low, Joe would stop the procedure and Sam would start ventilating with the BVM in order to re-oxygenate.

Without moving his eyes from the back of the patient's throat, Joe asked Eric to hand him the tube. He took it with his right hand and gently slid it in the right side of the patient's open mouth, down the throat and into the trachea and then removed the blade.

"Okay, it's in, great job everyone," he said.

Sam attached the bag valve to the end of the endotracheal tube and squeezed in a breath every six seconds. We saw the chest go up and down as Joe listened with his stethoscope.

He looked up and said, "Perfect, keep it just like that Sam."

When someone is intubated, we no longer use the mask portion of the bag valve mask. The bag valve will connect directly to the endotracheal tube.

Eric then finished dressing the large scalp laceration as Joe grabbed the radio mike and updated the trauma center of our four minute ETA (estimated time of arrival).

The hospital we were going to is Regional General Hospital. In the pre-hospital arena it is known as Regional or RGH. They are a Level One facility and thus capable of providing any level of care and handling any type of emergency.

Joe started a second IV in the left arm and hung another bag with normal saline. He now did a reassessment from head to toe and called out the findings.

"The right pupil is blown, possible frontal skull fracture, chest sounds are clear and equal, and the bruising over the upper left abdomen is getting larger," he noted aloud.

When one pupil is of normal size and the other is dilated, this can be indicative of intracranial swelling. We call it a "blown pupil." This is an ominous sign. The combination of the head injury and shock would not have a good outcome.

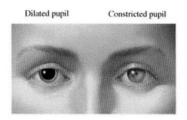

Dilated pupil   Constricted pupil

Eric and I stabilized the right femur fracture by aligning it with the left leg and then taping it to the spine board. His skin color is changing right before us; becoming paler and clammy.

I looked at the LifePak 12 and called out the latest numbers, "Heart rate 140, blood pressure 60/44, SpO2 is not reading."

Joe nodded as he looked at the patients face and sighed heavily.

We arrived at RGH where Dr. Mike, one of the emergency department physicians was there to greet us. He and Joe followed us as we got the patient into the main trauma room, Suite 12.

Our patient made it to surgery within eleven minutes of arriving at RGH. His condition deteriorated and he went into cardiac arrest. After an aggressive resuscitation attempt he was pronounced dead at 0016 hours.

Our patient's name was Damon. He was 37 years old. We later learned he was married and worked offshore on drilling rigs. He was heading home at the time of the crash. It seemed we had done everything we could to save this man.

Joe talked to me later and said, "Always remember this: You can't always judge your results based on your efforts. If that was the case, they'd all live."

This would be another valuable lesson.

At the next EMT class, I was given the opportunity to talk to the class about that case. You could have heard a pin drop while I was describing the scene, the sights, and the sounds. At the end of the of presentation I brought up the observation of the ring, and how I wished I could have let his wife know how hard we tried, and how compassionate we were for her husband during the short time he was with us. It brought about discussion how there's so much more to EMS than just treating the patient. We're dealing with people's lives and the lives of their families.

This call would make us all look at our roles as EMT's in a new light.

CHAPTER 3

SUPERSTITIONS

Superstitions play out in all aspects of life, so why should EMS be any different? For instance, making plans after working a 24 hour shift is one way you can count on that shift sabotaging those ideas. Be it a lack of sleep or a late call towards the end of the shift, it's a given.

Brandon took a few shifts off and this left an open slot to work alongside Joe. Since I had completed my EMT training last month, I was eligible to sign up for these shifts and my construction job afforded me the opportunity to work around these days.

This was a great opportunity to learn from the master. I watched everything Joe did from the way he approached patients, set up the ambulance, wrote his reports, kept the mirrored shine on his boots to the creases in his uniform and found myself emulating these traits.

We had several calls during one of the shifts and only got about three hours of sleep due to calls through the night. Our last call got us back to the station at 0600. We decided it wasn't worth going back to bed for an hour since station policy was crews had to be up by 0700 to finish chores around the station and ensure paperwork was completed for the 0800 shift change.

At 0700, the tones went off nearly giving both of us heart attacks in our near slumberous states.

"Medic 41, Rescue 41, respond code one for a female with back pain… 114 Carlos Way…time out 0701 hours."

As we responded I thought, "This'll be about perfect, transport to the hospital, back to the station by 0800, then off to the golf course for my 0900 tee time."

We arrived at the residence and after knocking at the front door, we heard the patient yell out, "Come in, I'm here."

Our patient is a 35 year old female lying on the couch; she's apologetic and claiming she can't move because of several vertebrae that are out of alignment and causing severe pain. She stated she's under a doctor's care and he's requesting she be brought to his clinic at a hospital in a neighboring city.

This would be a forty-five minute trip, each way. (I made a mental note to myself about not making plans after a shift ever again.)

After the exam and discussing plans on what we would like to do, Joe explained to her the best option would be to place the gurney next to the couch and gently slide her over. To make that happen we would need to move a large coffee table that was in front of the couch. She was insistent we not touch or move the table and became quite adamant about it. Joe pleaded it would make the transfer the easiest and assured her we would move it back, exactly as it was found.

After several minutes of this back and forth negotiating, Steve motioned to Eric and in an instant they lifted the table and walked about two feet when all of a sudden the room went silent as everyone stared at the floor where the table had been.

There are three large sealed bags of what looked like weed, a flat digital scale, a box of baggies and a large coal black automatic pistol with two clips next to it.

After what seemed like an eternity of awkward silence, the patient spoke up and said, "Everyone relax its medical marijuana."

There were several glances among everyone in the room and Joe finally said, "Oh, okay, we figured it was something like that."

We lifted her to the gurney, replaced the coffee table exactly as promised and transported as requested. There was no further discussion of this incident and the patient acted like it never happened. We are not law enforcement. We are obligated to report on-going criminal acts such as child or elderly abuse but our role is otherwise largely the patient advocate. We may not agree with life styles but this is one of the many challenges to EMS and professionalism.

Then there's most dreaded word in the industry, the "Q" word. I don't even like to say it, and everyone cringes when it's spoken around the station. It's guaranteed to generate a call--even multiple calls if you say it too often or too loudly.

It would all start somewhat innocently.

Someone would casually blurt out, "Boy it's been *quiet* today," and if looks could kill, everyone start's putting boots on, getting bathroom stops out of the way, grabbing a quick bite to eat...too late, tones.

"Medic 41, Rescue 41, respond code one to the Port Dock for a back injury. There will be a tug boat approximately ten minutes out and will meet you at the public landing...time out 1630 hours."

By now I've learned you try not to guess what could be going on. You keep an open mind and expect the unexpected. When information is

36

passed on from person to person, it has the potential to change from what is actually going on. So, a back injury--how bad can that be?

We arrived at the public landing and after about fifteen minutes the tug boat is approaching with a couple of the crew members waving. We acknowledged them and waited until they docked and motioned for us to come aboard.

The deck supervisor greeted us and said, "We were towing a disabled boat with a large steel cable when the cable broke. It whipped back to the tug and struck one of my guys in the back; it hit him pretty hard and knocked him flat on the deck, now he's complaining of back pain, we just tossed a couple blankets on him and called for you guys."

Joe nodded to the supervisor as we followed him towards the back of the tug boat.

The patient is lying in an open area with arms behind his neck as if he's enjoying the break from work. He says his back is pretty sore and it "feels cold and wet back there."

Sam began removing several blankets covering the patient when it became shockingly apparent he is nearly cut in two. He has a three inch wide opening from just left of his spine and extending around to the mid-sternum at about the nipple level.

As he breathes you can see his lung expanding and deflating and what looks like a beating heart. The boat crew had obviously not seen the extent of the injury nor did the patient and these were both good things.

In a near whisper, Sam asked Joe, "Did I just see what I think I saw?"

Joe said, "Yep, you did."

Joe told the patient, "My friend, I'm going to put you on a helicopter."

"Okay, cool," he replied.

Joe looked at Steve and made a "whirl sign" with his hand to which Steve acknowledged. Steve walked to the dock and was talking into his portable radio ordering the helicopter transport through our dispatch.

Sam put an oxygen mask over the patient's mouth and nose while Eric and I used two large trauma dressings to cover the gaping opening. Joe put a 14 gauge IV in the right mid-arm which the patient asked him jokingly if he was putting a large steel rod in.

A 14 gauge is the largest IV needle you can put in a vein. It's important to place the biggest IV possible in trauma patients. The bigger the IV, the faster fluids can be infused if needed to offset bleeding.

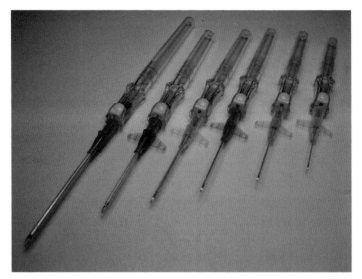

These are the IV needles we use. The orange is the 14 gauge, the largest we can insert into a peripheral vein. The gray is a 16 gauge, green is an 18 gauge, pink is a 20 gauge, blue is a 22 gauge and the yellow is a 24 gauge. (When you donate blood they use the 16 gauge)

Steve got the landing zone set up and as the helicopter was landing, I noticed I was the only one not under cover from the down draft of the rotors. This was something that would usually happen to someone in EMS only once. After the dusting and nearly being blown over, I understood why Joe hunkered over the patient, Steve hid behind the boat motor house and Sam and Eric protected the kits.

The patient was flown to the RGH and quickly taken to surgery. Amazingly, the graphic presentation was just that. He lost very little blood, his lungs remained intact. There were two cracked ribs, no heart damage, no spleen injury, just a "half-the-body" cut.

He spent the night in the trauma ICU and went home three days later with an impressive story and more impressive scar to go along with it.

Full moons will cause the most hardy to think twice about urban myths of stranger than strange experiences. Whether you're in an ambulance, police car or dispatch center, the full moon syndrome has made true believers out of skeptics and led to story after story to go along with it.

One full moon night, we're all sitting around the station dinner table talking about nothing in particular, everyone secretly wondering what this particular full moon night would bring, and everyone got their answer with the tones melding into the conversation.

"Medic 41, Rescue 41, respond for a suicidal person with a gun, 1425 Learner Rode, law enforcement is also responding...time out 2300 hours."

This wasn't an infrequent response; most of the time it was only a cry for help and resulted with a trip to the hospital and mental health evaluation. On this night things would not be so predictable. After Joe advised the dispatcher we were staged a block away, she immediately responded back and said we were requested to the scene and the patient had shot himself.

We pulled up in front of the residence and there's several police officers standing in the front yard.

It's a cool night; there's a foggy mist in the air, you can see your breath and the moon is creating eerie shadows.

One of the officers is kneeling next to the patient who's lying in the grass just outside the front door. We recognize this cop as Officer Jensen and have worked together on previous scenes.

As we are walking up to the patient, Joe is in the lead.

Officer Jensen looks up at Joe and says, "I think he's gone."

As Joe examines the patient closer, we find he shot himself just below the chin and it exited through the back of the left upper neck. The entry wound under the chin is about the size of a nickel. The exit wound on back of the neck and is about the size of a tennis ball. This is a graphic and surreal image. There's very little bleeding, no breathing, and no *obvious* carotid pulse Joe could detect.

There's also a distinct heavy aroma of alcohol emanating from the steam that is rising from this gaping wound. The alcohol presence makes me wonder, "*Would he have done this had he been sober?*"

Joe tells Officer Jensen he concurs with the conclusion and adds, "We won't be doing anything for this guy tonight."

Officer Jensen then reached up to his lapel mike and said, "Six Nora-One…this is a confirmed DOA, send the ME" (medical examiner) and dispatch quickly confirmed the transmission.

He looked at Joe and said, "I'm going inside the house to check with the roommates and see if we have any other information."

"Roger that," was Joe's response.

Joe took a few moments to examine the injury more closely with Eric and Sam and me as he gently moved the patient's head to the right. It's a devastating presentation. He then placed the head back to the neutral position and said, "Guess we're out of here too."

As Joe starts to walk away, Sam suddenly puts her hand on his shoulder and squeaks out a shrill. This causes Joe and the rest of us to quickly look down at the patient.

He turns his head towards us and with his eyes half open, nearly sits up with elbows behind him and speaks in a slow, deep and reverberating sounding voice and says, "Am I gone like the cop said?"

This froze all of us in our tracks. No one could speak for several seconds. Finally, Joe spoke up and said, "Can you hear us?" The patient closed his eyes and laid back down, obviously breathing with steam rising with each breath.

About then another officer walked up, unaware of what had just occurred. Joe looked at him with wide eyes and urgency and said, "Tell Officer Jensen we're taking his DOA to the hospital!"

Seconds later Officer Jensen came running out of the house and asked Joe, "What the hell's going on?"

"He woke up," Joe exclaimed.

Jensen stared at him trying to process a thought and said, "HOW?"

"He just did!" Joe exclaimed.

We seemed to go into an overdrive mode as if trying to make up time lost. Brandon and Steve brought the gurney and back board and after getting him secured we were into the ambulance. As soon as we went en route to RGH, he woke again and is now trying to get up, this time becoming physically aggressive. This created tense moments as we didn't want to fight with him potentially making the injury worse. We would need to RSI this patient, quickly.

Joe applied the rubber tourniquet to the left upper arm and searched for a vein. After finding a suitable one he inserted a 14 gauge. Eric had drawn up the RSI drugs and had the syringes ready. Sam's ready with the BVM and I'm standing by with the suction unit.

Joe has the intubation equipment ready and gives Eric the nod to push the drugs. I watch as the patient responds by letting out a deep sigh and then quickly stops breathing.

Joe gently inserted the curved laryngoscope blade into the mouth and down the throat. As he got to the epiglottis he encountered a significant obstacle. There's swelling throughout the back of the throat caused by the GSW (gunshot wound) making the view to the trachea obscured. After several seconds of manipulation and a hint of cyanosis (blueness) around the patient's lips, Joe was able to pass the tube into the trachea. This is one of the few times we would see Joe let out a sigh of relief after an intubation.

Now that he was intubated, things started getting even more bizarre, blood pressure at 130/86, heart rate at 74, SpO2 at 98%, and sugar is 88. Everything's in the normal ranges; in fact, it was like there was nothing wrong with the patient, except for having this gaping GSW to the front and back of the neck.

Arriving at the emergency department we're directed to Suite 12. The trauma team listened intently to Joe describing the scene as if we were all sitting around a late night campfire listening to a tall tale or horror story. You could see the chill it created on several faces and could overhear chatter about a "full moon" and people nodding with raised eyebrows.

The patient went to surgery and amazingly had non-life threatening wounds and no serious internal damage. There was actually a flap from the exit wound they replaced and closed with simple sutures. He awoke the next morning and had no recall of the event. His alcohol level was at nearly five times the legal limit at .38, which was obviously a major contributing factor.

Nothing is ever "black and white" in EMS.

CHAPTER 4

PARAMEDIC TRAINING

District 4 opened up a residency program in which I was able to essentially work full time and could put my entire focus on learning as much as possible and working towards climbing the EMS ladder.

After a year of working as an EMT, I was now eligible to take the next step in my training by attending paramedic school. It's expected that when you arrive at paramedic training, you're a seasoned EMT veteran. The strongest paramedics out there were the strongest EMT's! I had full support from Joe and everyone else at the station and was very excited to take this step.

Paramedic training focuses on Advanced Life Support (ALS)--things like cardiology. You learn to interpret EKG rhythms, be able to recognize, assess and treat almost any cardiac emergency. The 12 lead EKG is now a pre-hospital standard in assessing a patient presenting with chest pain. We can see the heart attack happening in real time right in front of us.

You'll be trained in advanced airway placement such as endotracheal intubation. This is one of our more invasive skills that require a great amount of training and perseverance. We'll spend many hours and rotations in the O.R. under the guidance of the anesthesiologist trying to develop habits that we'll carry in to the uncontrolled pre-hospital arena. This is also a procedure that demands great confidence in ones abilities.

You're trained with enough pharmacological knowledge to be dangerous if used improperly. We're carrying anywhere between thirty and fifty different drugs. All of the ALS skills have to be used with respect, confidence and caution.

Paramedic training takes on average one year. This will be one of the most intense years of my life. My time will either be spent in class, completing clinical rotations in the hospital, on an ambulance or studying, which takes up just about all the hours in a day. (Notice eating and sleeping aren't included.)

Entering into this commitment requires a great deal of forethought and anticipating any potential problems that may arise during that year, and dealing with them before getting started. It's not a good year to start a relationship, get married, have a baby, hold down two jobs, travel on vacation, build a house, or party. There are no shortcuts. Every minute is valuable and every rotation crucial.

One of my clinical rotations involved spending two eight hour shifts in the morgue. This was actually very educational and most of my fellow classmates came away with positive experiences. During my last shift at the morgue, it wouldn't be a typical day.

A local ambulance service was dropping off a recently deceased male and I was assisting in the transfer to the morgue gurney. I happened to notice it didn't look like the ambulance gurney and morgue gurney were matched up properly. To my horror, the morgue gurney started to roll away. The body began to fall between them and I sprang forward in an attempt to keep him from going to the floor. I ended up with the body falling on top of me as we both fell to the floor.

We're now embraced; our heads cheek to cheek, at that moment the deceased body expelled a large amount of air that was trapped in the stomach. It came out in a slow, deep, demonic whisper into my left ear.

I think my heart stopped for several terrifying seconds and have no doubt that very moment is the most scared I've ever been in my life. It was quite a few days before I could think of it rationally.

When you finish school, it can take upwards of two years walking around like you have your shoes on the wrong foot. You need to develop your style, to use your skills, to learn what your limits are--your strengths, your weaknesses--and it takes every bit of this time or longer to get it figured out.

A very good medic I know had just finished his training and was eager to save every patient and alleviate suffering the world over. He and his partner were called to evaluate a female that was part of a domestic dispute scene.

The police were called by the boyfriend and when they arrived he told them his girlfriend had taken all of her amitriptyline medication.

Amitriptyline is a powerful anti-depressant and not used as much nowadays. It's a dangerous medication to OD (overdose) on, as there's no antidote and if it's allowed to remain in the system, death is almost certain.

When the medic crew arrived, the boyfriend was handcuffed and in the back of the police car. He was very animated and agitated about not being taken seriously and eventually had to be restrained.

The girlfriend (Mandy) was beautiful, full of life, blondish brown hair with green eyes, almost five foot six and 110 pounds. She's sitting in the front room of the home and very calm, rational and engaging. My friend introduced himself as a paramedic and listened as she went on to describe the boyfriend as controlling, jealous and easily upset in the relationship. She said they'd been arguing and eventually went in the bathroom and told him she'd taken all fifty of her amitriptyline tablets. She claimed to have them down the toilet as she'd never be stupid enough to take all that medication. She was very convincing of this story.

After twenty minutes on the scene, Mandy agreed to go with the crew to the hospital to be evaluated but assured them it wasn't necessary. During the transport the medic allowed Mandy to sit on the bench seat where they talked and it was an otherwise uneventful twelve minute transport.

After arriving at the hospital, the medic escorted Mandy into the emergency department. She was allowed to sit in a waiting area to be checked in. This is where she went unconscious and had a grand-mal seizure and then proceeded to go into cardiac arrest. She was pronounced dead ninety minutes later after an exhaustive resuscitation attempt by the staff in the emergency department.

Mandy had taken every pill.

Dealing with mental health patients can be challenging. You have to be respectful but always keep a high degree of suspicion when pills are involved or suicidal ideations. My friend talks of this case when he teaches EMT's. In fairness, it was a difficult case; even a seasoned medic may have been led astray. There are some very convincing people out there.

I also had some powerful experiences while going through school. The ambulance rotations were the longest to complete. I had to have eighty hours of actual patient time. This translated into months and months of ambulance shifts.

One afternoon we received a call for a shooting victim. The dispatcher indicated the patient was a teenager and had been shot with a .22 in the right shoulder. He was conscious and breathing and police were on scene. As the paramedic student, my role was to observe as much as possible and participate where I could to help the medics. During those ambulance shifts, I looked like a Sherpa because I had to carry most of the equipment

On this day I was working with my paramedic mentor, Nick, and his partner Sheppard. Nick had been a paramedic for seven years and I was fortunate to be assigned under his tutelage. We arrived on scene and found two patrol cars at the residence. One of the officers met us at the front door and we followed him to the kitchen.

The patient's name is Scott and he's 17 years old. He's five foot seven inches tall and weighed about 145 pounds with dark hair and brown eyes. He's seated at the dining room table holding a small towel against his right shoulder. I will never forget meeting him.

"Scott, can you tell us what happened?" Nick asked.

When Scott answered he did so with very subtle clues about his condition.

"My friend Jason…accidentally shot me," he said.

"Well, we need to take you to the hospital; can you tell us where you hurt?" Nick asked.

"My shoulder…my chest is burning a little…it's a kind of hard to breathe," he said softly and nearly inaudibly.

Nick pulled the towel away from the shoulder. There's a very small hole between the clavicle (collar bone) and the humerus (upper arm bone) and just a trickle of blood.

He looked at the back and surrounding regions of the chest and said, "Looks like it's still in there, no exit wound I can see."

With a hint of urgency and concern in his voice he said, "Mark, go ahead and get a dressing on that wound and we need to go."

I applied a 4 inch by 4 inch occlusive gauze over the wound and taped it. We had Scott on the stretcher and in the ambulance after a five minute scene time. We're transporting him code three, lights and siren. I started him on oxygen through a face mask and Nick was starting an IV on the left arm.

What I noticed next would stay with me forever.

Scott's lips changed color, or "*lost their color.*" They're now candle wax-looking and nearly translucent. He also has small beads of sweat formed on his forehead. He's breathing faster and his heart rate has increased from 100 on the scene to 126 per minute now.

Nick asked me to check the blood pressure. I felt a distinctive fear in the pit of my stomach as I seen the numbers…64/36, "*We're losing Scott.*"

Two minutes later he went unconscious. He became a ghostly pale color, cool and clammy. Nick quickly intubated him and had me start providing breaths with the bag valve.

We both looked at the EKG at the same time to watch the final beat of Scott's life go across the screen and then flat line.

Nick looked at me with urgency and said, "Start compressions Mark. Let's go!"

We continued this effort for four minutes until we arrived at the hospital. There were an army of people working, the pace was blurring, a controlled chaos. The emergency physician was joined by a trauma surgeon who opened Scott's chest and tried in vain to clamp the damaged areas. After forty seven minutes of this heroic and aggressive resuscitation attempt, Scott was declared dead.

This was an incredibly graphic experience for me; from listening to Scott tell us what happened to seeing him dead on the E.D. gurney.

Nick arranged for us to attend the autopsy, which I really wasn't sure if I wanted to see. I'm glad I did because it gave some closure to the terrible tragedy. Scott's fate was sealed from the time he was shot.

The bullet entered through the right upper chest, ricocheted off the first rib and travelled through a pulmonary artery and went through part of the left ventricle of the heart. It continued on going through the liver and lodged just above the bladder. The destruction was devastating and obviously fatal.

To this day Scott's presentation follows me on trauma calls. When I see subtle signs such as a slight increase in breathing, small beads of sweat over the brows, the ever so slight changes in lip color, red flags go up like fireworks.

Scott's friend Jason was not charged with the death. The investigation revealed it was a terrible set of circumstances and both families agreed with the findings. Scott and Jason had been lifelong friends since before first grade.

Nick gave me a very good foundation to build my style as a paramedic. The year in school can be very overwhelming. It's a lot of information and practical experiences that hopefully starts you in the right direction.

I was just about three quarters of the way through my ambulance internship and Nick was letting me be more involved in actually running the calls with him at my side. One morning we were dispatched to an attempted suicide. A female had been found in a car running inside a garage. She was alive and that was all we knew.

Nick looked back at me sitting in the jump seat and said, "Mark, you want to run this one?"

Before I could even think about it I said, "Sure, no problem."

We arrived and parked next to two sheriff's deputy patrol cars. The garage door was raised and the car in the garage had the driver's door open. The deputies and mother were kneeling in a semi-circle around a patient lying on the grass in front of the house and they're waving us to their location.

The patient was a 15 year old girl named Sara. Her mother worked the nightshift at a local Convalescent Home. She came home and found a note Sara left indicating she was going to kill herself. She found the car running in the closed garage as described in the note. She raised the garage door but couldn't gain entry to the vehicle as the car doors were locked. There was also a hose going from the exhaust pipe to driver's window rolled up tightly holding it in place. Sara had gone to great lengths to ensure her wishes.

The mother called 9-1-1 and one of the deputies went into the garage. He busted the car window and they were able to get Sara out of the car and out onto the front lawn. As we walked up to Sara, the first thing I noticed was how young she looked, and almost peaceful. She didn't seem to be in pain or any distress. She was maybe five feet, around 90 pounds, blonde hair at the shoulders. She wore a small black tee shirt, white shorts and no shoes.

I was also surprised at how pink her skin looked. This is an effect of carbon monoxide poisoning. The skin can become almost cherry red. It's a dangerous and misleading appearance as the carbon monoxide will replace the oxygen in the cells with deadly results.

She's unresponsive to voice or a tap to the shoulder. Sheppard immediately put a mask over her face with high flow oxygen. Nick was hooking the EKG monitor up and looking at the rhythm when Sara suddenly arched her back, briefly convulsed and then went into ventricular fibrillation.

Nick charged the monitor to 200 watts and shocked her. I quickly started CPR and Sheppard was providing breaths with the BVM.

Nick put an IV into her left arm and administered epinephrine. After two minutes we stopped to look at the rhythm, still V-fib. We shocked her with 300 watts, she arched and then back to compressions.

Nick then asked one of the deputies' to switch with me on the compressions and then said, "Mark, get her intubated."

This would be my first intubation in the field and under tremendous stress. All of my previous intubations had been in a controlled environment, in the O.R. with an anesthesiologist standing right there guiding me. I got everything set up and was ready. I used the large curved blade, placing it gently down Sara's throat and within an instant there was the epiglottis and then the vocal cords. Sheppard handed me the tube and I slid it in like I did it every day. As pleased as I was at the moment, my mind immediately went back to trying to figure out what we were going to do to get Sara back to life.

We worked relentlessly and continued these efforts throughout the transport. We arrived at the hospital where the exhaustive attempts to save Sara went on for forty five minutes. I stayed in the room the entire time. One of the hospital security guards and I were trading out on chest compressions.

My heart sank when the physician spoke up and said, "Folks, unless anyone has any suggestions, we're going to stop the resuscitation."

You could have heard a pin drop. I looked at Sara and stared at her lifeless expression for several moments.

I felt a hand on my shoulder, it was the physician's. He said, "You did a great job there my friend, great job on the intubation and your compressions were perfect…it's never easy when you can't get them back…"

I knew on that day that I would be okay as a paramedic.

CHAPTER 5

FLYING SOLO

It's such an accomplishment to complete paramedic training. What it doesn't do is give you that magic potion to know everything and do everything you're capable of doing for some time. In fact, I ended up having a lot of the same feelings I did when finishing the EMT training: "Did I learn everything I was supposed to?"

I had to trust all of that information is up there (hopefully) and with patience it'll come together and make me the paramedic I know I can be. It'll be a lifetime of learning and I will learn something new almost every shift.

After finishing paramedic training, it was good to get back to being around the station with Joe and Brandon and Steve and Eric and Sam. They were very congratulatory and I was very appreciative of their confidence and support they had given me.

I finished the program just in time as District 4 had been planning to expand coverage due to an increasing call volume. The plan was to hire another paramedic and put a second ambulance into the system. I was offered this position after going through a rigorous testing and grueling interview process and became the proudest and newest paramedic hire at District 4.

The new ambulance would be known as Medic 42.

My new partner is Jim Rocha. We call him Rocky. He's 26 years old and a seasoned EMT. He's been working at another station in the district for the last five years. When he heard we were planning to put the second ambulance in service, he applied and the rest is history.

Rocky is married to Rachel, a nurse in the emergency department at RGH. They have three dogs they call their kids--Hank, a black lab; Abby, a black and white springer spaniel / lab mix and Kelsey, a golden retriever.

Rocky and I were excited to be part of the new staffing. With our ambulance ready and me as a brand new paramedic, the tones went off for my very first call on my own, look out world!

"Medic 42, Rescue 41, respond code one for a fall victim at the Sunny View Retirement Villa, 108 Sparks Circle, possible head injury...time out 0900 hours."

We went en route and it took less than five minutes to arrive. We're greeted by one of the nurses' aides and led to room 16 where our patient had fallen. She's lying on the floor next to her bed with another aide holding a small bandage over the right eye.

Amazingly she smiled as we walked in and waved, almost as if we were only there to pay her a visit.

I knelt down beside her and said, "Hello, my name is Mark, I'm a paramedic and this is my crew. Can I ask what your name is?"

"Millie," she said, "And nice to meet you. I fell and bumped my head."

I nodded and said, "I noticed that," and then explained everything we needed to do and will take her to the hospital for a check by the doctor which she was happy to hear.

Rocky and Sam took over for the aide and assessed the laceration over the eye. It's a "crow's foot" laceration. It is called that because the laceration pattern resembles a crow's foot. It has stopped bleeding and they placed a sterile bandage over it and taped it in place.

She had no other injuries that we could find and the cause of the fall was a witnessed stumbling versus a dizzy episode or other severe complaint. Steve and Eric lifted her to the gurney and we made it to the ambulance without any problems.

In the ambulance I let her know I was going to start an IV in case we needed to give her any medications and she said that would be okay.

I decided not to hang an IV bag, but use a plastic plug which fits into the back of the IV and can still be used for injections. I chose the back of her right hand for the IV and placed it successfully on the first attempt. I inserted the plug and taped it. I then covered her up and sat back thinking I was going to be pretty good at this stuff.

We had the most pleasant conversation during the transport. I learned how she was a telephone operator back in the '30s and '40s and what a fascinating person she was. We arrived at RGH about ten minutes later and nothing had changed. Rocky and I wheeled her into the emergency department and got a room assignment to Suite 7. Rachel was working; she took my verbal report as we were pushing the stretchers together for the transfer.

I pulled Millie's blanket back so we could see what we were doing; we all stood aghast, staring at the basketball-size circle of blood all over the sheet and now dripping to the floor. The plastic plug from the IV had fallen out and blood had been oozing out of the IV for the last ten minutes.

Rachel handed me another plug which I immediately inserted into the back of the IV, "tightly" this time.

She then gave me a glare to which I had nothing to say other than, "Have a good day, see you later, take care, bye," and then walked out of the room. Rocky looked at me and was shaking his head whispering something about rookies.

The lesson learned here was to *never hide the IV under the covers, ever!*

Millie did fine despite my best efforts to bleed her out. She had her "crow's foot" laceration sutured and was sent back to Sunny View.

Rachel still pretends to check my IV's when I bring a patient to her and then offers a wry smile. The learning curve as a brand new paramedic is frightfully high. Every call challenges you because it's now a different person calling the shots--you. It's such a departure from when I was following the directions from Joe.

Over the next month we had several mental health calls where we had to stage due to weapons involved. As usual we'd get cancelled as the problem was defused by police.

We went out one afternoon for a subject that called 9-1-1 and said he was going to shoot himself and was also reportedly quite intoxicated. The police learned he did have a weapon, a shotgun, and this prompted us to stage a couple of blocks from the scene.

We were staged for almost thirty minutes when the silence broke with the chilling dispatch.

"Medic 42, Rescue 41, respond to the scene, the subject has shot himself, police are requesting an immediate response, time out 1245 hours."

We were on scene within thirty seconds. One of the officers came out of the front door and waved at us with a sense of urgency. I grabbed the airway kit, Rocky grabbed the main kit, Sam has the oxygen and Eric has the LifePak 12, Steve was pulling the gurney and will be right behind us.

Walking into the house was like walking into a hellish nightmare. The air is pungent with a thick bluish haze of gun smoke. There's a large hole in the ceiling and the walls are covered with a red splattering.

The patient is lying face down. An officer is holding him by the back of his hair. There's a pool of blood at least twelve inches in diameter and two inches deep with thick clumps of tissue and bone on the carpet in front of the patient's face.

The officer looked at me with deep concern in his voice and said, "Before you look, he's still alive."

I thought, *"Okay, maybe a severe nose or mouth injury…"*

The patient placed the shotgun under his chin and as he reached for the trigger he leaned forward, this caused the blast to blow off his *entire* face from the jaw, the nose, the cheekbones, the eyes and up through the forehead. He has a large cavity where his face *used* to be.

Then it became even more shocking when he reached up with his right hand and probed where his face used to be. He's fully conscious and alert.

I said, "Eric, Sam, trauma dressings, now!"

There's a portion of the face still attached and hanging off to the right. Part of the nose and cheek are with it. Eric gently placed it back where it looked like it fit and encircled it with the large trauma dressing. This stemmed the flow of blood and the patient is managing his airway by remaining on his stomach.

Steve turned towards the door and said, "I'll grab the back board" and I quickly followed with, "No…no back board; we're going to keep him in the position he's in.

He has an airway in this position."

Steve nodded affirmatively and said, "Roger that."

When I was going through paramedic school, our medical director came into the class on day one and without saying anything, wrote these words on the board…"PRIMUM NON NOCERE"…which is Latin and part of the physician's Hippocratic Oath…it means "FIRST, DO NO HARM"….in other words, do what's best for your patient. It may not fit the rules; it's called making tough choices.

Transporting him on his stomach may not have been the most appropriate, but I believe we would have encountered significant airway issues if we were to lay him flat on his back. Gravity would be the main factor in keeping his airway clear of secretions. Sam's providing oxygen by holding a mask next to the hole near where his mouth used to be.

As we were moving him to the ambulance I asked one of the officers to alert RGH through dispatch and request a trauma team standing by. He was talking into his radio as we continued on.

The transport to RGH was as it was on scene, the patient kept his airway open without assistance. Sam hooked up the LifePak 12 and the numbers were surprising considering the horrific presentation, blood pressure 100/88, SpO2 96%, heart rate 116.

The alcohol aroma in the back of the ambulance was a constant reminder of how this all began.

I put rubber tourniquets on both upper arms and would use the first vein that popped up. I noticed a large one on the right mid arm. After getting the 14 gauge into it and the IV line secured, Eric checked the sugar which the glucometer displayed as 99.

Sam got close to the patients right ear and told him everything we were doing. She then asked him to "squeeze her fingers" if he understood. He immediately complied. She told him he would be hearing a lot of activity once we arrived at the hospital and that someone would be near him at all times. He squeezed her fingers again and held on this time.

We had several nurses and one of the physicians meet us on arrival to RGH. He spent two hours in the O.R. and will spend the rest of his life dealing with the action of a split-second decision.

He was transferred out of the county shortly after the initial surgery and there has not been any update on how he ended up.

His presentation left a significant impact on all of us. To see a person with an injury this significant regardless of the cause is difficult to make sense of. It creates an emotional and empathetic scar we will always carry.

His alcohol level was .28. A large percentage of our violent calls and suicidal calls have this common denominator, alcohol.

EMS generates a lot of paperwork for each call. The patient care report form is a permanent record of what you did for your patient. Report writing is a skill and it's something that evolves throughout your career. There is a saying in EMS, "if it isn't written, it wasn't done." Documentation can make you look very silly or be complementary of your excellent patient care.

I had a habit of using the word *"appears"* in my charts. This was all changed one day by Dr. Stein in the E.D. He is one of our pre-hospital medical advisors and reviews our charts. We'd brought a patient into the emergency department and transferred patient care to one of the nurses when he called me over to his desk.

"Hey Mark, how's it going?" He asked with a sly grin and obvious agenda.

"Okay…I think," was my suspicious and less than positive reply.

He then explained the query, "I was reading some of your charts and came across one that said *"patient appears to be very short of breath,"* was she?"

He handed me the chart and patiently watched as I squirmed while not only reading the chart but trying to formulate a brilliant response.

"Well yes, she had labored breathing, circumoral cyanosis (blueness around the lips), increased respiratory rate and shortened sentences when she spoke," I said trying to sound convincing.

This brought a large smile from him.

"Now why didn't you write that instead of *appears?*" He said, "The word appears means you don't know."

To this day I do not use that word in my charts…I write what I see. Rocky came over to join in on the conversation and was halted in his tracks by our station tones coming across his portable radio.

"Medic 42, Rescue 41, respond code three to Chuck's Family Restaurant for a seizure… 2036 Henley St…time out 1445 hours."

Chuck's was a family restaurant and catered to large parties and special events. It was always crowded and today would likely be no different. We arrived to find a man with a white shirt and tie out front to meet us. His name tag read "Jerry-Manager."

Rescue 41 was pulling in right behind us.

"Thanks for getting here so quick, we have a guy who took a pretty bad fall and had a seizure," the manager said after Rocky and I got out of the ambulance.

Sam and Eric were getting equipment when I asked him, "So did he fall first or have the seizure first?"

"Well, he's with a group here for a birthday party. They started cutting the cake when he suddenly screamed out, arched nearly totally backwards, and then went face-first into a table like a tree falling. When he hit the floor he was seizing which lasted a couple minutes, he's busted up pretty bad too," he said.

This was starting to sound worse and worse as he went on.

We went in and as anticipated the place was packed to capacity. The patient is lying face down in the middle of the room surrounded by a small crowd of curious onlookers. He's not moving and there are two ladies kneeling next to him.

I walked up and one of them said, "Hi there, this is Richard...he goes by Rich...he had a seizure...he hit his face something terrible on this table, and he's bleeding very badly...do you have a tissue?"

I said, "Well, thank you very much for staying with him. We're going to do some things and we'll take care of him."

I looked at Steve and motioned for him to hold cervical immobilization by putting my hands to the sides of my neck and he was immediately in position. Rich's head was turned to the left. There's bleeding from a laceration across his forehead. He has significant swelling around the left eye, an obvious broken nose, blood coming from the mouth and teeth embedded in the lower lip. He also has the familiar bite marks to the tongue and was incontinent of urine which are both common during a grand-mal seizure.

In this presentation it's critical we maintain cervical immobilization throughout the transport. This MOI (mechanism of injury) carries a high potential for a neck injury and any undue movement could put him in a wheelchair for the rest of his life.

Sam has small trauma dressings and is assessing the facial bleeding. Rocky has the long spine board ready and is standing by.

Rich was starting to wake up and now we had another problem.

After a seizure, it's common to experience disorientation. This is called the postictal phase of the seizure. During this period the patient doesn't understand what's happening and can be combative and incredibly difficult to manage. Rich is easily over six feet and every bit of 230 pounds.

He's now making serious attempts to get up by trying to get his legs under him and putting his hands forward.

I got close to his ear and said, "Rich, please don't move, you've had a seizure and we're taking care of you."

Steve was doing an excellent job at keeping Rich's head in line but it was getting tougher by the second. Eric and Sam and Rocky were now all trying their best to passively restrain Rich and this was getting out of control quickly. Rich is screaming and growling and grunting with all this and has managed to roll over, sit up, and is now trying to stand. His face looks like he was hit by a train; he's spitting blood and doesn't seem to be affected in the slightest by our attempts to control him. People around us are getting up and moving away, chairs are tipping over, kids are crying.

One lady screamed out, "For God's sake, just leave him alone...let him get up."

After several minutes of this, one of the young female waitresses came over to me and said, "Ah, there's a lady a couple tables over whose getting light headed from seeing all the blood. Can you come over and talk to her?"

My look to her obviously answered her request because she turned around slowly and walked off.

Steve managed to call on his radio to dispatch that we needed additional help. The request must have sounded urgent because within a minute there were four police officers walking through the door. They quickly came over and the lead officer thought we were fighting.

He asked me, "Do you want me to *taze* him?"

With a panicked look I said, "Oh no, please no…he's had a seizure and just out of it, we need to try to protect his neck."

With the additional help we managed to get Rich flat on his back and secured to the spine board. Eric was managing Rich's airway with occasional suctioning and Sam applied dressings to the bleeding facial lacerations. I got an IV started and gave him versed through the IV, which made him calm down considerably. Versed is a powerful muscle relaxant that worked great for this scenario.

Rocky called out the blood sugar, "124" he said.

Walking out of the restaurant we had looks of empathy, appreciation, scorn, shock, pretty much the whole gambit of expressions.

On the way to the hospital we were able to assess the injuries more closely. The large full thickness laceration went across the forehead from brow to brow. The left eye is completely swollen shut and the swelling around the orbit is deep and dark purple. His nose is grossly displaced to the left. The two top front teeth were knocked out and embedded through the lower lip. We're seeing good movement in all the extremities which is always a positive sign. Vitals were good, blood pressure at 146/94, heart rate 106 and the Sp02 is at 98%.

About twenty minutes after arriving at RGH, we went to Suite 6 to see Rich. He's a mess to look at. He looked at us through his open right eye and said, "Hi…did you guys bring me in?"

I said, "Yes we did. I'm Mark and this is Rocky. The other crew went back to the station."

"Thanks, I heard I was kind of out of it and hope I didn't hurt anyone," he said humbly.

Rocky and I looked at each other and smiled. Rich's cervical spine X-rays were clear. He has a left orbital fracture, broken nose, sutures to the forehead and jaw, and a date with the dentist. He was admitted for observation overnight and released the next day. They determined his seizure was caused by missing a couple of doses of his seizure medication.

Seizures can be very challenging to treat. Not only do we have the primary consideration for the cause of the seizure, but secondary injuries can be devastating as well.

CHAPTER 6

TOUGH DAYS

Taking the step from EMT to paramedic has been an incredible experience. I've had some challenging calls and got to make some critical decisions. This created an inherent anxiety as I thought I would ease into it with easy calls and graduate to the tougher ones. One thing about EMS is you don't choose your calls, they choose you. And no matter what you're dealt, you play the hand and make something good out of it.

Steve made a large pot of his award winning spaghetti for lunch which was just what we all needed. We are very fortunate to have Steve on our team. His cooking is in another category. We finished getting the kitchen back to some type of order when the tones had everyone headed for the truck bays.

"Medic 42, Rescue 41, respond code three for an unconscious male in the bathroom…457 Daniel Street…time out 1305 hours."

As Rocky is navigating us through the sea of traffic, I'm trying to form a "battle plan" and had thoughts of an elderly person, maybe a heart attack and collapsed in the bathroom, how long they been down, who found them, and on and on.

Dispatch interrupted this train of thought with an update, "Medic 42, Rescue 41, police on scene advising possible overdose, CPR in progress."

We arrived four minutes later. After grabbing all of the equipment and walking through the front door, it was puzzling to see the patient on the floor in the middle of the living room with the officers kneeling next to him and nothing going on.

"We were told you guys were doing CPR? What happened?" I asked with curiosity.

One officer looked at me and said, "We got here and found him lying outside the bathroom and blue, we couldn't find a pulse. We dragged him here and after a few compressions, he started coming around and didn't like us pushing on his chest."

The patient is starting to get blue in the face again. Sam opened the airway kit and grabbed the BVM. She created a seal over the mouth and nose as Eric is squeezing the BVM. With a couple breaths the blueness is replaced with a more normal looking pink color.

The officer then told us, "His girlfriend called 9-1-1 and said he OD'd on heroin and was on the bathroom floor. She told the dispatcher she wasn't sticking around because she had a warrant for her arrest and there would be a couple kids left on scene that would need cared for."

They're both sitting on the couch side by side watching the drama play out, emotionless. The boy is about 4 years old and his sister about 3; they're dressed only in tee shirts and underwear.

The place doesn't look like somewhere you'd want kids being raised. There's a mountain of dirty dishes rising out of the sink, empty pizza boxes stacked seven high on the kitchen floor, a permeating stench of rotting food and trash and a cat darting throughout the house as if it's tail's on fire. This resembles a scene out of a movie, but it's very real and incredibly heart breaking.

Heroin is a devastating drug; users develop a strong addiction that's difficult to kick. We've responded to overdoses as young as 12 and as old as 70. There's no discrimination for the reaches of the drug and subsequent addiction--rich, poor, young and old. It has no boundaries. Heroin overdoses suppress the respiratory drive and if the patient isn't discovered quickly, they die.

I lift the patient's eyelids back and his pupils are constricted, pinpoint. This is a hallmark sign of narcotic influence, in this case heroin. They look like two periods in a sentence. There are also IV track marks up and down both arms and the backs of both hands.

He has no visible veins in the arms for IV access but I do notice a very large external jugular vein on the right side of his neck. I slide a 14 gauge catheter in and plug the IV tubing into the back of the IV. I then tape a safety loop in the IV tubing to his right shoulder. You never want to have an IV get pulled out after a difficult start, especially with this guy not having many sites to choose from.

Next was to prepare everyone for the magic antidote, narcan. Narcan is a narcotic antagonist which means it counteracts the effect of the heroin and usually wakes the overdosed person rather quickly. Sometimes they can be quite unhappy about having their high reversed and come up swinging. The last thing they remember is putting the needle in their arm, feeling the quick effects of the drug, now they're surrounded by cops and medics. Another side effect can be vomiting after the administration. This can be minimized by administering it slowly.

When I was going through paramedic school, one of the instructors told us about a heroin overdose patient they were treating. They gave narcan and the guy woke up with a nasty disposition, fought through three police officers and four EMS crew members before bolting out the front door. He was eventually found on the next block, hiding in a doghouse. The home owners couldn't figure out why their dog refused to go in his doghouse until they realized it was occupied by a new tenant, the patient.

Rocky drew the narcan up and handed me the syringe. Everyone is in position in case the patient gets combative or vomits. I slowly push the contents of the syringe and within seconds the patient opens his eyes, looks around as if he's waking from a bad dream and says, "What's going on?"

I tell him to relax and that we are taking care of him, and we think he may have overdosed. He responds with the classic line, "Sir, I didn't do any drugs."

I ask about the needle marks on both arms which he looks at as if he's never seen them before and responds with, "Dude, I didn't put those there."

I then tell him not to move around too much because he has a very large IV in his neck. He cautiously tries to look at it and responds with, "Dude, I didn't put that there either."

I said, "Well, you're correct on that one, I did."

I informed him we need to take him to RGH for evaluation and he pleads he's okay and doesn't need to go. This isn't an option because the narcan will not last as long as the heroin. This means he could end up unconscious again and die if no one was around to help. The officers told him he had the choice of jail or the hospital, he chose the hospital. The transport was uneventful. He spent several hours in the E.D. before being discharged.

The children were placed under temporary custody of Child Protective Services.

We got back to the station a little after 1500 hours. Sandy was standing in the truck bay holding some type of pamphlet and seemed very pleased to see us.

"You have that look like we're just in time for something," I said.

"Oh, you are indeed, I have a couple of members from a local citizens group that would like to interview you and Rocky for their monthly news magazine," she replied with a sly grin.

We either weren't supposed to do the interview or it was just bad timing. The tones took care of any further conversation, I smiled at her and waved as Rocky and I got back into the ambulance.

"Medic 42, Rescue 41, respond for a gunshot victim, 1529 31st Place… time out 1507 hours."

It'll take us three minutes to arrive. Dispatch advises we can respond in; the patient is conscious and breathing.

Upon entering the residence, there are two police officers standing next to a tall skinny mirror that is leaning against a wall and a large hand gun on the floor in front of it.

It looks like there's a bullet hole in the hard wood floor in front of the mirror and small puddle of blood surrounding it. Both officers have note pads out and are busy writing in them. The ubiquitous smell of gun smoke is unmistakable.

We can hear moans and cries of pain coming from the bathroom. As we walk down the hall, there are two more officers standing outside the bathroom who make way for us. One of them points in the bathroom and says, "This is Daniel, he's 40 years old."

Daniel is sitting on the edge of the bath tub with his right foot inside the tub where there's a large pool of blood surrounding it. He has a GSW (gunshot wound) to his right foot. The bullet went through the top of the foot and exited through the bottom. The entry hole is about the size of quarter and the exit wound is just a little bigger. The bleeding is moderate and he's in some intensive pain which I am not surprised about.

"Hello," I said, "My name is Mark. I am a paramedic and we're going to help you…how did this happen?"

He looked at me with obvious disgust and said, "It was a stupid accident, end of story."

I said, "Okay, well, we should get you to Regional and get that looked at."

"Do we have to go there?" He asked.

I said, "Well, it is the closest and it's a fully capable trauma center."

He looked down at his foot and nodded.

Sam and Eric did their usual excellent job dressing and splinting the foot. We have two injuries to treat here, one being the GSW and the other being the potential fractures of the bones in the foot. They shaped a cardboard splint to the foot with thick padding and small pressure dressings to both entrance and exit wounds.

On the way to RGH I placed a 16 gauge IV in the back of Daniel's left hand and plugged in a bag of normal saline. He consented to my offer of pain medication and I started with 4 mg of morphine and increments of 2 mg every few minutes. After ten minutes and 10 mg of morphine he became a bit more relaxed.

The picture got a bit clearer after I asked him what kind of work he does.

He looked at me with a humiliated glare and said, "I am cop. I'm the county gun safety instructor and defensive driving instructor."

We stared at each other in an awkward silence. I didn't know what to say to that one. Then it got worse when he admitted he was practicing a quick draw technique with his *"unloaded 40 cal."* This wasn't bad luck, this was NO luck. I was glad to arrive at RGH.

Daniel was off with the surgeons and after an overnight stay at RGH, went home to recover. He was expected to make a complete recovery, at least physically.

We got back to the station after 1700 hours, the day flew by. Sandy left and we didn't have any idea about the status of the citizen's group interview, hopefully Joe took care of it. We got the rig restocked; paperwork completed.

Last month we cleared out one of the offices used as storage and created a small workout area. We now have a station gym. We got a tread mill, some free weights and tried to use it every shift.

We wouldn't need the workout today.

The tones went off as Rocky and I looked at each other with shrugged shoulders and started walking toward the ambulance. Steve, Eric and Sam right behind us.

"Medic 42, Rescue 41, respond code three for a male subject and possible heart attack, he is unconscious and family is attempting CPR, 3705 Magnolia Street...time out 1710 hours."

We went en route and Rocky said the address sounded familiar. He thought he'd been there before and hoped he was wrong.

I asked him why and he said, "You don't want to know."

Nothing good ever comes out of that statement.

A few moments later dispatch updated us, "Medic 42, Rescue 41, family members are unable to get the patient on the floor, they're advising the front door is open and they're in a back bedroom."

Rocky frowned upon hearing this additional information and said, "Oh boy, call for additional help, trust me."

I did as Rocky recommended and we arrived three minutes later. Engine 61 would be dispatched as mutual aid from the neighboring county; ETA would be nine minutes.

The front door was open as advised; we walked down a short hallway to the back bedroom. The sister and a caregiver were frantically trying to do CPR with the patient in bed.

The shock of this scenario was difficult to take in and almost overwhelming. The patient weighs over 625 pounds. He covered the entire queen sized bed. His eyes are half open, his face is a terrible deep blue color and there are piles of vomit around his mouth and neck.

The caregiver yelled out, "He was eating dinner and started turning blue, please help us, he's only 26."

We had to come up with a plan, and fast. We decided to roll him off of the bed to the floor. Steve and Rocky and Eric started rolling and pushing him to the left side of the bed. There was no way to control him going to the floor but we had no other immediate options.

He ended up falling heavily on his stomach which served as an unintended but successful abdominal thrust expelling a half-eaten roast sandwich.

We immediately removed the mattress, box spring and frame from the room. We then rolled this massive patient onto his back where Sam began compressions.

Steve and Eric had to clear the mouth of the remaining food and vomit before they could provide ventilations with the BVM.

Sam and Eric switched after every thirty compressions due to fatigue. They literally had to stand next to the patient in order to compress his chest. Kneeling next to him was not going to be an option. His chest is above the level of Sam's knees!

Rocky managed the LifePak 12 and applied the combo-pads to the chest. One on the right upper chest and one on the left lower chest: they looked like pediatric patches on his enormous chest.

After two minutes of CPR we checked the rhythm. It's V-fib. Rocky charged the LifePak and delivered a maximum shock without the resulting jump we were more accustomed to seeing at this wattage. Eric was next up on compressions.

I had just enough room on the floor to get the laryngoscope blade into his mouth and immediately encountered a nightmare view of more un-chewed food, blood, and vomit. The suction unit is operating at full speed and barely able to keep up. After roughly twenty seconds I had most of it clear but now had to withdraw and re-oxygenate his tissues.

It was time for another rhythm check, still V-fib. Rocky gave another maximum shock and Sam took over on CPR. For the second intubation attempt I have a clearer view. I need Eric to press and hold the front of the throat while I passed the tube. His large neck and tissues in the back of the throat prevented a clear view without the external manipulation.

Steve is now providing ventilations with the bag valve. The chest is so massive I cannot see it rise after each squeeze of the bag. I can hear air going in with my stethoscope over the front of the chest.

We can hear voices calling out and realized it was the Engine 61 guys with a crew of four. They were a welcome sight. Their captain is Willie Neeves. I asked him and his engine driver Russell to start planning an exit for us and leave the other two guys to help Eric and Sam on compressions.

"You got it sir," he said and then quickly left the room.

After another two minutes the rhythm was still V-fib: Rocky delivered the third maximum shock followed by the continued marathon of compressions.

This time after sixty seconds of CPR, one of the Engine 61 guys said, "Hey, he's moving his arm."

Sam then pointed and said, "Look at his neck!"

We can see a strong pulse pounding at the left carotid artery.

I put an 'X' over the carotid artery. Steve is continuing to ventilate every six seconds with the bag valve.

We don't have a blood pressure cuff large enough to go over his upper arm. I attached it to the lower arm above the wrist. This wouldn't be as accurate; however, it would give me a ballpark number.

164/110 is the reading, heart rate 110; oxygen saturation levels of 90%. This was promising; now how long would all of this last?

I placed an 18 gauge IV in his left wrist as Sam looked down at the glucometer and called out, "Sugar at 164."

Captain Neeves then came into the room and his look said it all.

"We aren't going through the front door. He won't fit. If we do we'll need another twenty-four inches, minimum, and the back door's the same," he said.

The sister and caretaker were behind Captain Neeves with pleading looks and asked how he was doing.

I said, "We have his heart started again, he's still very critical and we're doing everything we can."

I then explained our dilemma, "We're having some trouble trying to get him out of here; we may have to cut the door."

The sister said, "Do whatever you have to, just help him."

Captain Neeves looked at me and said, "We have the chain saw; we'll get to work."

"Roger that," I said.

Rocky and Eric fastened two spine boards side by side and with great physical difficulty, we managed to roll the patient and get the boards underneath him. You couldn't see any part of the boards beneath him. Now another major problem, the bedroom door opening wasn't wide enough to get through.

Captain Neeves hadn't started cutting the front door yet when Steve gave him the news. The new plan was to cut an opening in the bedroom wall, pull the ambulance around the side of the house and in theory load straight into the back of it.

The Engine 61 crew shut the power off to the house and then began cautiously cutting the outside wall. Within several minutes there was an opening we felt we could get the patient through. Rocky positioned the ambulance outside the bedroom wall.

The move required a near-herculean effort but we got him through the wall opening and onto the ambulance floor. Everyone wore exhausted yet determined looks. Neighbors stood outside on their porches watching the drama unfold. It wasn't often the side of the house had to be cut open and used as a door.

A quick reassessment showed we still had the strong carotid pulse. The pupils are equal and reactive and he's starting to take some breaths on his own. The blood pressure at the wrist is 160/100, heart rate is 116 and the Sp02 is 92%. We're going in the right direction.

We're off to RGH with everyone kneeling on the floor. Sam's managing the bag valve, Eric is monitoring the EKG, and I'm amazed we pulled this off. I radioed ahead to RGH and requested they meet us with the largest gurney in the hospital. That was met with silence and then a curious sounding, "10-4."

The total on-scene time was eighty three minutes. The patient was admitted the CCU and nothing short of a miracle to have no damage to his heart or brain. It was determined his arrest was secondary to a fully obstructed airway and subsequent asphyxiation.

The next day Rocky and I went to the CCU to check up on Harold, our patient. He was awake, slightly reclined in bed, and smiled as we walked in.

The first thing he said was, "Did you guys bring my glasses to the hospital yesterday?"

Rocky looked at me as we both chuckled and I said, "No, we must have left them at the house, sorry."

Back at the station I made a call to Captain Neeves.

"Thanks for coming over and saving the day. We couldn't have pulled that off without you," I said.

His reply was gracious and humbling, "Anytime for you guys, one of these days we'll be calling you to come save us, so we're happy to be of service....have you heard anything on how he's doing?"

I said, "Yeah, he's a little upset we forgot his glasses at the house; other than that, pretty well."

Captain Neeves chuckled and said, "I guess we'll consider that a win."

It's the first of the month and a busy time around the station. We have drugs to check for expiration dates, inventories to update, major cleaning projects and vehicle inspections. Of course, calls take precedence and sometimes keep us away from the station the entire day. We've had shifts where you hit the ground running and never make it back to the station till late in the night. You run from call to call and fit food and paperwork in where you can.

Today was one of those days. Our last call was for a 62 year old male with severe chest pain. His name is Walt and we transported him with a heart attack three months ago.

We got to Walt's house and Sam asked him if he was currently taking any medications. He handed her a shoebox full of medications for numerous medical issues, high blood pressure, emphysema, diabetes, high cholesterol, gout, digestion issues, blood thinners, kidney stones and of course *Viagra*.

I then asked him to describe the pain for me he said, "Well, you remember when you took me in last time, well now it's worse."

When a patient says something like that, it better raise a red flag. His EKG confirmed was he was having his second heart attack, right in front of us. He then asked me what the EKG looked like.

I said, "Well, it shows a couple of changes and…"

He interrupted and said, "Don't BS me…just tell me…"

I said, "Well, remember the way it was last time we saw you, it's just as bad."

"Great," he said, "Just lovely!"

We were getting ready to leave the house and he pleaded with me to let him have a smoke.

He said, "C'mon man, they won't let me have one once we get to the hospital, please…" Needless to say he wasn't happy with me for not granting the request.

Walt spent very little time in the emergency department. He was almost a direct admit to the coronary cath lab. Two stents later and after being admitted to the CCU (Coronary Care Unit), he was still moaning and griping about not having a cigarette.

Stents are small mesh devices that open blocked coronary arteries and restore blood flow and basically stop the heart attack from causing permanent damage. Time is the key, getting someone to the hospital as quick as possible is the goal. Our mantra in the pre-hospital arena is "time is muscle."

CHAPTER 7

SAM'S BIRTHDAY

Eric and Steve were discussing Sam turning 24 next week, on the 13th. They suggested we have a surprise party here at the station and then Steve touched on the fact that the 13th was Friday and it was bound to be "*one of those days.*"

Sammy was born and raised here. She has an apartment she shares with her cat Boots. She's an avid gun enthusiast and recently took first place in her division and second place overall at a regional shooting competition with fifty of the area's top shooters. This wasn't unusual for Sam as she's well-known at the local range and rarely bested.

We had a "top secret meeting" with Sandy and Rocky to put a plan in to action. Rocky would have Rachel invite E.D. staff and Sandy would take care of the decorations, food and cake.

Friday the 13th came upon us and Sam didn't show up for shift. She came in thirty minutes late due to a power failure in her neighborhood sometime during the night.

"This is a great way to start the day," she said and it went downhill from there with the first tones of the day and a startling dispatch.

"Medic 42, Rescue 41, respond code three for a female that has been run over at the First Savings Bank, 1111 Main Street, low cross of Broadway…time out 0833 hours."

We went en route quickly and were on scene within four minutes. Several bystanders were waving us to the drive-through section of the bank.

A bystander and eye witness told us this 20 year old female dropped her bank card while trying to initiate a transaction at the drive up ATM. She pulled ahead and instead of parking and getting out of the vehicle, she noticed the card ended up in the middle of the lane and decided to back up with the door open.

As she leaned out to look where she was going, she fell out of the small truck ending up in the path of the left front tire which narrowly missed her head as it rolled along the left side of her neck, down her chest and abdomen and then pelvis.

We find her conscious and working extremely hard to get a breath in. An impressive part of all this was the tire track along her body. You could follow where the truck rolled over her.

Sam quickly had oxygen flowing by mask over her nose and mouth.

A quick assessment reveals she has no air movement on the left side of her chest and "rice crispies."

This finding was due to a pneumothorax (collapsed lung) and air that has escaped from the lung is now trapped in the skin tissues and feels like *rice crispies* as you palpate or press over the chest, an ominous presentation. Her color is also terrible with ashen colored face and blue lips.

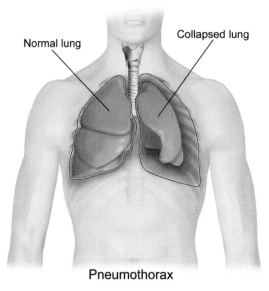

Normal lung

Collapsed lung

Pneumothorax

She not only has the pneumothorax, but has developed a tension pneumothorax. This is collapsed lung that has trapped air in the chest cavity and creating pressure like a balloon making it nearly impossible to breathe and severely restricting blood flow back to the heart. This is considered an immediate life threat and something you can die from very quickly.

I told Rocky to hand me the "big needle." It's a 12 gauge 3-inch long needle and would be inserted into the chest to relieve the pressure and save her life. Rocky and I had discussed treating a tension pneumothorax and agreed we would call it the "big needle." This needle is so big that you could use it to sip a milkshake if you didn't have a straw, almost.

I cut her shirt to expose the chest leaving the bra intact; we have the public watching and try to protect dignity where possible. I located the 2nd intercostal space (between the upper ribs) and in-line with the mid-clavicle (collar bone) and got down to her ear and said, "I am very sorry, this may hurt a bit but it'll save your life," she blinked at me with a frightened look.

I pushed the large needle through the skin, which was tougher than I thought it would be. This was the first time ever doing this procedure on a real person. The needle penetrated the chest as she winced at the pain, followed by the rush of air that seemed to go on for thirty seconds.

The immediate relieved look on her face said it all and with the faintest whisper said, "Thank you."

I nodded and said, "Excellent, let's get you to the hospital now."

Eric and Sam and Steve got her secured to the long spine board and we were in the ambulance after a five minute scene time. The transport to RGH would take four minutes. I still had some work to do in this short amount of time.

She is remaining conscious and very alert. I still cannot hear lung sounds on that left side but she is breathing easier. The chest and abdomen are heavily bruised with the tire imprint becoming more pronounced. The pelvis is intact and heavily bruised. Her color is better in the fact that the blueness is gone but now she is cool, quite pale and clammy, in shock.

Eric had two IV bags ready to go as I was applying the rubber tourniquets to both of her upper arms. I found a vein in the left arm and put a 14 gauge in which she seemed to grimace at more than the 12 gauge-3 inch needle in the chest.

"Heart rate 126, blood pressure 84/54 and Sp02 at 92%," Eric called out.

"Roger that," I said. We need to get her to the surgeons at RGH. We have gone as far as we can go.

Pulling up to the emergency department entrance is always comforting when you have a critically injured patient. We know the trauma team was waiting and ready as we come walking through those doors.

Our patient's name is Tiffany. She had a chest tube put in on the left side and off to the O.R. After repairs to a ruptured spleen and bowel in the abdomen, she was admitted to the trauma ICU. She also has a non-displaced pelvic fracture and will not be driving for the next few months, but she's miraculously alive.

We also found out today is her birthday also, *Happy Birthday Tiffany.*

I wanted Rocky and Sam and Eric and Steve to be aware of several critical items we carried in case they were ever needed along with possible scenarios where these items would be used and individual roles to be filled.

One was the 12 gauge 3-inch long "big needle" used for relieving the tension pneumothorax which we used for Tiffany and had life-saving results.

Another rarely used item was the OB kit. This was something none of us wanted to use, and hoped it stayed in the cabinet. It really doesn't have anything needed to deliver a baby, some sterile drapes; clips to clamp the cord, a little stocking cap for the baby and it's more of a confidence booster but still, better left on the shelf.

When I was going through paramedic training I was riding third on the ambulance when the call came in for a female in labor and imminent delivery. We got to the scene and determined she was not crowning indicating we had time to transport. So we headed off to the hospital. We were about two minutes into the transport when she let out a wail as her water broke. The entire back of the ambulance was covered by this, the walls, the ceiling, everywhere! Then within thirty seconds a baby boy joyously came into the world. After arriving at the hospital and assessing the collateral damage to the back of the ambulance, it turned into an hour of cleaning. I made a mental note; do not deliver a baby in the back of the ambulance.

There's a story, probably an urban myth as there are many in EMS, that a crew somewhere in the US was faced with an imminent delivery, they pulled over to the shoulder, unloaded the gurney, delivered the baby outside, loaded everyone back up and drove off. Not sure if this is true or not, but I understand if it is.

Another of the critical items is the cricothyrotomy kit. This is a small compact kit I would use to create a surgical airway should I not be able to establish one through manual jaw manipulation, bag valve mask assist or endotracheal intubation. I would then move on to the surgical airway. This is very rarely used. In fact with good airway skills, a paramedic shouldn't have to ever use this option, although it is carried for a reason.

The other critical item is the burn sheets. These are large sterile sheets we use for large surface area burns. We cut as much clothing away as possible, place one burn sheet on the gurney, place the patient on that one, and then cover them with the second one. This is another one of those items we could go forever and never use, and be fine with that.

The last critical item is the 10 inch by 30 inch trauma dressing. When you have a patient that has a wound that is 10 inches by 30 inches, you have big problems. So obviously this dressing is not used too often, but when it is, it's needed very quickly.

I labeled these items as the "Extreme Event Items." We would talk about them often, and if they were ever needed, as they were today, we wouldn't have delays in remembering where they were located. Every morning during the vehicle inspection, these items were checked.

We finally got the morning rig checkout finished at 1030 and decided to wash the ambulance. It was washed every day and sometimes twice a day, depending on the weather. It was not that uncommon to get one side soaped up and get dispatched...then the mad dash to remove as much soap and get going.

The rest of the morning was slow with only one other call. At one of the local bakeries a pastry chef nearly severed her thumb while slicing a pineapple in half. (We hoped this wasn't where Sandy ordered Sam's cake.) The patient collapsed immediately after the incident and would pass out if there was any attempt to sit up or look at the injury. As long we kept her lying flat she was okay. Another successful outcome!

Before we left the hospital Rocky was visiting with Rachel as she was getting ready to leave the hospital. Her 12 hour shift was over and she wanted to get ready for Sam's party this afternoon. The visit didn't last long as our station tones came across the portable radio.

"Medic 42, Rescue 41, respond code three for stabbing victim, police are on scene requesting immediate medical response to the their location… 828 4th Avenue, the Qwik Stop Shop…time out 1230 hours."

I acknowledged the dispatch as Rocky said, "Hey, that's just a couple blocks from here."

I nodded affirmatively and said, "Roger that, we should be there directly."

Rescue 41 advised they were a minute out as we arriving on scene. There are three patrol cars parked in front of the store.

I got out and grabbed the main kit with Rocky on my heels and we're following a blood trail leading in to the store that doesn't look possible given the amount. It's at least a foot wide with deep puddles of thick clots.

Once inside, it's even more grisly as two officers are frantically trying to control bleeding on a male in his early twenties. He's bleeding profusely from the neck; despite them holding a large towel firmly against the left side of his neck, blood is spurting around it. They are kneeling in a pool of blood four feet in diameter and at least two inches deep. It's hard to believe the patient not only had blood left, but was still conscious.

One of the officers said the clerk called 9-1-1 after a car skidded to a stop in the parking lot in front of the store. The patient was pushed out of the vehicle as it sped off. He stumbled into the store with both hands holding his neck, blood spurting between his fingers and said, "Please help me."

Police units were on scene within a minute of the call and seconds later working feverishly trying to save his life.

I grabbed two 8 by 10 dressings and am ready to remove the towel the officers were using. I see a full thickness laceration four inches long and one inch wide from just below the left ear to the clavicle, and it's freely spurting blood with each heartbeat. I stuffed one of the dressings into the wound and folded the other in half pressing it against the first one. This stopped the flow for now.

I then took a large elastic bandage roll and started it over the dressings and then wrapped it across the chest and under the right arm pit and after several passes the bleeding is controlled.

I looked at the patient and he's staring at me, paralyzed with fear. I gave him half of a smile and said, "I'm going to take care of you, hang in there."

He blinked offering half a smile back unable to mask his obvious fear.

Steve and Eric and Sam walked through the door with gurney in tow.

I yelled to Steve, "Call RGH and get a team standing by. We'll be there in less than five with no further updates."

Steve nodded and said, "Roger that."

Eric took over ensuring the bandages were holding and Sam provided oxygen with a mask. We lifted him onto the gurney, and then quickly into the back of the ambulance.

Rocky shouted out, "Hang on, here we go."

I threw a rubber tourniquet on the patient's right arm and quickly set up an IV bag of normal saline. I couldn't believe what I saw, the biggest vein in the middle of the right arm. I put a 14 gauge into it and plugged the IV tubing into the back of it. This could be the difference between life and death for this guy.

He remained awake throughout the three minute transport. His color is terrible, ghostly pale, cool and clammy skin. He has no radial pulse which tells me his blood pressure is in the cellar and he is breathing over 40 breaths per minute, classic hypovolemic shock, no blood!

As we pulled into the RGH emergency entrance we could see police officers, security personnel and nurses in trauma gowns--we had the cavalry waiting. The doors were opening almost before we stopped and the two security guards briefly paused with shocked looks at the gruesome sight and amount of blood.

"Suite 12!" I heard someone yell out, and we were flying in there. There are two trauma surgeons in the E.D. and they took over for Eric before we even had the patient off our gurney.

"What size IV you got in there?" The first surgeon asked.

"A 14 gauge and that's the only site we had," was my reply.

"Great," he said, "Let's get him to the O.R.," and off they went.

Rocky and I stood there watching them head across the hallway.

"What just happened over the last nine minutes?" Rocky mused aloud.

I looked at him and said, "I'm not sure but I think we just had a call. I also think we may have just saved that guy."

"Very cool," was Rocky's response.

It took us nearly an hour cleaning the ambulance. Steve, Eric and Sam stayed at the E.D. and helped out. We really appreciated this, as every time we thought we were done cleaning, we would find more blood.

We got back to the station and Sandy told us the E.D. wanted us to call them. I called and spoke to Brenda. She is the emergency department and trauma nurse supervisor. She wanted to give us the update that the patient made it through surgery. He had repairs to the left carotid and jugular and part of the subclavian artery. He had his entire circulating volume replaced six times during the surgery.

She also said he was awake in the ICU. He had been interviewed by the detectives and didn't know the people in the car or why they stabbed him and didn't think he could recognize them. He also had no desire to look at police photos. Guess it's just one of those things that happen to some people on some days.

We now had some major restocking to do. We have enough supplies to run several calls back to back but Rocky will take advantage and restock when the opportunity arises. We also happened to notice the training room door was suspiciously covered with yellow caution tape and a sign that said "Keep Out."

Sandy was very evasive about answering any questions and said that it should be ready for use by 1600 hours followed by a sly grin and a wink. We had forty-five minutes to wait.

Rocky and I went out to the ambulance and were joined by Steve, Sam and Eric. We discussed the stabbing call and all conceded to the intensity of it. We talked about how we never got a chance to take a blood pressure, or look at an EKG tracing, and really none of it would have made any difference in our care or priorities.

I said, "You notice they didn't even take a blood pressure in Suite 12, they went straight to the O.R.--priorities."

We all felt good about the way things went and believed we would do it the same way again if we had a similar incident in the future.

Sandy's voice came over the intercom.

"Attention all station personnel, please report to the training room for a mandatory meeting," she announced.

We headed that way and "innocently" put Sam in the lead. We went through the door and the lights were out. Once we made it in a few steps the lights came on with a room full of people. Sandy, Rachel and several others from the E.D. yelled out and started singing, *"Happy Birthday to you, Happy Birthday to you, Happy Birthday dear Sa-am, Happy Birthday to you,"* and then applause and clapping. This was perfect!

Sam looked around the room sporting the biggest grin along with some rosy red cheeks. Everyone's smiling and lined up for the "bro hug." Sandy had done an awesome job: the decorations and balloons, the cake was an incredible triple layer red-white and blue design with twenty-four candles lit up. (We're lucky we didn't burn the station down!)

Rachel brought the kids and they were the life of the party. In fact they thought the party *was* for them. Hank was offering "kisses" for anyone that would take one. Abby thought it was her job to "shake" the hand of everyone there, and Kelsey was making sure anything that was dropped was immediately "cleaned up."

This was just what we needed after today, Friday the 13th…Happy Birthday, Sam.

CHAPTER 8

STREET SIGNS

One of the appealing aspects of working in the Emergency Medical Services system is that you never know what your next call will be. It's truly like having a new job every time you come to work.

Rocky and I have gone almost two weeks without any critical patient's and in fact, the most serious run we had was this morning, a little girl at the Middle School with a fractured lower arm as the result of a fall with an outstretched arm. When we arrived she was sitting in a chair in the school nurse's office. The left arm looked like the letter 'S' just above the wrist.

Rocky whispered to me, "How are we going to figure out which arm it is?"

"Maybe it's the one that looks like a snake?" I said.

We transported her to RGH where she was outfitted with a nice pink cast and discharged home to recover.

On the way back from the hospital Rocky and I thought we were following our next call. We witnessed a very shocking display of serious road rage. The vehicle in front of us is tail gaiting the vehicle in front of him with an inch of space between them. The aggressor driver is incredibly agitated and can be seen screaming and quite animated with "hand gestures." The driver in front of him is in a near panicked state and finally pulled over and stopped. The angry driver drove by him at a snail's pace with a death glare before speeding off.

Now we're behind a younger female who was driving 30 mph and the posted speed limit is 45 mph. She had a cell phone to her ear and oblivious to the rest of the world. We had a line of at least eight cars behind us. It's almost comical, except to the drivers behind us. That's when the tones went off and Rocky and I both of grinned because we would get to go around her.

"Medic 42, Rescue 41, respond code three to SR 3 and Wyatt Loop, motorcycle rider down, possible fatality…time out 1535 hours."

Rocky flipped on the lights and hit the siren; the poor gal threw her hands up with her cell phone flying into the back seat, and then stopped right where she was. Rocky had to nearly lock the brakes but managed to go around her as we sped off.

It would take about seven minutes to arrive on scene; Rescue 41 would be on scene before us. We got an update from dispatch; a state trooper on scene is reporting this as a hit and run…motorcyclist down in the road, unconscious with a leg amputation.

This was important information that prompted me to call to RGH. I spoke to Brenda and gave her heads-up that we'd probably be needing the trauma team activated and ETA of at least twenty minutes. She thanked me for information and said she would advise the team.

Rescue 41 was arriving on scene seconds later and Steve quickly got on the radio confirming this would need the "full trauma activation."

I acknowledged Steve's update with, "Roger that, ETA 30 seconds."

State patrol had traffic stopped in both directions which created a fairly major back up with people standing outside their cars trying to get a look at what was going on. We arrived and Rocky positioned the ambulance close to the patient but also giving us a quick exit route from the scene.

The patient is lying face up in the middle of the road. His motorcycle is fifty feet away against the guardrail and smoking heavily.

I can see Steve using the portable suction and suctioning blood from the mouth. He also has one of the state patrol officers holding the patient's head immobile.

The left leg has been amputated above the knee at mid-thigh and there's a large pool of blood around the stump. Eric has a 10 by 30 inch trauma dressing and wrapping the stump. The bleeding was moderate considering the violence of the mechanism: the leg had been torn off and remaining stump is shards of bone, muscle and tissue.

Sam is walking towards us carrying the leg which was thrown several feet away.

I walked up to Steve and without losing focus on what he is doing said, "Hey Mark, he's been unresponsive since we got here. His tongue is nearly severed and creating quite a challenging airway. I also think he may have a flail chest on the left."

"Roger that," I said and began the initial assessment.

This is a seriously injured patient and his airway will be a priority. A quick listen to the chest and it sounds equal on both sides. He does have at least two ribs that are unstable on the left side. A flail chest is a very significant chest injury meaning multiple rib fractures in more than one place.

There's no radial pulse which tells me his blood pressure is less than 80.

Sam took over for the trooper and is holding cervical immobilization. Rocky cut the clothing away and has the long back board ready. Steve continued to maintain the open airway and suctioning as needed. Eric finished dressing the amputated stump, and bleeding was under control.

We need to roll him on his side in order to secure him to the spine board. Everything looks okay on his back and we secured him to the board. We made it into the back of the ambulance and were on scene less than six minutes.

I informed Eric and Sam we were going to set up for the RSI procedure. Eric immediately had high flow oxygen by mask over the patient's face.

Sam finished getting the LifePak 12 hooked up.

"Heart rate at 138, blood pressure 70/40 and Sp02 is at 88%," she called out.

"Roger that," I said.

After putting rubber tourniquets on both upper arms, I didn't see any veins popping up. I decided to look at the neck and removed the cervical collar. He has a large external jugular vein on the left side. I'm able to get the 14 gauge established and now have the IV bag of normal saline running wide open secondary to the high heart rate and low blood pressure. Sam carefully replaced the cervical collar. We can still see the IV and it is secured.

We're now set to start the RSI procedure. I pushed the etomidate and sux to which he responds quickly by letting out an exaggerated exhalation and then goes flaccid. As I place the laryngoscope blade into his mouth, it's difficult to control the tongue which is nearly severed.

My field of vision is seriously affected by blood that has pooled in the back of the throat creating thick coagulated clumps. Eric is cheek to cheek with me using the suction trying to keep my view clear. I finally see the epiglottis and the opening to the trachea. Sam hands me the

91

tube and we all breathe a sense of relief as it passes through the tracheal opening.   Sam's now managing the breaths at one every six seconds.

A quick re-assessment of the lung sounds and now they are diminished on the left side. It's not developing into a tension pneumothorax at this time, we will watch it carefully. With the flail chest, I was concerned about bleeding into the chest and maybe a spleen or liver injury.

We estimated blood loss on scene at well over a liter from the amputation. (The human body has an average of 5-6 liters)

Eric called out the latest numbers, "Heart rate 140, BP 68/40, Sp02 at 84%."

These numbers are going the wrong way, we're losing this guy. I looked at the patient's face and thought, *"Hang in there a little longer buddy, we're doing everything we can."*

I'd left a rubber tourniquet on the mid right arm. There is a large vein that has popped up. I got a 14 gauge in and we now have two good IV's. With both bags of normal saline running wide open, we have over a liter infused. The glucose is 104.

"Heart rate 134, BP 76/44, Sp02 at 90%," Eric called out with an optimistic tone.

"Okay, outstanding," I said, "Let's slow these lines down."

We have to be very careful with infusing too much fluid. If the blood pressure gets too close to normal, the internal bleeding will increase. We want the pressure just high enough to perfuse the brain and other vital organs.

We're about four minutes from RGH. I got on the radio and called to give the update. They advised they were ready for our arrival. Sam had wrapped the severed left leg in a sterile burn sheet. During the transport I hadn't realized that.

I finally asked, "Whys there a sterile burn sheet on the floor and what's in it?"

Sam looked at me like I was kidding and said, "That's his leg."

It was then that we all kind of looked at each other and reflected on how serious this guy was. We could only wonder how all of this happened.

I got down to the patient's left ear and introduced myself.

"My name is Mark. I'm the paramedic helping you. I'm sorry this happened to you. You're in great hands right now. Sam and Eric are here also. We're all taking care of you, hang in there."

Sam followed the lead, "Hey there, I'm Sam" and then Eric did the same, "Hey, I'm Eric."

We know that somewhere in there, he heard us, and knew it couldn't hurt.

We arrived at RGH and got the ubiquitous greeting from security along with half of the trauma team. It's hard to recognize everyone in their yellow gowns and full face masks, but we knew we had the right people to help us.

We followed this patient closely as we couldn't help but have empathy for him after such a violent incident. His name is Spence. He's 45 years old. He has a closed head injury which would not require treatment and he ended up losing the left leg above the knee. He got a chest tube on the left, spleen was removed and lacerated liver repaired. The tongue was saved and sewn back together. He would survive. This would include potentially months in and out of the hospital and rehabilitation.

Spence is married; his wife is a teacher at the School for the Deaf. We never did see Spence after that day. We didn't need to. Going home to his family was the outcome we wanted. We made a difference in someone's life today.

We also later learned a witness was able to get a license plate of the car that hit Spence. The state patrol located the car twenty-five miles down the road at a tavern and the intoxicated driver. Spence's blood was smeared along the driver's side of the car. The driver was arrested and denied any knowledge of the incident.

The EMS Council conducts a monthly meeting and it's being held at Station 4 this month. This organization consists of an elected board that reviews EMS policies and trends in EMS that potentially can be adopted in our county. We're hoping to sit in on it as it's generally informative about the direction of EMS and our input is always appreciated. Of course the calls took care of any thoughts of attending. We left the station at 0950 hours and seven calls later the day disappeared. We're headed back to the station and Rocky said he wanted ice cream. He mentioned a small place not far from here that "was calling his name." So we headed that direction. Actually, it sounded pretty good to me as well.

We're a few blocks from the place when we noticed a bicycle lying nearly in the lane of travel. Just to the right of it, beneath a stop sign, was a male lying on the ground.

Rocky spoke up first and said, "Now what do think this guy's problem is?"

"Not sure, but let's stop and see if we can do anything for him," I said.

There's no one around and the bike looked intact--no damage or indication he was hit by a vehicle. He is face down, right arm up, the left at his side. He's wearing a lime green tee shirt, black shorts and tennis shoes and is not wearing a bicycle helmet.

Rocky parked the ambulance next to the patient and turned on the overhead emergency lights.

I got out and walked over, scanning the scene for clues--nothing obvious. As I got closer I could hear moans with each exhalation and inspirational snore. This isn't a good sound as you walk up on a patient lying on the ground.

I called out, "Hi there...you okay? My name is Mark. I'm a paramedic. Can you hear me?"

No response.

Rocky knelt down and put his hand on the guy's shoulder.

"Man, this guy is sweaty, soaked," he announced.

Then we noticed a small pool of blood in the grass that was coming from the right side of his head.

"Mark we better get the rescue headed this way," Rocky suggested.

I grabbed the portable radio and advised dispatch of our location and requested a code three response from Rescue 41. They acknowledged my transmission and we could hear tones going out over the radio almost immediately.

After a quick assessment for injuries to the back, Rocky took control of the head and neck and we gently rolled the guy onto his back. His right eye is swollen shut, there's coagulated blood mixed with hair over the forehead and right side of the head. I can feel a strong radial pulse at 80.

We can hear the rescue's siren getting closer.

The pupils are equal and reactive, I hear clear breath sounds throughout the entire chest, everything felt intact, the abdomen is soft, and pelvis was stable and no other injuries we find at this time. Radial pulse remains at 80 and regular and breathing 20 times a minute. He has no ID or medical alert bracelets. Our working diagnosis here was head injury, but something didn't seem right about that.

Rescue 41 pulled up and a patrol car right behind them. We quickly secured him to the long spine board and were getting ready to load him in the ambulance when the officer walked over and asked, "Do you think he was hit by a car?"

"It's hard to tell," I said.

"We found him in the grass under the stop sign, and the bike doesn't have any obvious damage and there wasn't anyone around," I added.

"Okay, I'll take care of his bike and meet you guys at the hospital," he said.

"Roger that," I said.

Sam quickly got him on oxygen by mask.

Eric was hooking up the LifePak 12 and also exclaimed, "Man, this guy is drenched," and then called out vitals, "Heart rate 84, blood pressure 124/76, SpO2 96%."

I found a good vein on the right arm and got the IV in and asked Sam to check a blood sugar. (*This patient is why we check a sugar level on every unconscious person.*)

A few seconds later Sam announced, "Sugar is 24!"

That confirmed it. We have insulin shock.

Insulin shock can occur in a number of ways. They may not have had anything to eat after using insulin; maybe they've taken too much insulin or exercised after taking insulin or sometimes an illness. It can come on very suddenly, and even when the diabetic is aware of it, they can still slip past that point of being able to take care of it on their own.

We administered an amp (pre-filled syringe of medication) of dextrose 50% IV (D50). D50 is a large bolus of concentrated sugar water that quickly raises blood glucose levels and within seconds of it going into the

IV line the patient opened his eyes and looked around and said, "Did my sugar go low again?"

I said, "Welcome back, and yes, you were running pretty low…24."

"Oh great, my wife is going to kill me," he said.

I said, "It might be a good idea to wear a medical alert bracelet or something that gives us a heads up."

"I do wear one. Yesterday it broke when my dog and I were rough housing. My wife told me to get a new one immediately and I told her I would but haven't had time, I'm in big trouble," he said with a worried tone.

"So now that we have you back, do you hurt anywhere?" I asked.

He paused at that question for a few seconds and said, "Is something wrong with my right eye?"

"If we had a mirror I could show you why that is," I said with a grin.

"Can you tell us your name?" I asked.

"Donavan, everyone calls me Donnie," he said.

"Okay Donnie, sorry we had to meet this way," I said.

Sam did a repeat sugar check, "163" she said. I gave her the thumbs up.

Donnie answered all of the questions for determining if he was indeed back to his normal orientation, name, place, time and recall of the event.

He then said, "I was riding to the ice cream place and started feeling dizzy, and that's it."

I smiled and said, "Other than the dizzy part, my partner and I had the same idea…looks like the ice cream will be another night."

We dropped Donnie off at RGH. Steve met us with the rescue and picked up Sam and Eric. Rocky was visiting with Rachel as she'd finished her shift and was headed home. She had to get the kids fed. Rocky would ask people if they wanted to see pictures of his kids, and of course they would respond with "Oh yeah, of course." And then the strange look he would get when they found themselves looking at dog photos...pretty funny. They were one big happy family.

The next shift we came on duty and started out with an unexpected delay. We walked into the truck bay and the medic unit was not sitting level, the right front tire was flat. So the emergency call was placed to the district mechanic and he promised to have us up and running in less than twenty minutes.

This was okay since we had scheduled medical training from 0830-1030. Today we are reviewing our trauma protocols and specifically discussing head and chest injuries. Joe is leading the class and as always it will be an excellent presentation.

We finished the training and found the medic unit with a new right front tire and were ready for the day. It's close to lunch and Rocky and I were trying to decide what sounded good when the tones took care of further thoughts of food as they usually did.

"Medic 42, Rescue 41, respond code three for a motor vehicle rollover with ejection, patient is believed to be trapped underneath the vehicle... 4000 block of Hawkins Road...time out 1155 hours."

We both thought about it but Rocky spoke up first, "Wonder why his seat belt didn't keep him in the vehicle?"

A rhetorical thought at best. Over the years, we've never heard of anyone getting tossed out of the vehicle wearing their safety restraint, *as it was designed.*

Dispatch updated us the patient is trapped underneath the vehicle and bystanders were trying to "free the patient." A heavy rescue truck was dispatched from District 6 and would be about four minutes behind us.

As we're arriving, we see a small compact vehicle on its top with legs sticking out from the knees down. There are five guys "rocking the car" back and forth in an attempt to "roll it off the patient."

Each time it would roll back toward them, you could see the feet moving. Rocky and I were both in shock over this. At about that moment they had the car rolled over and the patient is lying there, face up, and the horrific presentation of traumatic asphyxia.

Traumatic asphyxia occurs when the chest is compressed and does not allow blood flow back to the heart. The veins in the neck become engorged, the eyes can bulge nearly out of their sockets, and the face can become a terrible purple-black color that's terrifying to witness. It also carries a very high mortality rate.

Walking up to the patient I notice his eyes are moving side to side as if he's trying to focus on something. The whites of his eyes are bloodshot; his lips are nearly black and face is a deep purple. The neck veins are swollen and the purple color extends to the collar bones. The right side of the chest is caved in and does not rise as he takes a breath. He also has a large full thickness scalping type laceration from the right side of the forehead to just past the right ear. This is a gaping wound that exposed a shiny white skull. This was a gruesome combination of injuries; I would need to RSI him ASAP.

Sam and Eric immediately had the BVM and oxygen and trying to get breaths in. This was difficult as the patient was fighting against their actions. Patients that are oxygen deprived can be unpredictably combative. This isn't something they are doing consciously; it's secondary to the brain not functioning rationally with the low oxygen. Steve's cutting clothing and Rocky is bandaging the head laceration.

I looked the patient in the eyes and asked, "Can you hear me?"

This was met with a couple of blinks, not sure if it was lucid or not.

As Steve cut the shirt off, the chest injury was as bad as we had feared. The entire right chest is heavily discolored with large abrasions. There are several ribs fractured. Each breath made the chest look like a see-saw motion...as he would take a breath, the right side of the chest sunk and the left side rose, and then vice versa on exhalation. This is called paradoxical breathing movement and a serious finding.

While the long spine board packaging was going on, I could hear the suction unit turn on and off.

Eric said, "Mark we're getting a lot of foamy secretions with blood mixed in them."

Bloody and foamy secretions are indicative of pulmonary contusions. This is actual bruising to the lung tissue and small air sacs which is a complicated injury as it interferes with the oxygenation process.

I applied two rubber tourniquets to both upper arms in hopes that veins would pop up by the time we got into the ambulance.

The Engine 61 crew had arrived and stabilized the car when Captain Neeves came over and said, "Mark, did you see the inside of the car?"

"Not yet, we've been busy with him. I can check it out now," and followed him to the car.

The driver's seat belt was buckled and obviously not used. In fact, the driver's compartment was the only area of the vehicle not affected by the crash. Had the patient made the choice to wear his seat belt, he'd likely have only minor injuries. Now he is fighting for his life.

Once in the back of the ambulance, the early application of the rubber tourniquets paid off. There's a large vein in the right mid arm. I got a 14 gauge in and secured the IV tubing with extra tape.

As always, we can't afford to lose a critical IV. You only need to lose an IV one time on a critical patient and you'll never let it happen again. Any scene outside the hospital is uncontrolled, chaotic and things can happen quickly. On some critical patient's you'll only have one chance at an IV; it is called a lifeline for a reason.

Eric did another assessment for breath sounds with his stethoscope and said, "I'm not hearing anything on that right side, and it's getting harder to get air in."

We both agreed it would be prudent to insert a "big needle" into the upper right chest. Eric handed me the 12 gauge 3-inch long needle. After double checking the landmarks, I inserted it and within seconds there was the expected rush of air followed by blood tinged foam.

We're now ready for getting the airway secured. The RSI drugs were pushed through the IV line and the response was immediate. After one minute I inserted the long straight laryngoscope blade into his mouth and down his throat. I needed suctioning twice as the bloody foam from the lungs was near continuous.

As soon as the tube was placed through the vocal cords into the trachea, Sam took over ventilating the patient and she is very competent at this. She's focused on ensuring the endotracheal tube stayed at the correct depth and breaths are delivered ensuring maximum oxygenation. This was a critical task requiring complete attention. Sam is one of the strongest EMT's I've worked with. There's a saying in EMS that paramedic's save lives and EMT's save paramedic's…Sam is the epitome of this proverb.

I hooked up the LifePak 12 and he has a heart rate of 140 and EKG shows frequent extra beats that shouldn't be there. It could be reflective of a cardiac contusion. This is a bruise or some trauma directly to the heart muscle itself.

The blood pressure is 60/40 and Sp02 level was 86%, numbers I expected but hoped not to see.

Despite our ventilation efforts, he still has the deep cyanosis, or blueness, to his face. His pupils are reactive and this is our first positive finding.

The trauma team was ready as we arrived at RGH. This guy needed a higher level of care and we had been behind the eight ball since this incident started. The next few hours would be critical.

He ended up with a skull fracture on his right side, four fractured ribs, pulmonary contusions along with a chest tube, a cardiac contusion, liver laceration, fractures to three of the thoracic vertebrae, and has a very long recovery ahead.

Witnesses to the crash report he was talking on a cell phone when he drove off the shoulder and over corrected. The vehicle started swerving and eventually rolled, he was ejected and the vehicle came to rest on top of him.

His name is Timothy. He's 34 years old and owns a landscaping business. He's married with four children. He did beat the odds associated with traumatic asphyxia. He didn't beat the odds of not of wearing the seat belt.

Rocky and I are always looking for ways to improve the setup in the back of the ambulance. There are times when you're with the patient for only a few minutes, but in that time your actions can make the difference in their outcomes. Your system and delivery of that system are never perfect. You have to be open to change and always looking for those edges that translate into advantages. We would spend many hours in the back of the ambulance ensuring everything was functional, clean and set up for optimal performance.

One of our station volunteers is a Boy Scout Leader and he brought his troop into see the ambulance. One of the scouts commented, "Everything is so clean and organized."

Rocky and I shared a satisfied grin and then the tones gave them an opportunity to watch us head out into the night.

"Medic 42, Rescue 41, respond and stage for a possible shooting victim, police are en route…1818 Alameda Road…time out 2050 hours."

This response would take about four minutes. Dispatch updated us that police were calling for immediate EMS response into the scene. They had a victim shot twice at close range with a shotgun.

Upon hearing this, I told Rocky, "I'm going to hop in the back and set some things up."

"Roger that…hang on," he said.

I got the LifePak 12 set up and ready to go, set up two IV bags and hung them from the ceiling, laid open the airway tray, set out the RSI drugs and had a bag valve mask out and hooked up to oxygen. I set out tape and made doubly sure the ends were folded over.

There's nothing worse than grabbing a role of tape on a critical call and not being able to find the end. It's amazing how something so small can shut a scene down.

I then grabbed two rubber IV tourniquets. I will place one on each of his arms and then once we were in the ambulance hopefully have IV sites to choose from. We never want to delay transport by starting IV's on scene when a patient needs a surgeon.

Climbing back into the passenger seat, I told Rocky, "Let's plan on taking a couple trauma dressings and the back board and we'll just load and go."

"Roger that, load and go," he said nodding approvingly.

We parked as close as we could get and still had an exit route from the scene. There are multiple police units on scene with officers creating a perimeter as well as several neighbors standing on their porches watching the scene unfold with natural curiosity.

One of the police officers met us and explained this scenario started with a hysterical female who called 9-1-1 and reported her boyfriend had just been shot by her ex-boyfriend. She told them they were sitting on the couch watching TV when the front door was kicked open; there stood the ex-boyfriend with shotgun in hand.

As the present boyfriend stood up to confront him, the first blast hit him in the right hip and put him to the floor. The second blast was to the left upper chest and shoulder--both massive wounds, either one potentially fatal.

Rocky and I walked up to the residence with Steve Eric and Sam right behind us. We had to step over two red spent shotgun shells lying just inside the front door. We could hear the girlfriend crying in the kitchen and calling out, "Kevin, honey, Kevin…oh my God…"

Kevin is lying next to the couch on his left side, moaning. There's a tremendous pool of thick coagulated blood on the floor around the upper chest and hip area. Rocky quickly cut clothing to expose the wounds. I placed a rubber tourniquet on each arm, just above the elbows.

I looked at the officer closest to us and said, "Have dispatch alert RGH, full trauma activation and we'll be there directly!"

With an affirmative nod, he spoke into his lapel mike and made the call….they'd be ready for us.

The chest blast hit just a few inches below the left clavicle. It had mercilessly torn through flesh leaving an opening several inches in diameter. There is bubbling coming from it as Kevin drew breaths in and out. There are smaller pellet holes beneath the primary wound extending to the mid-abdomen.

Sam placed the wrapper from the 10 by 30 inch trauma dressing over this wound and then folded the dressing itself over that and taped it in place. This was a great trick as it occluded this large sucking chest wound.

Sucking chest wounds are dangerous and need to be covered immediately. Left open they can seriously interfere with the breathing and oxygenation process. After they are sealed, we have to be alert for tension building which becomes a tension pneumothorax. If this occurred we would open one end of the sealing bandage and release the pressure.

The right hip wound was just as devastating. It left a hole about the size of a tennis ball. This one had shattered the head of the femur and hip socket and there are more pellet wounds extending to mid-thigh. Steve compressed another 10 by 30 inch trauma dressing over this wound and taped it in place.

Sam then immediately took control of the head and neck. Eric had the spine board ready. Steve and I are in position to roll him and we looked at Sam. She called out "one-two-three-roll" and he's secured to the board.

Kevin's eyes are open but he only responds with moans. His color reflects this incredibly violent assault with a pasty pale look along with "candle wax-translucent" colored lips and beads of sweat over the brow.

We carried him to the gurney and made it to the back of the ambulance in less than three minutes. Rocky closed the doors, ready for the four minute ride to the RGH trauma team.

"Hold on…here we go," we heard Rocky shout out.

Sam had the BVM ready in her lap and an oxygen mask over his face. I had two IV's going in within sixty seconds, one in the left mid arm and one in the right wrist, both 14 gauges. They were secured by taking the roles of tape that were set out and rolling them several times, not pretty but effective. Someone was watching out for Kevin to have the veins pop up the way they did.

Eric was attaching EKG leads while I am pushing the RSI drugs. Kevin quickly went motionless and stopped breathing as anticipated.

After a quick switch with Sam, I had the laryngoscope in my left hand and inserted the long curved blade down the throat and quickly found the epiglottis and vocal cords. Without losing the view I called for the endotracheal tube. Sam handed it to me and it passed easily into the trachea. We now had the airway controlled and IV's running. The EKG showed a heart rate of 126. We also managed to get one blood pressure, 80/54.

Rocky yelled out, "Thirty seconds, we're gonna be there."

"Roger that," I called out.

The back doors on the medic unit seemed to open before Rocky had us at a complete stop. I was surprised to see Dr. Sage, one of the trauma surgeons, in the front of the group.

He was commanding and focused, "Let's go, let's go," he said and we were headed to Suite 12. After a quick X-ray, Kevin was wheeled across the hall into the O.R. theatre.

I looked up at the clock in Suite 12. It was 2102 hours. This entire call had lasted twelve minutes. That's from the dispatch, the response, the scene, the transport and now into surgery. Kevin was in the O.R. for two hours and admitted to the trauma ICU. Forty-eight hours later his endotracheal tube was removed and he was awake. If we responded to this same call ten times, I'm not sure the outcome would be the same.

Kevin will walk with a limp for the rest of his life. He had a lobe of lung removed and he is a survivor of one of the most violent crimes a person can be part of…attempted homicide by a double shotgun blast at close range.

The ex-boyfriend fled the scene and was later arrested at a nearby bar. He ordered two pitchers of beer and one large order of fries and told the waitress, "This will be my last plate of fries and beer for a while."

I ended up having to testify at the attempted murder trial. I had to describe the shotgun shells lying in the front door and then the injuries we treated. The suspect sat in the courtroom and was about ten feet away from the witness stand. I could feel him staring at me as I testified, very intimidating. He was convicted of attempted aggravated manslaughter and sentenced to 25 years in prison.

Medic 42 was an older ambulance and due to be replaced. The new medic unit finally arrived and it was an exciting day. It is a modular type with a walk-through from the cab to the patient compartment. It has the new car smell and Rocky and I will put it into service tomorrow. Today we are moving all of the equipment from the old rig to the new one. It's a very long and tedious process. Everything has to be in the optimal location. It doesn't make much sense to put the airway equipment toward the back of the rig when the patient's head will be toward the front.

It's a brilliant blue and white, shiny wheels with an impressive emergency lighting package. You will see us coming and if for some reason you can't, you will hear us.

After a final check and double check everything was in place, we took it for a test drive around town. It is a privilege having such an awesome vehicle. We are all very proud of the newest vehicle in the Station 4 fleet.

We were backing into the station and Sandy is there with the camera. We are the envy of the station. She took several pictures of the rig and then with the crews standing around it.

Our photo op was cut short by the tones.

"Medic 42, Rescue 41, respond for a vehicle into the ditch, the driver is unresponsive…2300 Commercial Drive…time out 1045 hours."

This would be the maiden voyage in the new rig. We pulled out of the bay and headed for the location. This response would take about four minutes.

We arrived and noticed the car off the road as reported. The vehicle was nose-down in a very small culvert and looked like it pulled off the road as opposed to crashing. There's no damage and we see the male driver slumped over and leaning against the driver's door. His head is down with his chin against his chest.

"He doesn't look like he's doing too well," Rocky said as we both exited the vehicle.

Two county deputy cars are also arriving and have blocked the right lane.

A female was standing next to one of the cars that had stopped and began to explain what she saw as Rocky and I walked towards the patient's vehicle, "I was behind this car when it started weaving and then just slowed down and drove off the road…I went over and tapped on his window and he started turning blue…that's when I called you guys," she said with concern.

"Thanks and we appreciate what you did, the deputy will need to talk to you also," I said.

The car is running and doors are locked. The patient looks to be in his mid-30's, maybe 170 pounds, dark hair, button-up collared shirt, jeans, and a briefcase on the passenger seat. His face is blue and he's taking an occasional agonal (dying) breath.

This type of breathing is not *actually* breathing. The breathing reflex is powerful and can continue after the heart stops. It does not move air in and out of the lungs.

"We have to get in there now," I said to Steve.

"Roger that," he replied and went to the passenger window.

He used his handy-dandy window punch device and with a small tap to the left corner of the window it shattered. He reached in and pushed the door lock to the open position and the driver's door unlocked. Eric and Sam had the long spine board; Rocky has the main and airway kits ready next to the car.

As I opened the door slowly, the patient followed it without hesitation… he's in cardiac arrest. We got him out and onto the back board. Sam started compressions. Eric had the BVM and was providing breaths. Steve's cutting clothing and Rocky was applying the combo-pads and plugging them into the LifePak 12. We would perform a full two minutes of CPR before looking at the rhythm.

During that time I put a rubber tourniquet on his right upper arm and looked for IV sites. We're getting close to two minutes. I told Eric and Sam to plan on switching positions during the rhythm check.

"V-fib…we'll shock at 200 watts…clear…" The shock was delivered and the patient arched slightly. Eric continued the compressions.

I found a good vein in the right arm and put a 14 gauge in and taped it securely. I quickly scanned for medic alert bracelets or any clues as to why this guy had the cardiac arrest. He didn't look out of shape. We needed to make sure we weren't missing anything.

"Sugar is 104," Rocky said.

"Roger that," I acknowledged.

Rocky now had the intubation equipment ready and I moved to the patient's head. The airway is clean, no obstructions, blood or secretions. After a clear view of the vocal cords I watched the endotracheal tube pass through the vocal cords into the trachea. Rocky listened over the chest and stomach with a stethoscope and gave thumbs up on the positioning of the tube.

It was time for another rhythm check.

"V-fib…let's shock at 300 watts this time…clear…" I ordered.

Another shock delivered and arch from the patient. Sam immediately resumed compressions. I pushed epinephrine through the IV and opened the line up to ensure the drug had gone into the system.

We use epinephrine in cardiac arrest to try to stimulate cardiac activity.

On reassessment, everything looked good: the airway, the compressions, no injuries. We had to consider the way he slowed down and then went off the road. This could be suggestive of having a medical problem with the ensuing sudden cardiac arrest.

At the end of the two minutes we stopped to check the rhythm.

"We have a good looking rhythm here folks…Eric, check for a pulse," I said with optimism.

"Good strong carotid here," Eric confirmed and then took out his pen and placed an 'X' on the left side of the neck over the pulse.

"Okay, let's start getting ready to go," I said to everyone.

We were loaded into the ambulance and headed for RGH. The rhythm still looked good, heart rate 104, blood pressure 88/46, Sp02 92%. Pupillary response is good. We seem to be going in the right direction.

I looked at the patient and got close to his left ear. "If you can you hear me open your eyes? Can you squeeze my hand?"

I didn't get any obvious responses.

I updated RGH and we arrived three minutes later. We were led into Suite 6 where Dr. Stein took over care as we provided a detailed account of everything to this point.

"I agree with you guys about this being some catastrophic medical event. Good job guys," Dr. Stein said.

We had our first call with the new ambulance and it was positive. We were all pleased with how the resuscitation efforts went on scene. We got the kits and gurney back together. Steve arrived with the rescue and said one of the deputies was contacting the patient's wife.

Steve and Eric and Sam headed back to the station. Rocky and I went back into the E.D. and noticed the curtain was pulled around Suite 6. We went in and the patient had gone back into arrest. Dr. Stein was running the resuscitation; he looked over and didn't give us high hopes. They worked for thirty-two minutes before discontinuing the efforts.

He died before his wife arrived.

We found out several days later the autopsy revealed multiple coronary occlusions with a substantial myocardial infarction. He had a massive heart attack while driving.

His name was Ken. He was 36 years old, married and had a 12 year old daughter. He was a manager for a grocery chain and headed home at the time of the event. We also learned his father died at age 45 from a heart attack and his grandfather died at age 35 from a heart attack.

CHAPTER 9

LITTLE EMERGENCIES

It wasn't uncommon to have the public come and tour the station. We enjoyed these encounters as it gave us a chance to show off our equipment, our vehicles and give the public an idea of what we are here to do. There's an inherent pride associated with dedication to delivering the best EMS system for our community.

The small kids are the most fun with their inquisitive nature and classic questions such as, "Why does the ambulance have big tires?" or "You couldn't put a giraffe in one of those" or "Do you sleep on that bed?"

We let them walk from the back of the ambulance to the front and they are mesmerized with the experience, such curiosity.

Rocky would ask the group, "Who wears seat belts?"

All hands go up immediately with large, beaming smiles.

And then the honesty comes out. "My dad doesn't wear his seat belt and my mommy hits him," came from one of the smallest kids.

Rocky and I can't help but grin.

The tour no sooner left and the tones were calling.

"Medic 42, Rescue 41, respond code three for a child choking, unknown if conscious, caller is frantic, 1221 40th, low cross of Oriole…time out 1138 hours."

This response would take five minutes. If it's a fully obstructed airway, time would be critical. Of course traffic is heavy and as usual not everyone remembers the driving handbook. Cars are supposed to yield to emergency vehicles with activated lights and siren by safely pulling to the right and allowing the vehicle to pass.

Left hand turns seem to be the most sacred. Vehicles waiting for an opening in oncoming traffic will do anything they can to avoid the "pull to the right and stop" requirement. They "pretend" they don't see us and stand their ground.

We pass on the left, so when this vehicle doesn't pull over, it slows our response as we have to be cautious about going around them, thus avoiding a potential collision.

Some drivers panic and stop right where they are--no pulling to the right, just a dead stop. And then there are ones that will try to outrun you. They think that if they speed up, they can make it to where they are going before having to pull to the right.

We came upon a car doing 10 mph under the posted speed limit while responding with lights and siren. She had her cell phone to her left ear and was "talking" with her right hand, probably steering with her knee. After twenty seconds she was visibly startled as she looked in the mirror and "happened to notice us behind her," and then gave an angry scowl as we went around her.

We arrived on scene in a little over four minutes and grabbed all of the equipment. The front of the house looks like a toy warehouse with bikes and bats and soccer balls and wagons.

The front door opened and a young girl about 7 years old stood there and looked at us with squinty eyes and a scrunched up nose then said, "My mom said to come in; she's in the kitchen."

Walking into the house we counted no less than six children, from the baby on the couch to the 9 year old on the computer paying no attention to anything going on around her.

In the kitchen we see a 6 year old boy leaning against the refrigerator. He has Batman underwear on and a large black bath towel around his neck for a cape. He has his hands on his knees and looks as if he has just finished running sprints. He has "drool" running from his lower lip almost to the floor before it breaks stream.

Mom is washing her hands in the sink and says, "I think we got it."

I said, "Okay, got what?"

She explained, "His sister screamed out that he was choking, so I grabbed him and held him upside down and shook him several times...then I grabbed him from behind and gave him that *"Hemlock Maneuver"*...then I reached down his throat with my finger and dug around...and finally I got a bottle of ipecac down him, and I think we're okay now...thanks for coming out, anyway."

After hearing this story, I looked down at this poor little boy leaning against the refrigerator and totally understood his *"beat up, been through the ringer, don't want no more"* look. It turns out that the sister that hailed the wrath of mom over the choking claim was, "just kidding."

Rocky and I sat down with mom and talked about what happened. We then explained how this incident will still play out since administering the ipecac. We offered to take the child to the emergency department to be checked as a precaution. She declined and said she'd call us back if she needed any help.

As we were leaving, the poor little boy looked at me with a look that said, "Please take me with you, please."

I gave him a wink and a smile and an empathetic tilt of my head.

Rocky and I didn't say much on the way back to the station. I think we were so shocked at what we just heard, and had images in mind of this poor kid being "worked over" by mom, wondering what he did to deserve the madness and *never do it again!*

 Back at the station Eric and Sam wanted to review the equipment in the back of the ambulance. Of course, this was one of my favorite pastimes as it would usually pay off during a critical call. Rocky and Steve joined in and we started with the LifePak 12 and then to the main kit and some of the drugs: narcan for reversing narcotic overdoses, drugs for cardiac arrest, drugs for allergic reactions and everything in between.

Then out of the blue, Eric sprang his big news on us that he decided to go to paramedic school. He said he had been a student too long and was now sure this would be his career.

Sam and Rocky and Steve and I looked at each other speechless and before we could say anything the tones interrupted the moment.

"Medic 42, Rescue 41, respond code three for a child with food poisoning…3828 Merriman Drive…time out 1245 hours."

We all went en route and Rocky and I were puzzled by the dispatch. We don't get too many calls for "food poisoning."

Rocky then said with a more serious tone, "Hopefully they didn't call our last mom for advice," followed with a grin.

We arrived to a nice home with several cars parked in the driveway. We had to walk a ways to the front door.

A lady met us with a nervous smile and said, "Please come in. It's my daughter; she isn't feeling too well."

We were led into a sitting room where the patient was nearly slumped over on the couch. She was attended to by two ladies and with her pasty pale skin, colorless lips and lethargic look, she got my attention.

I walked over to her and knelt down.

"Hi there, my name is Mark, and I'm a paramedic. What is your name?" I asked.

"Heidi," her mother immediately answered.

It's really important that I hear Heidi speak for herself. This would give me valuable information as to her level of consciousness and the status and patency of her airway.

I said, "Thank you" and then asked Heidi, "Can you tell me how old you are?"

"She's 10," her mom quickly spoke up again.

I asked Eric if he could take mom into the other room and get some information. He immediately understood and said, "Ma'am, could I trouble you to give me some information," to which the mother smiled and followed him out of the room.

Sam has the main kit open and is working on getting an initial set of vital signs.

One of the other ladies explained they were having a small birthday party out back and after the cake was served, Heidi started feeling dizzy, and this started about ten minutes ago.

Sam looked at me and in a whisper said, "I am not getting a blood pressure or a radial pulse and her carotid pulse is 130."

I asked Heidi if she hurt anywhere and she shook her head "No" and then pointed to her throat. I noticed a rash below her chin and all across her upper chest and arms. I asked the lady if anything unusual happened and she said Heidi was stung by a bee about twenty minutes earlier.

"It stung her on the lower back when they were swimming," she explained.

A quick check of the lower back showed where she had been stung. There was a large red raised area. She also has hives or raised red blotches across her back. Things just went from bad to very bad. We're dealing with an allergic reaction that had progressed to anaphylactic shock. Heidi is a very sick little girl.

Anaphylactic shock is an exaggerated response to an allergic reaction. The blood pressure drops, the smaller airways in the lungs clamp down and tissues can swell around throat and close the airway. This has turned into a life threatening emergency.

I asked Sam to get me the epinephrine from the kit. I started Heidi on oxygen by mask and estimated she weighed about 60 pounds which would make her about 30 kilograms. Our epinephrine dose would be based on this weight. Pediatric medications were generally weight based.

I laid Heidi down on the couch as I watched Sam draw this up in the syringe. I confirmed the dosage and after cleaning a spot on Heidi's left upper arm administered the dose.

This epinephrine injection would counter act the allergic reaction and usually works very quickly.

Eric had come back into the room and set up an IV bag with normal saline. I thought the IV might present a problem but found a good vein on the inside of her right arm. She winced a bit and I don't blame her, it's a 16 gauge, a large IV capable of delivering a lot of fluid for the low blood pressure.

Sam was looking down at the glucometer and said, "Sugar is 100."

"Roger that," I said.

We had the IV running wide open. I administered 25 mg of benadryl for the hives and solu-medrol, which is a steroid to help with reducing swelling in the tissues. With the drugs onboard, we began to see her color coming back fairly quickly.

She became more alert and said, "I feel really shaky."

This was a good sign as it meant the epinephrine was working. After infusing nearly half the bag of IV fluid, Sam checked her blood pressure: 94/60. The pasty pale color had changed to a more normal looking pink. We slowed the IV and got ready to transport.

One of the ladies came up to me and said, "My daughter is allergic to bees...I had no idea that's what it would look like when they had the reaction."

I said, "Well, this was somewhat of an atypical presentation."

She fortunately didn't have the throat closing off. Who knows how much longer she would have gone before her heart stopped? She was pretty sick.

Heidi was one of the most pleasant patient's we've had in the ambulance: polite, intelligent, beautiful smile, a very brave little girl. It was very gratifying to see her go from near death to almost full recovery by the time we reached the emergency department.

We handed her off to Rachel in Suite 6. Rachel asked her, "Did these guys treat you okay?"

Heidi replied, "Oh yes, Mark even put this IV in my arm and I didn't even cry. I was stung by a bee and was very sick."

We all looked at each other and exchanged humbled smiles. Rocky took the opportunity to visit with Rachel for a few minutes after she got Heidi ready for the physician.

I was putting the finishing touches to the ambulance gurney. Rocky and I pride ourselves on having the gurney always looking crisp and sharp with the creases and seat belts aligned. I was about to wheel it out the door when the calm of the moment erupted with screams coming from Suite 16, the mental health room. I rushed over to the commotion and was shocked at seeing the attending nurse, Jennifer, on the ground and a male patient choking her from behind with his arm solidly around her neck.

The fear in Jennifer's eyes was unmistakable and she's in jeopardy of going unconscious any second. She's blue around the lips, eyes bulging and veins in her forehead engorged. I immediately jumped toward them and grabbed for the assaulting man's arm. I was able to gain a slight handhold on his thumb. While pulling and twisting it backwards, he had no choice but to release the assault.

At that moment several more people arrived, including Rocky, Brenda and two security officers. Jennifer was able to crawl away from us toward the door and was helped up and escorted out by Brenda. The patient was screaming and fighting as if he had no intention of stopping. Several more security guards appeared and now this was one huge dog pile with me at the bottom, entwined with the mental health patient. It was several minutes before he was restrained, back on the gurney and under control.

I got a small cut above my right eye, a jammed left pinky finger, lost two buttons off my shirt but otherwise okay. I found Brenda and Jennifer in the break room, along with several other nurses. Jennifer was okay but obviously quite shaken by the experience.

"Thank you Mark, I'm sorry you got hurt," Jennifer said with sincerity.

"Hey, I'm just glad you're okay and plus I needed a new shirt," I said as she gave me a hug.

This is a vivid and graphic reminder of how dangerous and violent someone can become in the blink of an eye. You must always keep an escape route available and remain alert for things to change in an instant. Any patient has the potential to react violently to their illness or situation.

Jennifer was fortunate this afternoon. This patient was well known to the E.D. He is bi-polar with violent tendencies but has been docile over the last few months. Brenda said that she's attended him before and is a very nice guy, most of the time.

Rocky and I got back to the station and Eric and Sam sounded like they were in stereo asking, "What happened to your eye?"

I told them Heidi clobbered me before we left, for the IV. For a split second they almost bought it.

Sandy called Rocky and me to her office.

"The E.D. called and wanted you to know that Heidi is doing excellent and they're keeping her overnight for observation. She has an appointment with the Allergy Clinic tomorrow," she said.

We thanked her for that. It is good to hear outcomes when you can get them, as it is not always the case.

After getting a new shirt and a bite to eat and catching up on paperwork, Rocky mentioned getting a workout at our five star station gym. This thought came and went at the sound of tones echoing throughout the station.

"Medic 42, Rescue 41, respond code three for a car versus bicycle, 4000 Rolling Circle…time out 1704 hours."

This response would be on the outskirts of our district. It would take ten minutes to get there, and traffic would be heavy. We decided to put the helicopter, Mercy Flight, on standby. Dispatch is advising they're unavailable at this time but would keep us informed.

We received an update on the patient. He's a 12 year old male that was struck in an intersection and is unconscious at this time. We're also being advised there's a nurse on scene providing initial care.

On arrival there's a large crowd gathered and two patrol vehicles that have blocked off the scene. One of the officers is waving us toward him. To his right is a vehicle in the intersection with the windshield caved in and blood and hair in the center of it. It's an ominous sight.

As we're walking to where the officer directed us, the boy is lying on the ground about fifteen feet in front of the car with the broken windshield. A female is kneeling near the top of his head. She's stabilizing his neck and has a small towel used for the bleeding. I could hear the boy breathing from a few feet away, very rapid, upwards of 50 per minute.

I motioned to Sam to take over cervical immobilization; she nodded and was quickly in place.

Rocky was bringing the backboard and Steve started cutting clothing.

The lady that Sam took over for introduced herself as Jackie, a nurse and said she worked in pediatrics at RGH.

"Hi Jackie, I'm Mark…a paramedic, what can you tell me?" I asked.

"Well, I heard tires screeching and people screaming. He's been unresponsive since I got here. I held pressure on the head laceration which looks like a depressed skull fracture; his radial pulse has been around 50-60 and he's had the tachypnea (fast breathing) the whole time," she explained.

"Okay Jackie, thanks for your help," I said appreciatively.

The quick assessment reveals the obvious depressed skull fracture near the right frontal and temple area, his left pupil is blown which is reflective of significant intracranial swelling.

The chest sounded clear, abdomen was soft, pelvis was intact and he had been incontinent of urine. There's an obvious closed mid-shaft right femur fracture and his radial pulse is right at 50.

Sam started him on high flow oxygen by mask. Eric is getting the depressed skull fracture covered with a light dressing. We don't want to apply too much pressure to this wound as we could damage the underlying brain tissue. Steve and I are putting the traction splint on the right femur.

I told Rocky to set up for the RSI. He gave thumbs up and disappeared. We got the patient secured to the spine board and were ready to go.

Another quick check of the scene: witnesses said the kid rode his bike from the top of the hill, went in front of the car, which was traveling at about 25 mph. The collision threw the patient over the hood and into the windshield, and then forward as the car slammed on the brakes. There was no helmet used. The bike was demolished and about ten feet from where the patient ended up.

We are on scene less than seven minutes.

I assigned Sam to the LifePak 12. Eric was drawing the RSI drugs up. First I would need to gain IV access. I found a great vein in the left arm and got a 14 gauge into it. The normal saline IV bag is plugged in and secured.

"108 on the glucose," Sam called out. I nodded affirmatively.

We were ready for the RSI. The etomidate was administered through the IV line and within seconds the expected decrease in breathing was noted.

"Call out numbers for me Sam," I said.

"BP 160/104, heart rate 54, Sp02 98%," she announced.

I then pushed the sux. Within forty-five seconds he was ready. The laryngoscope blade was carefully inserted down his throat and I quickly found the epiglottis, then a good view of the vocal cords and tracheal opening. Without moving my eyes from the back of the throat, I grabbed the endotracheal tube and slid it into the mouth from the right side and watched it go smoothly into the trachea.

As always when you elect to put someone asleep and implement this procedure, there's an inherent risk. The biggest reason for failure is not being prepared. Everyone has to be on the same page and attentive throughout the process.

"You can never get complacent with the RSI procedure."

The next numbers from Sam were BP 164/100, heart rate 60, Sp02 98%. I instructed Eric to ventilate with the bag valve once every five seconds and watch the heart rate and Sp02.

The reassessment didn't change. His left pupil is still blown. There is minimal bleeding from the open skull fracture and the breath sounds are still clear, the skin color is pink, warm and dry. His primary injury is the head injury.

We alerted RGH to activate a full trauma team for us and gave them a seven minute ETA. On arrival we had the greeting we had hoped for. Joe and Brandon were there to give us a hand. They had just finished a transport before we arrived.

"Hey Joe...Brandon...good to see you guys," I said.

Joe nodded and said, "We're going to Suite 12."

Once in Suite 12 the team sprang into action and a flurry of activity unfolded. If there was ever going to be a favorable outcome, it would be directly related to this level of care. The neurosurgeon wanted the boy in CT scan in five minutes, and off they went.

He was taken to surgery with an epidural bleed. This is bleeding under the skull that creates intracranial pressure. The prognosis was favorable but guarded. His name is Martin and he's 12 years old. We would hear later that he was riding home after playing video games at a friend's house.

This was a tough case for all of us.

Later at the station we were critiquing our roles and reflected on how much less severe the injuries might have been with the use of a helmet. It certainly couldn't have made them worse.

We have a specialized course that's a requirement of being a paramedic. It's called Pediatric Advanced Life Support or PALS. This is a two-day course and sixteen hours of in-depth training on how to deal with pediatric respiratory issues, kids with shock and any other emergency problems kids come up with. This course has to be taken every two years. It's one of my favorite courses. RGH has some of the top pediatric physicians in the country. They put the course on and we always walk away with the best training.

The next set of tones would challenge our PALS skills.

"Medic 42, Rescue 41, respond code three for an infant that is unresponsive…701 Andersen Road…time out 1430 hours."

The infant isn't just a small person. Everything is different: the heart rate, the breathing, the anatomy. It's challenging dealing with smaller equipment and drug dosages, and fortunately we don't see too many really sick kids.

Arriving on scene was almost like we were at the wrong house--no one to greet us, no one looking out the window, nothing. We grabbed all of the equipment and walked to the front door and knocked.

After several seconds the door opened and a male in his early 20's stood there and said, "Come on in...the kid won't wake up from his nap."

"Okay, well, my name is Mark. I'm a paramedic and we can check him out," I said.

We walked into a near dark room with the curtains closed and no lights on. There's a playpen in the center of the room, a loveseat and folding lawn chair. A small TV on the floor with a gaming console next to it and games spread out. The male led us down a hallway into a bedroom with a crib and small chest of drawers.

He said, "I put him down for his nap a couple of hours ago. My girlfriend called and said to wake him up and now he just sleeps."

I asked, "How old is he?"

"He's like 14 months," he said and then shrugged his shoulders.

"Has he been sick or not acting normal lately?" I asked.

"Nope....just put him down for his nap and now he won't wake up," he said almost coldly.

When we first looked into the crib, the baby (his name is Keenan) is on his back, his arms and legs are abnormally extended which is indicative of serious brain swelling and he is breathing at nearly 70 times per minute which is over twice the normal breathing rate. I opened his eyes and the right pupil is blown, the other at normal size and shape.

I had Sam start oxygen as she placed a small mask over Keenan's mouth and nose.

"Has he fallen or hit his head?" I asked the male in a general, non-accusatory manner.

"Why would you ask that?" He answered with a raised defensive sounding tone.

"It's just something we need to ask to make sure we don't miss anything," I said.

He just looked at the floor and didn't answer.

At that point we all had a bad feeling about this presentation. I told Eric to get the LifePak 12 hooked up and I made the decision to RSI little Keenan.

Eric said, "Heart rate at 60, blood pressure 150/110, SpO2 98%."

Little Keenan has a brain injury and rising intracranial pressure.

I need IV access and will use an intraosseous needle (IO) for the IV in the left leg. Veins are tough to find on small children. IO involves putting a special needle into the center of the tibial bone (lower leg). The IV fluid and drugs are absorbed into the circulatory system through the cavernous blood network in the center of the bone. It's used the same as an IV would be used.

Sam called out, "76 on the sugar."

"Roger that," I said, "Sugar 76."

We estimated Keenan at about 20 pounds or 10 kg. As I pushed the RSI drugs, they went to work quickly. The laryngoscope blade is much smaller and the intubation was quick and uncomplicated. We controlled Keenan's ventilations during the transport and had the pediatric team standing by at RGH.

It was devastating to learn that Keenan had a massive intracranial bleed and was diagnosed with "shaken baby syndrome."

Little Keenan was declared brain dead.

In the most difficult decision of her life, the mother consented to organ donation and Keenan gave several children the ultimate gift, a chance at having a normal life.

The male at the house admitted physically shaking Keenan to make him stop crying. He was arrested and convicted of manslaughter and sentenced to seven years. We all had to appear in court and testify, which made the case very tough.

You cannot choose your calls in EMS. With some you will have miraculous results, and some you will live with for the rest of your life.

Keenan will always be in our thoughts.

CHAPTER 10

THAT'S SHOCKING

Our LifePak 12 was due for service and actually had to go to the "LifePak Hospital" for a couple of days. We're using our stand-by monitor, the LifePak 10. This is a good monitor and more than capable of filling in during the interim. After ensuring everyone was up to speed with the new monitor, we were good to go.

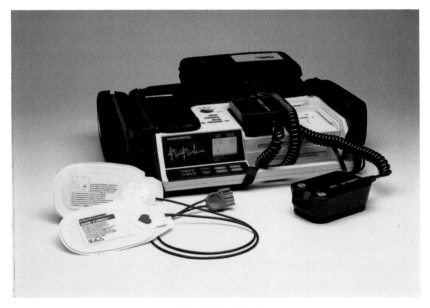

The LifePak 10

Eric started his paramedic training and was full of questions on a daily basis. I felt like I was back in school again. Some of the material he was talking about sent shivers down my spine recalling how tedious it was. One day he asked me to help him with the Krebs cycle and I about became ill. The Krebs cycle would nearly be the demise of many a student over the years and I was almost one of them.

It described the anaerobic metabolism process and energy production in the body which is quite complicated. Anatomy and Physiology are fascinating but a lot of information. He would ask a question and then both he and Sam would look at me like I was going to give them this straightforward, easy to understand answer. It included a lot of umm's and ahh's and on and on.

Finally the tones saved me from further humiliation.

"Medic 42, Rescue 41, respond code three for a 75 year old male with chest pain…88 Franklin Place, low cross of Gracie…time out 0907 hours."

Traffic was light and we made it on scene in just over three minutes.

We exited the vehicles when the wife came busting out the front door screaming, "He passed out, I can't move him, please, please hurry."

Nothing good comes from a start like this.

I made it in the house first. The patient is sitting in a recliner. He is slumped to his left, eyes half open, cyanosis to the lips and making an occasional agonal gasp; he's in cardiac arrest, clinically dead. Between Rocky and I, we got him to the floor and Steve began compressions.

His wife was crying and pleading, "Oh my God, this can't be happening… please help him."

A neighbor walked in and immediately hugged the wife and escorted her out of the room.

Sam was cutting the shirt off and Eric was at the head with the BVM. Rocky was setting up the main kit and I was getting ready to check his heart rhythm.

After two minutes of CPR, I told Steve to stop compressions; it's V-fib, I had Sam take over compressions while I got the LifePak 10 ready to shock.

The LifePak 10 has paddles which I grabbed from the machine. I applied the conductive gel to the shiny flat surface and rubbed them together as I told Sam to stop. I placed the paddles on the chest, said clear and shocked; a jump and small groan from the patient followed and Sam resumed compressions.

I thought this would be a good opportunity to secure the airway. Eric moved to the side as I got into position and then slid the laryngoscope blade into his mouth. I just got a view of the epiglottis when the upper dentures came lose and wedged toward the back of the throat. I had to withdraw the blade and after easily removing them, continued and quickly found the opening to the trachea. With the tube in place and secured, it was time to check the rhythm again.

"V-fib, let's shock at 300 watts," I said. Once again after applying the conductive gel to the paddles the shock was delivered.

Steve took over on compressions.

I applied the rubber tourniquet to the left arm and was starting the IV; I almost missed it as the patient suddenly lifted his right arm and tried to push Steve's hands off his chest.

I said, "I think we have some signs of life here, folks," and Steve stopped his compressions.

I checked the left carotid and sure enough it was strong, the EKG looked good as well. I put the signature 'X' over the carotid.

Eric continued to ventilate through the endotracheal tube with the bag valve and got ready to move to the gurney when Sam said, "Ahh Mark, I think we just lost him."

I looked at the monitor and sure enough we were back in V-fib. This time Eric said he would start the compressions while Sam took over on ventilations. When we see V-fib happen, we can go straight to the shock, which is what I did.

Only this time we had a little unintended post-shock event.

As I delivered the shock, I had too much conductive gel on the paddles because a large blue arc went across his chest and it ignited a rapidly moving small "chest fire."

Steve quickly grabbed the towel off the stretcher and tamped the fire out and Eric continued compressions. What it did was basically give us a smoother chest to work with and there was no actual burn to the chest.

This would forever be known as the "guy we caught on fire while trying to save."

We all had crinkled noses and squinty eye looks with the heavy burnt hair smell that permeated the room.

During the two minutes of CPR, I administered 1 mg of epinephrine through the IV and then it was time to check the rhythm. V-fib, another shock after carefully ensuring no excess gel and resume CPR.

After about thirty seconds, he started moving, it was the same as before--good pulse, good rhythm--but this time it stabilized. The crew was getting him into the ambulance as I spoke to his wife.

"We have his heart started again. He's very critical and hasn't awoken, we'll continue to work very hard and take him to RGH," I explained to her.

She said, "Thank you very much. Please let him know I will meet him there, his name is Glen."

At that time the neighbor pulled up in the driveway with her minivan.

During the transport I did as the wife asked.

"Glen, I know you can hear me. Your wife wants you to know she'll meet us at the hospital. We're taking care of you and we'll get you there safely," I said.

We noticed his heart rate went up a few beats after that, then back to normal. I think he heard me.

Glen went to the catheterization lab and had two stents inserted. He was admitted to the CCU and the next day his endotracheal tube was removed and was awake. The cardiologist was optimistic. No one ever asked us about the "*chest shave.*"

We would be happy to get our LifePak 12 back.

It is always gratifying when we can send a person back home to their families after a catastrophic medical emergency or traumatic event. Bystander CPR has made some of the biggest differences in outcomes. We are always trying to get the public to embrace immediate bystander CPR and quick response to 9-1-1. It's frustrating to arrive on a scene where a person has collapsed and find people standing around, not sure of what they should be doing and afraid they will make the situation worse.

I had just finished getting my boots polished and everything put away when the station became alive with activity. The tones reverberating through the ceiling speaker had something to do with it.

"Medic 42, Rescue 41, respond code three to the airport, lower level, south entrance, for a male subject collapsed, CPR is believed to be in progress...time out 1600 hours."

We knew we would have plenty of bystanders willing to jump in and do CPR if needed; hopefully that would be the case today. Arriving at the given location we noticed a police officer waving at us and parked right in front of the entrance.

The officer said, "I think he's okay now; they shocked him a couple times."

This drew an odd look from us and we proceeded in as directed.

Next to one of the baggage claim areas there's a small crowd and a male lying on the floor with a coat under his head for a pillow. He had his shirt ripped open and we could hear prompts from an AED: "*Stand clear, do not touch the patient, analyzing rhythm, no shock advised, it is safe to touch the patient, resume CPR if needed.*"

Considering you don't apply the AED unless the patient is without life signs, we were curious about the story here.

A bystander who was "in-charge" described how they were standing at the carousel waiting for the luggage to come around when the patient grabbed his chest, went down to one knee, rolled over and had a seizure. He then turned blue and had no pulse. They immediately began CPR and yelled for an AED. The AED was brought to them and deployed. It delivered one shock and they resumed CPR; after the second shock the patient started moving and actually woke up.

The patient's name is Barry and he just flew in from Hawaii. Kneeling next to him I said, "Barry my name is Mark, I am a paramedic. How do feel at this moment?"

"My chest is sore, but otherwise I feel okay. Did I die?" He asked softly in disbelief.

I said, "Well, it sounds that way. What do you think about us taking you to the hospital and make sure it doesn't happen again?"

He said, "That sounds good to me…Mahalo."

In the ambulance Eric started him on oxygen with a face mask. I found a good IV site on the left arm and put an 18 gauge into it. Sam has the LifePak 12 hooked up and is calling numbers.

"Heart rate 96, blood pressure 164/102, Sp02 96%," she said.

The 12 lead EKG shows acute changes in the inferior (lower) portion of the heart. With oxygen, nitro and aspirin, he said he was feeling better but was still quite humbled by everything that was going on.

Nitro is a medicine we use to relieve pain that is suggestive of being cardiac related. It helps to relax the blood vessels around the heart and allows more blood to get to cardiac muscle cells that are starving for oxygen. We use it with caution when someone is having a heart attack as it can precipitously lower the blood pressure. It is given under the tongue either in spray form or a tiny white dissolvable pill.

Barry remained silent during the transport. At one point I asked if there was anything I could do to make him more comfortable.

"I've been having a *pain* the last couple days," he said.

"I just thought it was the different diet, this could have happened at any time over the last few days," he reflected with mortal concern.

"Well, things are looking stable now, let's just get to Regional and have the cardiologists figure the rest of it out, just try to relax if you can," I said.

We got to RGH and had called a cardiac alert which had the cardiac team ready and within minutes Barry was off to the cath lab. After two stents he was admitted to the CCU and discharged five days later.

Sam put a "Fracture Assessment and Splinting class" together she was going to present for the crews today. We've made three attempts at the class without success and now for the fourth try made it as far as the training room before the tones turned us right back around to the truck bays...maybe next shift.

"Medic 42...Rescue 41, respond code three for a male subject short of breath, he's with police at 401 Main Street...time out 1444 hours."

Pulling up to the scene, we found two patrol cars and an officer waving us to the back car. They had the rear door open and we could see an individual sitting in the back.

As we walked up the officer said, "Hey guys, we stopped this guy on his bicycle because he had this large back pack and we noticed the copper sticking out. He couldn't come up with a good reason to have it all.... he then started complaining of trouble breathing and chest pain...and saying something about being shocked this morning...we figured you better check him out..."

I said, "Okay, we'll take a look at him," and walked to the back of the patrol car and knelt down.

"Hi there, my name's Mark; I'm a paramedic, what's the problem this afternoon?"

"Can't...breathe...chest...hurts," he said with an obvious degree of distress.

"Alright, why don't we get you in the back of the ambulance and see if we can figure out what's going on...sound okay with you?" I said.

"Sure," he said softly.

He's sweaty and his color is a terrible pasty pale. He is definitely sick.

He said his name is Tony. He's thin, maybe six feet and 140 pounds, long greasy hair in a ponytail at the base of his neck. He has tribal-type tattoos up both sides of his neck and two "teardrop" tattoos at the corner of his left eye. He is devoid of hygiene and quite aromatic.

In the back of the ambulance we noticed he's breathing fast, around 36 times per minute. His pulse is 124 and irregular. His Sp02 is reading 89%. His pupils are dilated and he's having trouble sitting still. Sam has placed an oxygen mask over his face.

Tony said, "My chest is burning…it started…after I got shocked."

I said, "How did you get shocked?"

"I was helping…a friend move his dryer…and I accidentally bumped into a wire," he said.

"I see, well where'd it get you?" I asked.

He pointed to his left shoulder, and then his right shoulder.

I said, "You pointed to both…did you get shocked in both of them?"

This time he put his right finger on his left shoulder and then made a line from there across his chest and then pointing away from the right shoulder. This was getting a bit confusing so I said, "Let's get your shirt off and show me what you're talking about."

As he removed his shirt, we all stared at his shoulders. On the left shoulder, he has a round charred area the size of a golf ball. It has a small open wound in the center. On the right shoulder is another charred golf ball sized burn but this one has a larger, more ominous looking open wound, like an exit wound.

I looked at Eric and said, "We may want to take a look at the monitor and check his rhythm."

Sam got the wounds dressed with sterile bandages and taped in place.

One of the officers motioned for me to step outside the ambulance. He said they received a report from Public Utilities about someone breaking into one of the substations today and steeling copper wiring. They also found evidence something came in contact with high voltage at one of the junction boxes. This made more sense and is a miracle Tony wasn't killed if this was him responsible for the break-in and subsequent electrocution.

At this point it really didn't matter; we needed to ensure he was transported and evaluated further at RGH. I stepped back into the ambulance and Eric was just finishing inserting an IV.

"Look at the monitor," Eric said.

He's having irregular and regular changes and everything in between, probably just what you'd expect after your heart takes a massive shock. He's still having trouble sitting in one place. His blood pressure is 180/114; heart rate is 114 and breathing 32 times a minute and the Sp02 is 94%.

Tony later admitted to stealing copper wire and nearly being killed at the substation. He had twenty-eight dollars' worth of copper from the heist. His condition ended up being critical with severe rhabdomyolysis which is a critical condition where his muscle tissue was breaking down and affecting his kidney function secondary to the massive electrocution episode. He was admitted to the ICU in where he spent the next week.

He has since been released and not heard from again.

CHAPTER 11

THE CLUB SCENE

In EMS there really isn't one day of the week that's necessarily busier than the other. We've had Tuesday and Wednesdays that have generated more assaults and traumatic calls than some Friday and Saturday nights. Weekends can be a wild time when you add elements such as alcohol, full moons, hot weather, a holiday and sometimes "just because."

It's Friday night; it's been a nice summer day, festive moods, what could go wrong here?

Tones…

"Medic 42, Rescue 41, respond for an assault victim bleeding from the face, police are responding, suspect is reported still on scene, stage in the area, 1801 Main Street…The Happy Time Tavern…time out 2005 hours."

We are within a block of the establishment when dispatch advises, "Step it up; patient has been stabbed in the face and has severe wounds."

Steve and I both acknowledged the update. I then requested dispatch to advise RGH of our status and I would update them ASAP.

Arriving on location is an overload to the visual sensoria…four police cars, all with lights flashing, crowds of people walking everywhere, a chaotic and fluid scene. An officer walked up to me as I exited the ambulance.

"You got a guy that's been slashed through the face and he's not doing too well," he said with obvious urgency and concern.

"Okay, we'll get our stuff and follow you," I said.

Rocky had the main kit, Sam had the airway kit, Eric had the oxygen and Steve was bringing the gurney.

Once inside the establishment, the lighting was darkened and less than optimal. Several officers are trying to help the patient who is on his hands and knees slowly crawling to nowhere in particular with blood streaming from his face. One of the officers is holding a large bar towel to the front of the patient's face, it is soaked with blood.

I put my hand on the patient's left shoulder and got next to his ear, "My name is Mark. I'm a paramedic. Stop moving and we'll help you," I said.

There's a steady stream of blood and part of face is hanging off. The slash wound starts near the left temple, goes through the left eye which is gouged from the socket and now a coagulated disaster. It continues through the nose, through both upper and lower lips and then splitting the chin open widely.

His breathing is uncompromised for now; the bleeding is the main priority and needs immediate control.

Eric and Sam each had a 10 by 30 inch trauma dressing. Sam applied the first one to the left side of the face which encompassed the flap. Eric then folded his dressing sideways and wrapped it from the left ear to the right ear, which covered most of the face but left the mouth open for breathing.

Rocky applied a large elastic bandage roll to secure the dressings in place and the guy ended up looking like a mummy. Spots of blood are leaking through but the major flow has been controlled.

Since we also covered the right eye during the bandaging, it's important to communicate with the patient as to what's going on. He's now temporarily blinded and can easily become overwhelmed by everything and potentially become combative. We need him to cooperate completely at this point.

Sam put an oxygen mask over his mouth and was next to his right ear explaining what was going on around him. I finished a quick head to toe assessment and found this to be the only injury. His radial pulse rate is 120. We have him on the gurney in a semi-sitting position.

As part of the investigation, one of the officers had grabbed the patient's wallet. He handed me the patient's driver's license to take with us to the hospital. The patient's name is Michael; he's 24 years old and a good-looking kid. I doubt anyone in his family or circle of friends would recognize him at this moment...neither would he, actually.

Once in the ambulance I got a 14 gauge IV placed in the left mid arm. Sam is continuing to explain what is going on. Eric has the LifePak 12 hooked up and calling numbers.

"Heart rate 116, blood pressure 108/88, SpO2 94%," he said.

These are good numbers considering the magnitude of the injury. We estimate blood loss on scene at over a liter.

I gave RGH the update and requested the full trauma team. We arrived and were directed straight to Suite 12. We stayed in the room while they un-wrapped the dressings. The wound is massive for a facial assault. The left eye was gone, that was graphically obvious. Now it was off to the O.R. and attempt to save the rest of his face.

A suspect was arrested and charged with the aggravated assault. Witnesses report both the patient and suspect had argued and nearly fought several times throughout the night. Finally the suspect left the bar and retuned with a large hunting knife, walked up to Michael and with one violent swing changed his life forever. We cannot fathom how one individual can be capable of such violence and how angry someone would have to be to harbor such rage.

Michael lost the left eye. He bears a scar through the face that he will see for the rest of his life.

On Saturday we planned a crew dinner. Gourmet chef Steve would prepare his hamburger and "secret recipe" fries that could give any fast food establishment competition. We never left the table unsatisfied and would have leftovers for the next several shifts.

Some of these leftovers would become ecological experiments in the fridge. I've never been able to figure out how such a great meal could become so hazardous after just a few days. It also seems like this process was accelerated in our station. There were times when special permits probably should have been issued to even open the fridge door.

With everyone's palate satisfied and kitchen cleaned, thoughts of relaxing were erased with the tones.

"Medic 42, Rescue 41, respond for an intoxicated female needing transport to the hospital, police on scene…608 11th Ave….time out 1930 hours."

When someone needs transported because of alcohol, they can have life-threatening levels. We also need to be aware that alcohol can mask underlying medical problems.

We arrived on scene with two patrol vehicles parked in front of the residence. The patient is slumped over in the back of the second patrol car.

An officer met us and explained, "We got an intoxicated female, 22 years of age. Her friends said they got together to celebrate a birthday and report everything seemed fine when she arrived. She had a couple drinks and kind of went downhill from there, mumbling incoherently, couldn't stand up and just not acting right."

Sam and Eric went over to the patrol car and started waving Rocky and me over as we were talking with the officer.

"What's going on?" I asked as we walked up to them.

"She is o-u-t, out, no response," Eric said.

Sam added, "When we first got to her she was having snoring respiratory efforts; we repositioned her head and she's breathing okay now."

I said, "Alright, let's get her in the back of the rig and see what's going on."

The patient is petite, maybe 110 pounds, 5 foot 4, along with an obvious alcohol aroma. There are no obvious signs of trauma, no medic alert bracelets or any other clues about what might be going on. Sam and Eric were able to easily lift her to the gurney.

Once in the back of the rig, the only response we could get was a slight withdrawal from a sternal rub. This was looking more ominous as we moved through our assessment.

Sam had the LifePak 12 hooked up and it's showing a regular looking rhythm, heart rate is 90, BP is 96/54, and SpO2 is 97%.

Eric extracted a drop of blood from a finger for the glucose check and said, "Guess what, everyone…it says LO."

This now made sense and explained the behavior. I will administer an amp of D50 IV and this should bring everything back to a normal baseline.

I let Eric set up for the IV since he was counting IV starts for paramedic school. They need over one-hundred successful IV starts during the year of training.

He secured a rubber tourniquet to her left upper arm and after a couple "taps" to her vein things went from "zero to a hundred" in an instant.

The patient began screaming and wildly swinging both arms. I happen to be in the right place at the right time and caught a right cross squarely just under the left eye. It immediately started swelling and felt like it came from more than a 110 pound female. She then started kicking violently and for a few brief seconds it looked like we would all be taken out by this female acting like the Tasmanian devil in the back of the ambulance.

None of this is intentional on her part. It isn't entirely uncommon to have a diabetic become combative with their sugar level being so low. Between Steve and me and Sam, we were able to gain control of her while Eric managed to secure an IV in her left arm.

I administered the amp of D50 through the IV line and before I finished injecting it she was starting to relax and then opened her eyes. She looked around as if trying to focus on where she was, who we were and why we were all looking at her with such caution and me with my left eye nearly swollen shut.

I spoke up and gently asked, "Can you hear me...are you back with us now?"

She closed her eyes and moaned, "How low was I?"

"Well, less than 20," I said, "Do you remember what you were doing?"

"Well, I think I was at Sherrie's and it's her birthday," she said through cobwebs of confusion.

I said, "Yep, you got it...so I am correct that you are an insulin dependent diabetic?"

"Uh-huh…I am so sorry," she said almost in a whisper.

We now have an entirely different patient. She is cooperative, polite, friendly and unaware of how much of a struggle we have just endured from her.

I am now unable to see out of my left eye due to it being completely swollen shut and can't wait to explain to the emergency room staff how "a 110 pound female nearly KO'd me."

"Well, at least we got you back to the right time zone. Can you tell us your name?" I asked.

"Debbie," she responded with her hand over her eyes.

"Can you tell me why your sugar got so low?" I asked.

"I have been having a lot of trouble and they can't get the dosage right," she said.

"Well, my recommendation is that we take you to Regional and see if they can help you through the rest of the night," I said.

"My doctor's going to kill me, he said I am NOT supposed to be drinking alcohol," she said.

"Well, let's just go one step at a time," I said.

She kept her hand over her eyes and nodded.

I then asked, "Do you have a medic alert bracelet or anything like that?"

"I carry a card in my wallet," she said, "Maybe I need the bracelet too…" which got affirmative nods from all of us.

The trip to RGH was uneventful, Rachel was there to take the report and of course several of the nurses had to come over and see my periorbital ecchymosis, medical terminology for black eye.

Every call has the potential to go "sideways" in an instant. This response is a vivid reminder of this.

After getting back to the station my focus was on reducing the swelling over my eye. I spent an hour holding a frozen bag of peas over my left eye and it seemed to be functional again.

The activity around the station is relaxed. We're listening to Steve snore while fully reclined in the recliner. Eric is flipping through the channels and as usual can't find anything worth watching. If there is, we'll get interrupted in the middle of it anyway. The EMS call Gods have a way of seeing to that. We've rented movies and taken them back without opening the covers.

They would ask us at the video store, "Did you guys like the movie?"

We'd give the pat answer, "Oh yeah, it was great, all the art work on the package...next time we're going to try to actually watch it."

Eric finally settled on the news, and even that wasn't immune to the tones.

"Medic 42, Rescue 41, respond for an officer involved shooting, 2380 Division Street, in front of Brett's Pool Hall...time out 2205 hours."

Responding to an officer involved shooting can be a very tense and dramatic scene. Something obviously went terribly wrong when deadly force is used.

We received an update: the patient would be in an orange pickup truck in front of the Pool Hall.

As expected, we arrived to a very chaotic and highly charged scene. There are at least five patrol cars and yellow police tape being strung up everywhere. An orange pickup truck is in the center of it all. The left front bumper of the truck is against a utility pole and there are skid marks that indicate it slid and stopped exactly as it sat. The driver's door is open with a leg dangling as if it were the first step in getting out of the vehicle.

An officer met us and explained, "This guy reportedly tried to beat another guy with a pool cue. The bouncers got into it with him and called 9-1-1…we arrived to find him running from the place. He jumped into this truck and drove straight at us, almost ran over one of the other officers….we fired and he stopped here and I think he's still alive."

As we're approaching the truck, I count at least four bullet holes through the windshield, all on the driver's side. Then as we get to the driver's door, the horrifying aftermath of being on the other side of a barrage of bullets is graphically revealed. The patient is lying across the bench seat and the first thing I hear was deep choking gasps he is struggling with. The bench seat is covered in what looked like his entire blood volume.

I called out, "Can you hear me…I need you to open your eyes and look at me…"

There's no response.

The most obvious bleeding is coming from up around his head. He took one of the rounds to the jaw which then traveled through the left side of the neck, just below the ear and there's heavy dark bleeding from this area.

I noticed a tee-shirt on the floor of the truck and placed it over the wound. He has a weak radial pulse at 130.

I yelled over my shoulder to Rocky, "Get the gurney and let's finish this in the rig."

"Roger that," he replied.

Steve came with back board and gurney and said, "Rocky's getting things set up in the back."

Between Eric and Sam and Steve and me, we got him secured to the spine board and onto the gurney. I see a second GSW in the left upper chest and this round is still in there as evidenced by no exit wound. Sam placed her gloved hand over this wound in case it was a sucking chest wound.

Any penetrating wound to the chest has to be treated as if it were a sucking chest wound regardless if there is no "bubbling" during the breathing process. This means immediately covering the wound.

Eric was at the head of the gurney and we're headed to the rig. He's holding pressure along the jaw and neck wound with a 10 by 30 trauma dressing and keeping the airway aligned while Steve is walking along side us using the suction intermittently.

This was a large and deep wound that was difficult to compress. Gunshot wounds have little mercy. We didn't see any spurting so it was primarily venous in origin. Had it have been arterial, he certainly would have bled to death prior to our arrival.

I'm estimating blood loss in the truck at well over a liter.

I would need to secure this airway before we could leave the scene. Sam cut the shirt off as Rocky placed an occlusive dressing over the hole in the chest and taped it in place. Eric continued holding direct pressure against the neck and I'm in position to insert the laryngoscope blade and get a tube into the trachea.

I gently opened the mouth and inserted the blade. I just got a view of the vocal cords when the patient opened his eyes, brought his right hand up, grabbed the laryngoscope out of my left hand and threw it against the back door of the ambulance just missing hitting Sam in the head as she instinctively ducked.

This really caught us off guard. The last thing we expected was him to wake up and become aggressive. We all yelled out in a collective "whoa there" as we quickly held both of the patient's arms at his side while I searched for an IV site. I found a vein in the left forearm and slipped a 14 gauge in.

Now I can administer the RSI drugs. After the etomidate went through the line, he went limp and let out an exhaustive breath. Next the sux was pushed and this brought on immediate paralysis. After ensuring he was out, I re-introduced the laryngoscope blade. The blown-apart jaw created a challenge of keeping the field of vision clear with steady bleeding and clumps of coagulated blood. I watched the tube go through the vocal cords and into the trachea and Sam attached to bag valve and began providing breaths.

We are en route to RGH and I radioed ahead and had the trauma team standing by with an ETA of three minutes.

I cut the rest of the clothing off and the two wounds were all I could find. There's an overwhelming and near intoxicating aroma of alcohol that permeated the back of the ambulance.

Eric hooked up the LifePak 12 and called out numbers, "Heart rate 134, blood pressure 76/40, Sp02 88%," he said.

During the reassessment I am puzzled by hearing clear and equal breath sounds given the hole that is just above the left nipple. I noticed significant dark blue swelling under the left armpit. Perhaps the bullet travelled laterally and didn't penetrate the chest cavity?

We arrived at RGH and two security guards instinctively stepped back as the ambulance doors opened with blood flowing on to the ground. Suite 12 was set up with the awaiting trauma team and after an X-ray they were off the O.R.

We later learned the chest bullet had indeed travelled laterally and did not penetrate the chest cavity. The neck and jaw were repaired and would be functional.

Blood alcohol level was .28, over three times the legal limit. He was also positive for methamphetamine, heroin and oxycodone and had recently been paroled after seven years in prison for attempted murder and would eventually end up back in prison for another ten years.

The last several shifts had been extraordinarily busy. We planned to have a day with no scheduled station activities. This would allow everyone to catch up on personal projects and hopefully get a workout in before lunch. These plans were short-lived by the first call of the day coming via the tones.

"Medic 42, Rescue 41, respond code three for an unconscious male, behind the Half Moon Tavern…1250 Bates Road…time out 0822 hours."

It took us three minutes to arrive. We pulled into the parking lot and were directed to the back of the establishment. We found three police cars and officers walking around the perimeter of the lot. One of them was waving us toward a small group of hedges.

It's a grisly presentation, an unconscious male so savagely beaten about the face that he has no recognizable features.

One of the officers explained, "A lady had been walking her dog and it alerted toward the bushes where she noticed the legs sticking out. She immediately called 9-1-1," he said.

He also said they found a car out front that belonged to the patient. They believed he may have been at the tavern last night, brought out here, assaulted and left for dead.

Walking up to the patient I can hear rapid, labored type breathing. Sam went to the top of his head and held cervical immobilization. Eric and Rocky got the backboard ready and Steve was cutting clothing. He is unresponsive to any stimulus.

I started at the head for the assessment. He has so much dried and crusted blood along with matted hair it's difficult to assess the skull. He is bleeding from both ears; the eyes are so tightly swollen I can't open them. There's deep black bruising around both orbits, the nose is dislocated in two directions with packed and dried blood blocking both nares, the right cheekbone is sunken in, the lips are swollen at nearly twice the normal size, all the front teeth are missing and the right ear is nearly torn off. These massive findings are usually not associated with positive outcomes.

The chest rises and falls with breathing. The abdomen is soft. There's heavy incontinence of urine and feces. The lower extremities are unremarkable. The fists are swollen with multiple lacerations to the knuckles. I notice he occasionally displays abnormal extension of his arms and legs, as if he is trying to "stretch." This adds to the grave neurological evidence of a brain injury. The radial pulse is 50.

He was obviously in some kind of fight for his life, and still may have lost.

We packaged him onto the long spine board and loaded into the ambulance. One of the officers came over and asked, "How is he…you think he'll make it?"

"I don't know…he's about as bad as you can be beaten," I said and probably didn't sound too confident.

We started for RGH and alerted the trauma team. Sam was at the head and providing oxygen by mask and suctioning as she could.

"I have to hold his jaw forward for each breath," she said.

I would need to RSI this guy. I placed the rubber tourniquet on his left upper arm and quickly found a site that I put a 14 gauge into. A quick check of the sugar showed 104.

Eric had the LifePak 12 hooked up and called out ominous numbers, "Heart rate 54, blood pressure is 210/130, Sp02 92%," he said.

These are frightening numbers and reflective of a TBI (Traumatic brain injury).

I prepared for the intubation and told Eric and Sam that I might need both of their hands to successfully get him intubated. Eric pushed the RSI drugs and the patient stopped breathing and became flaccid. I had Sam open his mouth and hold it as wide as she could with regard to the swelling. I gently inserted the curved blade and made sure I was aware of where I was on the way down. Eric is peering in and suctioning clots of blood and removed three teeth. Once I got to the epiglottis, I actually have a reasonable view of the vocal cords which are stained red from blood. They should be white.

"Hand me the tube," I asked Eric.

He placed it in my right hand in the correct position, and I watched it go through the vocal cords. We noticed good chest rise and fall with ventilation. This was a difficult intubation. We're now just minutes from RGH.

We were met with our usual excellent greeting from the trauma team. The patient was off to CT scan within six minutes. The report was as feared, massive bleeding in several areas of the brain and he was taken to the O.R. After ninety minutes he was in the trauma ICU. At 1530 hours that afternoon he went into cardiac arrest and after a valiant attempt at resuscitation he was pronounced dead.

He never regained consciousness. His injuries were mortal from the onset.

Our patient's name was Junior. He was 24 years old and an unemployed laborer. The police arrested two individuals in connection with the beating and charged with manslaughter. The fight was over drugs and money.

CHAPTER 12

ERIC'S GRADUATION

Rocky had taken a couple of much needed shifts off. He and Rachel went camping with the "kids." He said they had a blast and didn't want to come back. I told him Sam would be more than happy to take over if he decided to do the mountain man thing.

"Don't tempt me," he said with a sly grin.

Eric was finishing his last paramedic clinical rotations this week, and then the arduous task of final testing which would take several days to complete. He conceded it had been a fast and furious year and wasn't sure he learned everything he was supposed to.

I laughed at hearing that and said, "Welcome to the club, almost every medic feels that way when they're done."

I reminded him, "Remember the saying about good EMT's becoming..." and he finished the sentence with "good paramedics, I know, I know"...

We were interrupted by the tones.

I said, "Let's go on a call and test some of those skills," as we headed to the truck bay.

"Medic 42, Rescue 41, respond code three to mile post 16, Hwy 7, motorcycle rider down, reportedly run over by a second vehicle…time out 0840 hours."

As we were watching the bay door go up I asked dispatch about having Mercy Flight on standby. It would take a solid ten minutes to get to this location. The air transport could make up valuable time and could make the difference in survival.

We were several minutes from the scene when we received an update from dispatch. Mercy Flight was requested for another location and needed a decision from us as far as flying or cancelling. I decided to have them activated to our call based on the information we had on the initial dispatch.

You always know you're getting close to the scene when you encounter the "parking lot" of traffic that was backed up. Frustrated motorists stared as we cautiously proceeded past them with the lights and siren.

Arriving on scene we see a state trooper waving us to her location. We could see the patient lying near her in the road and his motorcycle not far from him.

A second vehicle was stopped in the lane of travel just beyond where the patient was lying. There are heavy skid marks that follow the path of its tires and go right over where the patient is lying.

A second trooper is standing with a guy next to that vehicle. I found out he is the driver of that car and described how a vehicle overtook him at a high rate of speed and rear-ended the motorcycle rider causing him to lose control and crash. That vehicle fled the scene. The driver stated he couldn't stop as it all happened so quickly and ran over the downed motorcycle rider. He is visibly shaken while explaining the story.

As I walk up to the patient he is unresponsive to verbal hails or gentle taps to the shoulder.

The most graphic and obvious injury is the massive damage to both lower legs. They were violently run over and are now grotesque angulations of bone and muscle along with shredded pieces of leather.

That was the obvious. I was more concerned with what we didn't see. Rocky was at the head, holding the neck to prevent any movement. The patient is wearing a small "half-helmet" and it has a sizeable indentation to the back of it. Sam and Steve are cutting clothing which includes the jacket we recognize as associated with one of the local motorcycle gangs.

He's bleeding out of the right ear and nose and his breathing is irregular and labored. After a quick listen to the chest I cannot hear breath sounds on the left side and there is air trapped in the skin (rice crispies). He has a weak radial pulse at 120. His skin is pale, cool and clammy, he's in shock.

Eric is utilizing his strong airway skills every EMT should be adept at by providing ventilatory support with bag valve mask ventilation. Sam took over for Rocky at the head which allowed him to open the kits and start setting equipment up.

"Mark, each breath is getting harder, I think we may have a tension pneumothorax," Eric said.

"Okay, I agree, we'll put the 'big needle' in," I said.

Rocky handed me the 12 gauge 3-inch needle. I mapped out the land marks over the chest, second intercostal space, going over the top of the third rib, in the middle alignment of the clavicle. As I inserted it through the chest cavity the familiar hiss was audible for several seconds before going quiet.

"That did it, much easier to bag now," Eric said.

Steve took over on the BVM while Eric and I searched for IV sites. We both found suitable veins at the same time and put the IV's in simultaneously. Rocky handed us each IV tubing which we plugged in to the back of the IV's and taped securely.

"Good job," I told him.

"Same to you," he said back.

Our next step is to get the airway secured with the RSI procedure. Eric drew up the drugs as I quickly got the patient hooked up to the LifePak 12. The first numbers didn't look promising.

"Heart rate 128, blood pressure 70/40, SpO2 won't read," I announced to Eric as he was ready with the RSI drugs.

I told Eric to push the etomidate which caused a noticeable decrease in the breathing. Next the sux went in and after less than one minute I had the laryngoscope blade down the patient's throat. Once I got to the area of the epiglottis, I was surprised to see clots of blood around the vocal cords. I was able to pass the tube past them and now Sam attached the bag valve to the end of the endotracheal tube and started providing breaths at one every six seconds. We can all see good chest rise and I can hear air over the right chest. The "big needle" is still in place in the left chest.

Steve finished securing the lower legs with large trauma dressings and cardboard splints. The damage is horrendous. The legs remain attached to the body by skin alone. He had to "re-align" each leg to the correct anatomical position before splinting them. It would seem doubtful of any hope in saving these legs.

Our last task was to get him secured to the long spine board. As we rolled him onto his right side I checked the back and was shocked at finding a pistol tucked into the waist band.

Sam said, "Hey, that's a .380….I have one just like it."

I called over to the trooper and she took control of it. It was ready to go with one in the chamber along with a full clip. Glad we found that before sending him to RGH; we would have heard about that.

Rocky then called out, "Sugar at 134," he said.

"Roger that," I said and noted it on my scratch paper of notes.

Mercy Flight arrived and I had Eric give the report. They were on scene six minutes and were happy with that turnaround. The patient was in the hospital in ten minutes.

We accomplished a great deal in a short amount of time. Eric had done a great job and hopefully this would give him some confidence going into his final testing. It wouldn't be any worse than this scenario.

We later found out that both lower legs were amputated. He has a TBI and they are cautiously optimistic at the long term prognosis because of good pupillary responses. He had a chest tube put into the left chest and will reside in the trauma ICU for the next several days. He's alive though, and that's the most important update.

The troopers believe the hit and run may have not been accidental but an actual planned assault. It is an on-going investigation.

The following week Eric completed his practical testing and was optimistic about the written exams. He would have the results in a few days. He was grinning while talking about his major trauma practical scenario. It involved a critically injured motorcycle rider that needed to be electively intubated by using the RSI procedure.

He smiled and said, "They could have just counted our call last week; it was almost the same scenario."

He said the instructors commented on how calm he was and performed as if he had known what the practical was going to be.

He told them, "Nope, just had a good mentor."

I said, "Oh well, you'll have to introduce me to him some time."

"Very funny," Eric said and shook his head grinning ear to ear.

Our County EMS Medical Physician Advisor has a directive in which you're evaluated for a number of shifts after completing paramedic training--a sort of check ride before they hand you the keys to the ambulance. Eric will be spending a few shifts with me as a third on the medic unit and basically running the calls with a safety net.

Steve and Sam had a new member on their team. Dana Davidson will be filling in for Eric. Dana is an EMT and has filled in on both the rescue and the medic unit. She's been an active volunteer with the department for almost two years and in the process of finishing her nursing degree.

Dana's claim to fame was the day her neighbor came busting through her front door after her Old English Sheep dog developed a fully obstructed airway trying to swallow a golf ball.

The neighbor knew Dana was an EMT and part of the rescue squad. She was nearly hysterical with blind panic; she grabbed Dana by the arm and literally dragged her next door. Once inside, Dana found the dog, "Sheba," on the floor in the kitchen having a seizure. Sheba's gums were a deep blue, eyes rolled back in her massive head and no air movement.

The neighbor was screaming something about choking and golf balls... Dana finally pieced together the dog needed a chest thrust for a fully obstructed airway. She somehow lifted this massive dog up and performed several squeezes as the golf ball shot out bouncing across the floor.

After several seconds Sheba sat up, took a couple of breaths, coughed violently a few times and started wagging her tail like nothing ever happened. The neighbor was crying and hugging Dana, who later said, "I wasn't sure what just happened, but I think I just got my first save."

Dana became a local celebrity and ended up in the newspaper. There were pictures and a great write-up and we now have the picture of Dana and Sheba in our training room on our wall of fame.

It was the start of another Sunday morning; the station is busy with the crews getting the vehicles checked out and preparing for the day. Rocky closed the hood after checking the oil and yelled out, "Good to go here… anyone interested in donuts follow me…" Sam, Dana and Steve were hot on his trail.

Eric and I stayed in the back of the medic unit and talking about scenarios. The morning checkout can be a valuable time of day. It's an opportunity to review and understand every piece of equipment you carry. This would always pay off on some critical scene. You're only as good as your working knowledge of your equipment.

We had the main kit open and were discussing our cardiac drugs when the tones went off.

"Medic 42, Rescue 41, respond code three for an unconscious female, First Congregational Church, 1200 Main…time out 0850 hours."

This was a common Sunday morning call. Large gatherings, the crowds, the heat, standing in one place and the next thing you know you're passed out. The patient would usually be awake by the time we arrived and slightly embarrassed.

This morning would be different as dispatch updated us that CPR was in progress.

We arrived on scene and I told Eric he had the lead; I would back him up. I had the LifePak 12, Eric had the airway kit, Dana had the main kit, Sam had the oxygen bottle and Steve and Rocky were following with the backboard and gurney.

One of the parishioners met us at the entrance and said, "Thanks for getting here so quickly. I think her heart stopped and they're doing CPR on her. Follow me."

In the front of the church, near the sermon stand was the female who collapsed and two parish members are performing CPR. There are several parishioners standing nearby nervously watching and holding hands. The church is nearly full to capacity and most are kneeling with hands folded and heads bowed. If we ever had odds in our favor, it was here and now.

We were told this occurred during the part of the service where each member walked to the front of the church for communion. The patient turned to walk away and collapsed without warning. She immediately began to have seizure activity, turned blue, stopped breathing and lost her pulse. She's 78 years old and her husband and daughter are part of the group standing near her.

Eric directed Steve to take over on compressions and Sam and Dana to start with the BVM.

"Roger that," Steve and Sam replied nearly in unison.

I cut away the clothing in order to place the LifePak 12 combo-pads. Because adequate CPR was already being performed prior to our arrival, we stopped to look at the rhythm as soon as the screen came on.

"Asystole," Eric called out.

Asystole is flat line--no activity. This was not the rhythm we want to see. It does not get shocked as there is nothing to shock. Sometimes this confuses the public because they think every cardiac arrest gets "a shock" and then the patient comes back to life.

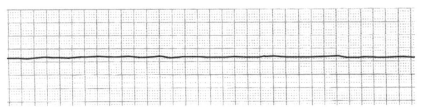

Asystole-Flat line

"Continue CPR, Steve," Eric said.

Rocky was getting equipment out of the main kit and had the IV bag ready to go. I established an IV in the left arm with a 16 gauge, plugged in the bag of normal saline and taped it securely. It was time to check the rhythm again.

"We have something to work with now, V-fib, let's shock at 200 watts," Eric said and then looked up and down to ensure no one was in contact with her before pressing the discharge button. The patient arched from the jolt which drew a collective gasp that echoed throughout the congregation.

Dana took over for Steve on compressions. Dana was performing as if she worked the rescue every day.

Rocky spoke up and announced, "Sugar is 110."

"Roger that, sugar 110," Eric noted.

Eric looked at me and said, "Let's give the epinephrine."

I said, "I agree, epinephrine going in," and pushed it through the IV line.

Eric then went to her head and prepared for intubation. He chose the curved blade, which would have been my preference as well. I watched him throughout the process; he gently placed the endotracheal tube as if he had been doing it for years as opposed to his first time as the medic in charge.

"Outstanding, sounds good right where it is," I said, as I listened over the chest to confirm he put it where it was supposed to go.

At the next rhythm check we were still in V-fib.

"Let's shock again, this time at 300 watts," Eric said and I delivered the energy which drew another collective gasp from the pews.

Shortly after the shock, I noticed the patient was starting to move. I held up my hand to stop Dana's compressions.

"We have a strong pulse," I said and there were soft claps throughout the church followed by cries of amen and shouts of encouragement for "Lila", the patient.

The LifePak12 displayed a BP of 160/100, SpO2 at 97% and a nice-looking rhythm on the screen. Things were looking positive at this point although we were still a long way from calling this a good outcome.

When we arrived at RGH, Dr. Stein looked at me and said, "What do you have here, Mark? Tell me a story."

I said, "Well, Eric was the paramedic running the show and he has the report."

Eric gave him the rundown from arriving on scene to getting her here.

Lila was admitted to the CCU. Seven hours later, she died without regaining consciousness.

When the nursing supervisor Brenda was telling us the story, she said she met with Lila's husband and daughter. They expressed such gratitude in being able to spend time with her in the CCU. They said that even though she didn't wake up, they spent the day talking to her and felt they were able to say goodbye.

We can't always judge our results by our efforts, but even in death we can make differences in people's lives. We never forget our patients or their experiences.

Eric and I had been working on our protocol review and it was productive for both of us. As paramedics we are not independent practitioners. We have a set of standard protocols that we follow for each scenario we might encounter. We also have the capability to call the emergency department for advice if needed. Patients have the right to refuse care and thus creating a difficult position we can end up in knowing that without the next level of care, they can have a bad outcome, and potentially die.

Tones interrupted the afternoon study session.

"Medic 42, Rescue 41, respond code three for a 63 year old male with chest pain…4511 Sparrow Place…time out 1600 hours."

I told Eric on the way to the call I expected a fairly quick 12 lead EKG after arrival. The 12 lead EKG was a crucial part of the assessment in a patient with chest pain. With the technology and capabilities we have with our equipment, we could literally see a heart attack happening in real time.

We arrived to find the patient's wife standing at the front door. She had a very obvious "irate" look as she greeted us.

'I'm the one who called…"*Mr. Denial*" is having chest pain and didn't want me to call you…he won't be happy you're here…he's been having chest pain all day, he's gone through at least a dozen nitro's, been sweating, breathing heavily and had a half dozen beers. He's also had two heart attacks and doesn't follow the doctor's orders and is stubborn as a jackass," she lamented.

"Okay, we can talk to him and we'll go from there," I said.

"Good luck," was her follow up response.

She led us into a day room where the patient was watching TV. As predicted he wasn't happy we were there. A small argument ensued between him and his wife regarding our presence that he quickly lost and conceded to talk to us.

He is at least 40 pounds overweight, has a three day unshaven appearance, a tee shirt at least one size too small with the lower third of his belly rolling out, a large ashtray on the stand next to him which is overflowing with cigarette butts, the trash can next to him is full with empty beer cans and remote control devices are spread out on the couch around him.

Eric knelt down in front of him and said, "My name is Eric, I'm a paramedic, and can I get your name sir?"

"Tom…and I can tell you right here and now I'm not going to any damn hospital so you're wasting your time," he said with a scowl.

"Okay," Eric said, "Can we at least check your blood pressure and look at your EKG?"

"Sure, knock yourself out, still not going anywhere," he said with determination.

Eric was talking with Tom while Dana was attaching all the 12 lead patches and Sam was checking the blood pressure.

"170/126," Sam called out.

Tom became notably irritated and said, "It's never been that high. Something's wrong with your blood pressure cuff or she can't hear too well."

Eric then showed me the 12 lead and it had clear evidence that he was having acute changes in the front part of his heart. This was a critical finding and needed to be evaluated in the E.D.

I stood next to Eric and said, "Tom, look, here's the bottom line: you need to go to RGH. Your EKG is reflective of changes that we are very concerned about."

"You can leave anytime, guys. I've heard this stuff before and all I do is sit there and they'll put me in the hospital overnight and nothing ever happens...I'm refusing and you can't make me go," he said angrily.

I was just about to try another angle when Tom suddenly developed a blank expression and took a deep gasp. His color rapidly went from pink to purple, eyes rolled back into his head, arched his back and was in full cardiac arrest in that exact moment.

Eric and I looked at each other as his wife screamed, "TOM," and then left the room crying.

Steve and Rocky got Tom onto the floor, where we quickly looked at the monitor screen and it showed V-fib.

Eric said, "Let's shock this, charging to 200 watts....clear," and then delivered the energy.

Tom lurched at the shock and let out a bellowed groan. Sam began compressions while Dana and Rocky were providing breaths with the BVM.

I got an IV established while the two minute round of compressions was being performed.

"Sugar is 160," I said.

"Roger that, 160," Eric acknowledged.

After two minutes of compressions, Eric told Sam to stop and looked at the monitor: V-fib, another shock, and this time at 300 watts, "clear" and the familiar lurch. Steve took over on compressions and I was about to administer epinephrine when Tom opened his eyes and with his right hand grabbed Steve's wrist to prevent him from giving another compression.

Eric told Steve to stop and got down almost face to face with Tom and said, "Can you hear me, Tom?"

"What the hell did you guys do to me?" He asked with a subdued and slurred tone.

The situation had become serious and dramatic and Tom wasn't so argumentative at this point. His wife came back in and with her hand over her forehead and cried out, "Is he okay?"

I said, "We have his heart started again and we really need to take him to RGH."

She said, "He's going and I don't give a rat's butt what he says about it, take him now!"

Rocky and Steve got Tom secured to the gurney and he remained stable for the transport to RGH. On the way in he seemed like a different guy than who we had the initial encounter with. I suppose that can happen when you die for a few minutes and then come back.

Eric had his focused look monitoring Tom on the way to RGH. He gave the cardiology team a very impressive report and had their attention talking about the sudden cardiac arrest. This would be a huge confidence booster for Eric.

It's challenging and difficult in knowing what you want to do, and having a medical directive to provide that care, and then have a patient refuse the treatment. My best advice is, if a paramedic ever says you need to go to the hospital with them, don't argue, take the advice, and go to the hospital!

Eric and I were going over one of his weekly evaluations. It's a difficult time after finishing school and actually starting to take the responsibility of being in charge and making tough decisions. Each day brings a new confidence. It's a very long process and one that can be extremely humbling.

We finished reviewing his last chart as the station came alive with our tones.

"Medic 42, Rescue 41, respond code three for a male subject down, reportedly not breathing…1200 Donation Street…Burgers and More… time out 1122 hours."

This should be a three minute response time but traffic was unusually heavy and it took us almost five minutes. We pulled up to the establishment and there's a patrol car out front and a young female employee waving us to the side entrance. As we're exiting the ambulance the employee shouted out, "The police officer's trying to get him out of the bathroom and the guy's blue."

This sounded like the officer definitely needed our help. We got in as quickly as we could and brought all the equipment with us. The Men's bathroom door was blocked open with a door stop and the officer was dragging this 20's year old male by his hands and walking backward towards us.

"I found him slumped over against the toilet, a syringe in his left arm and purple. The syringe fell out and is on the floor; he still has a pulse," the officer said.

Eric spoke up, "Dana, you and Sam take over on breathing. Steve, get me an IV bag set ready and Rocky, get the LifePak 12 hooked up."

Eric did a quick look at the pupils and said, "Pupils are nearly non-existent, pinpoint."

This pretty much confirmed we had at least some narcotic influence involved. Everyone was moving to their respective tasks and I applied a rubber tourniquet on the right arm to start looking for veins. Nothing was popping up.

Dana and Sam were getting good ventilations because his color was beginning to turn pink again. As I looked at their progress, I noticed a great external jugular vein on the right side of the neck and couldn't pass that up. I slid a 14 gauge into it and Steve handed me the IV tubing. I then made a loop with the IV tubing and taped it securely to the upper right shoulder. We won't be losing this IV.

Rocky checked the sugar, "100," he announced to anyone listening.

Eric had the narcan ready to go and cautioned everyone about potential fighting and vomiting after it was given. I decided to stay near the lower legs in case he started kicking.

Eric slowly pushed the narcan and after about thirty seconds the patient opened his eyes, looked around and then began making these dramatic motions like he was about to heave followed by two large episodes of projectile vomiting that sprayed all over Eric's right leg and crotch.

The accompanying sound of this heave echoed loudly, resonating down the hall and distinctly into the customer ordering area.

Then, a "warm and thick aroma" permeated the air; it was bad even by our standards. The poor young female employee started gagging as she turned and quickly walked off with her hand over her mouth. We saw several customers walk out and others are staring down the hall at us with mouths agape.

I thought to myself, *"Good thing I stayed down at the legs."*

Eric was the consummate professional and made sure the patient didn't aspirate or need additional help with the airway. When he noticed the patient was managing his own airway, he got up and walked into the bathroom, you could hear water running and the towel dispenser clicking and clicking.

I asked the patient his name and he said, "Bryce."

I said, "Hi Bryce, my name is Mark and I'm a paramedic. Can you tell us what happened this morning?"

Bryce's response sort of shocked me.

"Well it's kind of obvious, isn't it…I shot up some heroin and obviously OD'd."

I said, "We appreciate your honesty. You know we need to take you to RGH and get checked, don't you?"

Bryce didn't answer but just kind of stared off into the ceiling.

The ride into RGH was quite aromatic. Eric was looking quite humbled. The transport was uneventful and walking into RGH elicited double takes from everyone behind us as we walked by. We would not be the popular crew for the rest of this day.

The next couple of shifts were back to *routine* type calls, no critical patients. But then, no call was truly just a "routine call." We were sent to a poisoning yesterday and dispatch was giving us information that the caller was hysterical and having trouble providing information. It sounded ominous. We arrived to find a panic-stricken 26 year old female who met us at the door as we filed in past her.

"Who are we here for?" I asked.

"HEL--LO……ME…I've been poisoned…" she said.

"Okay…, my name is Mark, I'm a paramedic…can you tell me what's going on?"

"I was putting eye drops in my eye and some of the drops went over my lips and in my mouth…my girlfriend said it was deadly poison and I could die…" she said with complete drama.

At first we thought this may have been a prank but she was stone-cold serious. We have to remember what we consider an emergency and what someone else might are sometimes two different things.

I had her sit down and asked for the bottle of the eye drops. She pointed to the kitchen counter and Eric went to check them. He came back and said they were a generic over-the-counter brand, no poisonous ingredients. We took the time to calm her down and reassure her she'd be okay. After about ten minutes she was rational and actually laughing about it.

We have our share of calls that are at the least not *"true emergencies."* We were sent to a female feeling like she was going to pass out and after arriving she told us she felt fine. She said she made the fainting story up to get us to her house quicker. The real reason for the call was she wanted her blood pressure checked and knew we wouldn't respond just for that.

On another day we received a call for a diabetic not feeling well. When we arrived we could hear the patient yelling for us to "just come in." He was upstairs in bed. He's 42 years old, morbidly obese and admitted the real reason he called was he was hungry and didn't feel like walking down the stairs to make something to eat. He asked if we could get him some ice cream and bowl of chips and was as serious. We left without fulfilling the "order to go."

These would be some of the easier calls. As we sat around the day room table reflecting on some of these calls, the tones went off.

"Medic 42, Rescue 41, respond code three for a male subject trapped in machinery, possibly DOA, Perfect Packaging Industries…3800 Industry Way…time out 1703 hours."

We watched the bay doors go up and couldn't help but try to get mentally prepared for the worst. Obviously something terrible had gone wrong at this business. We'd been to calls for assistance here before, but nothing of this magnitude. This business used heavy automated industrial machines in the manufacturing of cardboard boxes and packaging.

We arrived at the front entrance and a site security guard met us.

"Follow me to the back entrance," he shouted with urgency.

Around the back of the complex we walked through a pedestrian door into a large hanger type area with large machines lining the walls. In the corner there were several workers focused around one individual who is leaning against the front of one of the machines.

We're told this machine is a large "flattener device."

It receives nearly finished cardboard product and sends it deep into the machine to be packaged. The machine was shut down for a regular maintenance and service check. During this process the front safety guards had been removed.

Our patient was performing maintenance and had his left arm well in to the main opening when he somehow triggered the auto-start mode. Before he could pull his arm clear, it pulled him flush against the machine, twisting and then violently snapping his left upper arm sending three inches of the humerus bone through the skin and now threatening to tear the arm off.

He then began to be strangled as his coveralls were so tightly wrapped around his upper chest and neck he had traumatic asphyxia, rapidly became a deep, almost black purple color from the upper chest throughout the face.

His eyes bulged with a look of absolute fear. He's making desperate attempts to breathe, without success. This is where literal seconds would count. The co-workers finally disabled the machine and are now frantically trying to pull him away from the opening.

Steve and Eric and I began cutting his coveralls with our scissors. We managed to cut enough away to where he now had to be supported as he was becoming free of the deadly grasp of the machine.

Rocky was setting the kit up. He has an IV bag ready and then began drawing RSI drugs up.

A few seconds later he's free. His left arm fell awkwardly behind him, leaving the exposed bone protruding menacingly. Sam had the spine board ready and slid it under him and quickly secured him.

Dana was providing breaths with the BVM. We could see chest rise. I took my pen out and marked an 'X' over the carotid pulse. I estimated it at 120 a minute.

Steve recruited one of the co-workers and they straightened the left arm and secured it with a cardboard splint. I put a rubber tourniquet on the upper right arm and was fortunate to find a good vein. I slid a 14 gauge in as Rocky handed me the IV tubing.

I looked at Eric and said, "Get ready on the airway; I'm going to push the RSI drugs."

"Roger that," he said and then got into position.

I pushed the RSI drugs and within a minute Eric was ready for the intubation attempt. I watched as he slowly placed the blade down the throat…he reached down with his right hand and pushed ever so slightly on the front of the neck. Then he asked Sam to place her fingers exactly where he had his…picked up the endotracheal tube and slid it down the throat.

Sam spoke up, "I felt it go past my fingers…I think you got it."

Eric nodded and said, "I saw it go through the cords, we're good."

A couple of squeezes from the bag valve by Dana and the chest went up and down.

I listened with the stethoscope and heard good sounds on both sides, "Great job, Eric," I said.

We loaded the patient on the gurney and headed for the exit. As he was being wheeled out, I got his name and basic information for the hospital.

"His name is Henry, he's 41, we're sending someone to get his wife," the supervisor said emotionally and with great concern.

"We'll be at Regional," and then I added, "We'll take good care of him."

Once we were en route to RGH we had Henry hooked up to the LifePak 12. He had a normal looking rhythm; heart rate is 118, blood pressure 160/100 and Sp02 94%. His color had markedly improved in the face. His eyes were completely bloodshot but his pupils were reactive.

Eric did a finger stick and checked the sugar, "104," he said.

We arrived at RGH and went to Suite 12 where the trauma team quickly took over care. Henry was in the best hands.

He was taken to the O.R. for repair of the left upper arm. He was admitted to the trauma ICU and followed by the neurosurgeons for forty-eight hours before attempting to wake him up. Henry regained consciousness and suffered no neurological deficits. He took a partial disability due to damage in the left arm and was retrained for a position away from the production line.

CHAPTER 13

SICK OR NOT SICK

Eric got his senior status as a paramedic in the county and was taking a few shifts off to recharge. Dana was enjoying the time on the rescue and was considering making it a full time position when a spot opened up.

I wondered if Eric's vacation planning had anything to do with the upcoming kid's fairs which can keep us quite busy.

RGH and several other organizations are all part of a large county-wide campaign to educate the public on keeping kids safe. Several local charities donated bicycle helmets, there are car seat clinics, and ways to "kid proof" the home from hidden dangers. We were always enthusiastic to be part of these campaigns.

Today we had a quick morning with a basic first aid presentation and "show and tell" at one of the Middle Schools and finished by getting called out at the end of the program.

"Medic 42, Rescue 41, respond code three for a 14 month old child not breathing, CPR instructions being provided over the phone...4455 Hawthorne Loop Road...time out 1304."

It was surreal driving off seeing all the happy smiling waving kids knowing that we may be going to one that would need heroic efforts.

Within minutes of the dispatch, we're updated the child regained consciousness and seemed to be okay. This was good to hear but sounded strange coming so quickly. We continued the response and not two minutes later were advised CPR was again needed. We're now only a couple of blocks from the residence.

As we're getting out of the vehicles, the mother quickly came out of the house holding the child, who didn't look to be in any distress; in fact, seemed unfazed by all of the commotion.

"He turned blue and stopped breathing," she said with a panicked tone.

"It scared me to death and I didn't know what to do," she added.

I said, "Okay, my name is Mark, I'm a paramedic, why don't we start at the beginning--what was going on before this happened?"

"Well he was on the floor next to his toy box and I looked over and he was a deep shade of purple," she said.

"Did anything come out of his mouth, like a toy or anything?" I asked.

"No, all of his toys are kids safe, we watch him very carefully," she said.

"What's his name?" I asked.

"Aiden," she said.

With mom holding him, I listened to Aiden's chest with the stethoscope, it's clear and equal on both sides of the chest, skin color is nice and pink, upper airway sounds good, he's smiling, moving appropriately--in fact, looked 100% normal in all areas of exam. She denied any recent illness, injuries, past medical history or any other problem that might explain the event.

I told Aiden's mother, "Well, I am at a loss to explain what happened. If it would make you feel better we could take him to RGH and have him examined…"

I didn't even finish the suggestion and she interrupted with, "Yes, yes, please take him there, and can I ride with you?"

"Sure, Rocky will help you into the front and we'll take Aiden with us in the back," I said as she handed Aiden to me.

"Thank you so much," she said, still visibly upset.

I had Dana and Sam come with us for the transport. This would give both of them experience getting vital signs and exposure to a "smaller clientele."

Dana was in the process of getting a blood pressure when without warning; Aiden went from pink to purple and lost consciousness. This was a shocking and alarming presentation. I immediately placed the stretcher in a flat position and grabbed for the pediatric bag valve mask. Then, as quickly as it started, he became pink and was smiling and looking up at me.

Dana was wide-eyed and Sam said, "Did we just see what we saw?"

I said, "I think so, although I'm not sure we saw what we seen."

At that moment mom leaned around from the passenger seat and said, "How's he doing…still okay?"

And I said, "Oh yeah, he's still the same…"

We hooked little Aiden up to the LifePak 12 and had oxygen ready. His EKG looked good; his Sp02 was 99%, everything perfect.

Thirty seconds later almost on cue, as we are all staring at him, he had a sudden blank stare and immediately became purple. I aligned his little jaw as Dana was about to place the BVM and after several seconds, he became pink again and smiling as before.

The repeated exam was the same: clear breath sounds, no obvious obstructions, no drooling, no unusual sounds, no explanations found.

We arrived to RGH and wheeled the gurney with Aiden on it and mom at his side to Suite 2, the pediatric room where Rachel came into take the report. I gave her the story and told her about the transport when all of a sudden Aiden made an impending *"I'm going to puke"* face and spit out a small flat purple plastic cover about the size of a dime.

We never could figure out what the piece was from, but somehow he found it and swallowed it. It must have lodged just above the trachea and would flap over, occlude it, then flap back on its own after a few seconds. Aiden was smiling and clapping like he was the star who just concluded his magic act.

Mom was crying happily and said, "I thought I was going crazy and seeing things."

Aiden could be the poster boy for "kid proofing" your home.

A week later it was unusually hot for the time of year. Anytime the weather changes for the good or the bad it tends to make the call volume change. Today would be no different.

After lunch, we're standing outside in front of the open bay doors watching traffic, enjoying the warm sunny day with the cloudless deep blue sky and hint of breeze when the tones broke this serenity.

"Medic 42, Rescue 41, respond code three for a 2 year old child that has fallen out of a window, she is unconscious at this time…1809 Tartan Lane, Apt. 16…time out 1333."

Both units went en route. We would take about four minutes to get there. This is a large apartment complex and we've had many calls to this location: heroin overdoses, assaults, a couple of babies delivered--quite the range of responses.

We arrived at the entrance to the complex and could see a patrol car parked ahead of us and small crowd gathered on the other side of it. As we parked we see two officers kneeling next to a very small child lying face up in the dirt. An adult female is next to the child with her hand over her mouth, crying.

Up above where the child had fallen from was an open window, the curtain blowing in the wind. The screen is partially pushed out and offering a grim description of what happened. The distance from the window to the ground was estimated at eighteen feet. A fall from that height can cause massive and potentially fatal injuries.

A little boy of about 6 years old standing a few feet away said, "Ashley pushed the screen when she was waving at me and she fell out the window."

Steve immediately took over cervical immobilization by holding Ashley's little head. Rocky went to retrieve the spine board, Sam and Dana and I started assessing.

Little Ashley has one of the largest hematomas to the forehead we have seen.

A hematoma is swelling under the skin, a large pocket of blood. This one is half again as large as her entire head. She looked like an alien bug. It's pushing down over her eyes and they are nearly swollen shut. She's bleeding out of her left ear and both nostrils. Her mentation is inappropriate with an intermittent moan and grunt and no lucid response. The pupils were difficult to see but equal and reactive, a good sign.

Her chest movement is equal, breath sounds clear, abdomen soft, pelvis intact and arms and legs look okay. We did notice she moved each leg and each arm, this was positive for no catastrophic spinal injury.

I can feel a strong pulse in her wrist and so our working diagnosis is TBI, or traumatic brain injury.

As we're packaging her to the spine board Sam said, "Mark, her breathing is very irregular and she's having some long pauses."

I said, "Okay, let's get set up to RSI in the back of the rig."

Rocky looked at me and nodded, "I'll get you ready," and was off in a flash.

This breathing pattern is associated with a possible neurologic or brain injury. Ashley was on the proverbial clock.

I had just a few seconds to meet with Ashley's mother. I learned she was the female standing next to Ashley as we arrived and is nearly catatonic.

"Ma'am, my name is Mark. I'm a paramedic and will be taking care of Ashley. We're going to RGH…she's very sick right now and we're going to take good care of her," I said.

"Thank you," she said.

"She's my… little girl….please…." and then couldn't speak after that.

I gave her a quick hug, hopefully some reassurance.

One of the officers said, "We'll drive her to the hospital," with an empathetic nod.

We were on scene for six minutes. It would take four minutes to get to RGH. This was time in Ashley's favor.

Sam had the oxygen at high flow by mask and pediatric bag valve mask standing by. Dana quickly hooked up the LifePak 12 and is now drawing up RSI drugs.

I put the rubber tourniquet on Ashley's right upper arm and a great vein popped up in the mid-arm and got an 18 gauge into it. A quick check of the sugar is 96.

I nodded to Dana and she started pushing the drugs; I was ready with the laryngoscope blade. Within one minute she was paralyzed and ready for the intubation. The laryngoscope blade is introduced into Ashley's little mouth. Everything is so small. I have a perfect view of the vocal cords and tracheal opening. The tube goes through easily and secured. Sam is now ventilating with the bag valve.

Dana called out vital signs, "BP 140/100, pulse 60, SpO2 99%," she said.

I called RGH on the radio and they were standing by with the pediatric trauma team. We would have the red carpet rolled out and Ashley would need every inch of it.

At the hospital it was impressive watching the team work, a controlled chaos of activity with people that are the best of the best. This was exactly the effort Ashley needed. When we left she was heading for CT and then to the O.R. with the neurosurgeons.

Two days had gone by with no changes. Brenda finally called with good news on the third day. Ashley was awake and made a miraculous recovery. She had extensive bruising to the brain and blood removed from a subdural hematoma--serious injuries to the head.

We're all very happy for Ashley's mother; in the short amount of time we spend with a patient we develop a connection. The system made a difference in their lives that day, and we were part of that.

It was that time of year to renew my Trauma Certification. In EMS, most of your certifications are good for two years. You then attend the course again in order to keep your certification current.

The Pre-Hospital Trauma Life Support class, or PHTLS, was being held at the District 6 Main Station. Its two-eight hour days that kept us current with trauma care trends. I successfully completed the course and over the next few shifts didn't have any trauma to practice the newfound knowledge.

Wednesday night ended the streak of no trauma starting with the tones.

"Medic 42, Rescue 41, Engine 61, respond code three for a motor vehicle crash, a rollover with entrapment, County Road 4 and Davidson Road… time out 2222 hours."

County Road 4 is a narrow and winding road. For some reason it was difficult to navigate when you weren't paying attention or impaired.

It took us eight minutes to arrive and Engine 61 was on scene. With the large gasoline spill from the overturned car, they deployed two charged hose lines and were in defensive positions to suppress any fire that might erupt.

Captain Neeves brought me up to speed on what they know so far.

"Evening Mark, we have one patient, he's been unresponsive since we arrived, we can hear him moaning and it smells like we have ETOH on board," he said.

ETOH is the acronym for ethyl alcohol. In other words, the patient has had *some* alcoholic ingestion; whether they're drunk or not can't be determined at this time.

Some other acronyms we use are HBD-has been drinking and AOB-alcohol on board. Sometimes it's less of a hassle when you're talking in front of the patient and you say, "He has AOB," instead of saying, "He's drunk out of his mind."

This will also potentially prevent the ubiquitous debate about how wrong you are and how they're perfectly sober and only had two beers.

Rocky's getting the ambulance setup up for a worst case scenario. This kind of teamwork pays off when you have a critical patient and seconds count.

Steve and Sam and Dana and I went to the vehicle. There wasn't much space through the passenger window and we could see blood pooling on the ceiling which was now the bottom part of the car. I was able to crawl partially in and determine the patient's breathing about 24 times a minute, has a strong right radial pulse and lacerations to the head. He doesn't respond to my voice or gentle taps to the shoulder.

Then I find a disturbing discovery, he has a traumatic amputation to the left arm above the elbow. I couldn't get a full assessment from this angle and noted it wasn't bleeding heavily. I also can't find the severed arm.

I crawled out and spoke to Captain Neeves, "We need to get moving on this. His left arm is ripped off."

About then one of the guys from Engine 61, James, walked over and said, "He doesn't have the left arm."

I said, "I just noticed that, we need to get going."

"I know, but he doesn't have a left arm," James reiterated calmly.

I looked at him with probably the most dumbfounded look and said, "Were you in the car already?"

He said, "No, I know this guy. He lost that arm in an industrial accident several years ago. His name's Greg, the left arm is a stump just above the elbow."

So now it made more sense. I was fortunate to learn this before going screaming in to RGH announcing a traumatic amputation that had occurred several years earlier.

The Engine 61 crew had the passenger door removed and we now have clear access to Greg. He actually has his seat belt on which presented a small issue, we didn't want to cut it and let him drop to the ground. With great difficulty due to the space, we're able to get him safely secured to the spine board and removed from the vehicle.

As we're loading him onto the stretcher, he opened his eyes and was trying to focus on what was going on.

"Hey there, can you hear me? My name is Mark, I'm a paramedic," I said.

With a slow and heavily slurred response he said, "Yeah...what happened?"

"Well, it looks like you rolled your car and we had to cut your car apart to get you out," I informed him.

"I wasn't driving," he said, which drew glances and grins from everyone standing within earshot. (I didn't ask him how he got seat-belted into the driver's seat while the car was upside down.)

"Can you tell us how much you've had to drink tonight?" I asked in anticipation of the response.

"Two beers," he said, as if no one saw that one coming.

The standard pat answer when asked about alcohol consumption is two beers. No matter what the level of intoxication is, it's two beers. If you multiply this by five you're generally in the ballpark for the actual number.

We thanked Captain Neeves for the great job and headed to RGH.

Sam's cutting Greg's clothing off and Dana is bandaging the laceration to the left arm. It's a full thickness and the length of the scar from the amputation. At first glance it could pass for a "new" amputation.

I'm more concerned about a head injury as Greg starts the repetitive questioning routine indicative of retrograde amnesia. This means the short term memory is affected causing the patient to ask "what happened" nearly every thirty seconds. I had Sam keep the *"what happened"* conversation going between them.

I found a good vein on the right lower arm and put a 14 gauge into it. The blood sugar is 88.

After getting the LifePak 12 hooked up, Dana called out numbers, "Heart rate is 104, blood pressure 136/88 and SpO2 is 96%," she said.

Once we arrived at RGH and turned over patient care, I spoke to Brenda and explained how I almost came in with the "amputation" before getting the full story. She had a shocked appearance and said, "I remember this guy, he came in three years ago after getting his arm stuck in a meat grinder."

"His arm was pretty much gone from just below the elbow and they had to make the stump just above the elbow," she explained.

Greg was treated and stabilized in the E.D. He was admitted for observation to the neurosurgery floor and discharged the next day. He is facing the DUI charges.

Eric came back to work after the much needed shifts off. Dana told him to take as much time off as he wanted, as she was enjoying her time on the rescue. We have a solid team and have worked hard to get where we are.

In between calls created opportunities to quiz Eric on the ALS drugs. Steve and Sam and Rocky would participate as the more we recognized each other's strengths and weaknesses, the stronger we became as a team.

Eric had a good working knowledge of the drugs and protocols. Sometimes the hardest concept was starting with simple solutions before moving on to more advanced directions. This was the genesis of the KISS theory, "Keep it Simple Stupid."

We had a 75 year old female that had fallen in the mall and ended up with a fractured hip. She was having moderately intense pain associated with it. We started an IV and gave her a couple of increments of morphine to ease the discomfort. Morphine being a narcotic can cause the respiratory drive to decrease or stop altogether. At first, she didn't seem to have any response to it, then it hit quite dramatically and she became lethargic and offered slightly less than a moan for responsiveness.

Then her respiratory drive decreased and she was down to a breath every ten seconds.

Eric quickly said, "Hey, we better give her some narcan…she's not breathing too well."

I said, "Wow, you got to the narcan quick…did you ask her if she wanted the morphine reversed?"

That stopped him in his tracks and he looked at me like I wasn't speaking English.

I leaned over, tapped the patient on the shoulder and said, "Hello… Barbara….can you wake up for me….hello…."

With a delayed response and droopy eyes, she smiled, "I'm here," she said over several seconds.

Later at the station we talked more about it. The morphine was working and she obviously wasn't having any pain. The narcan would have reversed the morphine effect and instantly put her back into the painful state she started with. Now, if the gentle hand to the shoulder didn't work, then yes, we could have considered narcan.

Shortly thereafter the tones were followed with an ominous dispatch.

"Medic 42, Rescue 41, respond for a drowning, Green Land Park, 10000 Clover Drive…time out 1505 hours."

Every year we'd have at least one drowning or near drowning at this lake. It's a popular spot and safe as long as you stayed inside the roped area. Teenagers would go beyond this and the water is very cold and distances deceiving.

It would take six minutes to arrive. About halfway to the scene dispatch advised the patient was out of the water and CPR in progress. They also advised this is a 17 year old male; believed he had been under water less than ten minutes.

Arriving at the park it was obvious where we were needed. There's a crowd of people jumping up and down, waving frantically. About twenty feet from the water in a grassy area, two guys are performing CPR.

The patient is blue, his face, hands, fingernails, all very poor color. His eyes are half open and there's emesis (vomit) around his mouth and neck. He's about five foot eight, 150 pounds, black hair and has black shorts on with no shirt.

Steve knelt down and took over compressions. Sam and Eric are at his head. Eric positioned the airway with a jaw thrust maneuver. This is how we will maintain his airway and not compromise the neck.

Whenever someone is pulled from the water after a near-drowning, we'll take cervical spine precautions. Perhaps this was a shallow water diving mishap. A percentage of drowning and near-drowning patients can have secondary spine injuries.

Rocky is getting an IV set up and drugs ready. I placed the combo-pads on the chest, one above the right nipple, the other below the left nipple and then plugging the adapter wires into the LifePak 12.

"Thanks for your help…can you tell us what happened?" I asked the guys that had been performing CPR.

"Well, he was trying to swim across the lake, got about halfway and yelled for help…he tried to come back and just went under…didn't come back up…he was gone for like eight minutes…I timed it…this other guy went out and dove for him…on the third time he was dragging him to shore…" he explained.

"Does anyone know him?" I asked.

"Tony," was the response from five or six people in unison.

The LifePak 12 shows electrical activity in the heart yet no corresponding pulse to go with it. This is a rhythm we can potentially fix. We need to figure out why the electrical activity isn't generating a pulse. One big reason for this is hypoxia. This is a low oxygen state at the cellular level that can prevent the heart from beating. It's probably secondary to the drowning.

I found a good IV site as Rocky handed me a 14 gauge before I asked for it. I looked at him and he shrugs his shoulders as if to say, "What? That's what you always use…"

He was right; it went right into the vein. We now had access for cardiac drugs.

Rocky then called out, "Sugar, 84."

Eric and I both nodded affirmatively.

I told Eric to get him intubated as soon as he was ready. As he was setting up, the rhythm check showed the same electrical activity and no pulse. I pushed epinephrine through the IV line as Steve and Sam switched places on compressions.

Eric slid the long curved blade down Tony's throat. He was just about to introduce the tube into the mouth when a large purging of lake water and stomach contents came up, covering him all down the front of his shirt. We quickly rolled Tony to his side while Eric held the head and neck in line and Steve suctioned what he could see. While he was on his side Rocky placed the spine board behind him and secured the straps.

Eric now went for his second attempt as Sam continued with the compressions. The blade went back down Tony's throat and this time he successfully got him intubated. We have good chest rise and I can hear equal breath sounds with evidence of some aspiration of water in the lower lung fields. Not much we could do for that now, we're administering high flow oxygen and the ventilations provided with the bag valve would hopefully clear this problem.

Eric and I thought for sure we would see something with these efforts. After two minutes of CPR we stopped to check the rhythm…it looks much better but we still can't feel a pulse. I pushed another epinephrine through the IV line and now we need Tony to work with us.

"Steve, take over on compressions," I said. Sam took over on the bag valve.

It's important to treat the patient, not the rhythm. In other words we need to ensure we aren't missing something. Reassessment is vital. Our efforts are aggressive and we're aware of each second ticking by.

After another two minutes of CPR, I had Steve stop. The rhythm is now looking much closer to a normal rhythm; it's showing a heart rate of 118.

"Check a pulse," I said to Steve.

"I can feel a strong carotid," he said enthusiastically.

"Roger that," I said with emphasis.

The second Steve said he felt the pulse; we all noticed a wave of pink color replace the blue throughout Tony's body. We definitely had circulation.

The small crowd standing near us shouted cries of encouragement to Tony and a couple of them embraced and wept.

"Let's get ready to move to the rig," I said.

Sam announced, "Blood pressure is 100/64, heart rate at 124 and Sp02 92%."

I looked at her and flashed a small grin and two thumbs up sign.

Tony was cautiously moved to the ambulance. I stayed behind for a few moments to find out if anyone was actually related to Tony. Turns out they were all just friends.

One of them said, "I called his mom…she's coming here."

"When she gets here tell her we are at Regional, and please, tell her to drive safely," I added.

During the transport I repeated a thorough secondary exam and didn't find any obvious changes. There wasn't any spontaneous movement or attempts to breathe but I didn't expect it at this point. It would take the system a while to come back. The most critical part was the heart was beating.

We arrived at RGH and were directed to Suite 12. After blood work and X-rays, Tony went to CT and then admitted to the ICU in critical condition.

We met Tony's mother in the emergency department. She was as expected from a mother who got a call with the news she did; scared, crying, and devastated. In between crying she thanked us and there were no words we could offer her. After a quick hug, she was escorted to the ICU.

Tony woke up twenty-four hours later. He had no recall of the event. Later that day he developed a high fever and a subsequent aggressive lung infection secondary to the lake water. He was re-intubated and critical for forty-eight hours. After the lung infection cleared, he rapidly improved and went home six days later without deficits.

CHAPTER 14

WINDOW DRESSINGS

Sam and Eric were hired into full time positions on Rescue 41. Our department was expanding to meet the ever growing call volume and this was a very proactive decision and direction. Every department across the country has to be frugal and inventive on how the funds are spent. Each year on average there's a 10% increase in responses. This can stretch any department's budget.

The city has an annual celebration event this week and it always increases our responses. Our alcohol-related call volume goes up, as if it isn't already a large part of our responses.

We would be involved in a major fight to save a life that started with a store owner who called 9-1-1 after a male subject punched out his front showroom windows. The suspect then walked down the sidewalk repeating this window assault to each business on the block. This sent several police units to the area for investigation. It didn't take long to encounter the "window boxer."

"Medic 42, Rescue 41, respond code three at the request of the police, 800 Main Street, male subject with massive bleeding…time out 1420 hours."

This prompted a quick exit from the station and three minute response to the location.

I looked over at Rocky and said, "I think I may double glove on this, sounds kind of ominous."

As part of industry standards, gloves are worn on all calls. Sometimes when you know you'll have a particularly bloody scene or a multiple patient scenario, you can wear two pairs of gloves. As the first set gets bloody, you remove them and have the fresh pair ready to go. I've tried the triple glove method but found it interfered with my dexterity.

We arrived to a very active scenario playing out where several officers are engaged in a violent physical confrontation with a male in his 20's who's covered from head to toe with blood. He's shirtless, heavily tattooed, in tattered jeans and combat style black high top boots.

The problem was the blood made everything very slippery, and the patient is highly intoxicated and enraged to the point of being dangerous to all on scene. He has blood pumping and flowing from several arteries in the wrists and upper arms. This created a pool of blood where the fight ended nearly four feet in diameter.

Between the officers and all of us, the patient was handcuffed. This struggle was far from over. As Steve, Sam and Eric were busily trying to stem the flow of blood; he continued to flail with no clue as to how serious his injuries were or that he's literally bleeding to death.

We resorted to stopping the flow with tourniquets which are rarely used in EMS. They're generally reserved for multiple patient scenarios or SWAT scenes where you cannot devote attention to bleeding because of hostile activity. The combativeness continued until I gave him two doses of versed as an intramuscular (IM) injections in the right upper arm. This slowed the physical activity but not the verbal assault to all of us in the ambulance.

Sam got the LifePak 12 hooked up and called out our first readings, "Heart rate 134, blood pressure 70/46, Sp02 won't read," she said.

Eric became a hero when he looked at me and said, "I think I can get an IV in this left arm."

I said, "Go for it, we'll try to hold him still and whatever you do...don't stick us with that needle," as we all nodded in agreement.

Eric found a site along the left bicep and inserted a 14 gauge. We used extra tape to secure it and will not lose this IV. This became the lifeline RGH would use to transfuse several units of blood after estimating he lost close to half his circulating volume. He couldn't have been closer to death.

The wounds were so extensive he went to the O.R. The tendon damage in the right arm was catastrophic and will limit his ability to extend the arm for the rest of his life.

In all he punched out the windows of five different store fronts. When the officers arrived they followed the blood trail which extended for nearly a full city block before encountering him. His blood alcohol level was .33, over four times the legal limit.

We all went back to the station wearing hospital scrubs, our uniforms covered in blood.

Interestingly, we don't see too many methamphetamine overdoses. Usually when we do it's to remove tazer prongs after a failure to comply order, or an evaluation after they're arrested for some crime, or unfortunately after a terminal event.

A few months back we responded for a 27 year old female found dead in her bed from a massive intracranial bleed brought on by methamphetamine use. We estimated she'd been dead for several hours. A neighbor called

9-1-1 after seeing two small children playing in the front yard, both kids naked. When police arrived they found the mother unresponsive and called for EMS. Obviously she was beyond anything we could do for her. The children, 2 and 3 years old were placed with the grandmother.

The next shift the calls started right after coming on duty. We had five calls before noon. After finishing our last call, we headed back to the station for some overdue and much needed nourishment. We made it to the front of the station before hearing the tones sending us back to the streets.

"Medic 42, Rescue 41, respond code three for a possible meth overdose, police on scene, 1111 Crawford, Apartment 6…time out 1655 hours."

This was another familiar complex that we have been to many times over the last few months for overdoses, assaults and alcohol-related incidents.

Arriving we found several patrol cars parked in front of apartment 6. An officer walked up to the ambulance and said, "Hi guys, we got called for an out of control male. Neighbors say he's been up on meth for the last five days. He fought us like a small tiger from the time we arrived, pulled a gun from under the couch and we ended up tazing him. He's got something going on now and doesn't look good."

Walking into the apartment looks like a small natural disaster took place. It's destroyed. Holes in the wall, furniture broken, plates and glasses shattered on the kitchen floor, burned areas on the carpet.

The patient is 35 years old, 5 foot 4 and maybe 120 pounds. He's lying face down on the floor with handcuffs behind him and rocking back and forth mumbling incoherently. He's breathing upwards of 50 plus per minute. His radial pulse is 160 and skin feels hot to the touch. His pupils are dilated which is consistent with methamphetamine influence.

I looked at the officers standing next to us and said, "This guy's pretty sick, we need to get him to RGH."

"Sounds good to us, we'll send someone with you," the sergeant said.

I said, "Roger that, but I'm going to have to have him on his back so we can treat him, we can secure him to the gurney."

"Okay, no problem, we'll help you," he said.

As we rolled him over, we removed the tazer probes; one just below the left side of the neck and the other above the left nipple. With seat belts and soft restraints, he's secured to the gurney and in the ambulance. Sam started him on oxygen with a face mask.

Eric was getting an initial blood pressure when he looked up at me with a confused look and said, "Mark, you may want to check this BP."

I said, "Okay," and traded places with him.

When a crew member asks for a blood pressure clarification, this means it is either way too low or way too high. This one would fit in a category all on its own.

I checked it and then had to double check it. I estimated it at 380/260. I checked the other arm and got the same reading. The cuff only measures pressures to 300. I had to pump the cuff an additional 80 mm/hg before being able to get the reading. To this day, it's the highest blood pressure I have ever heard of.

Eric ran a 12 lead and it shows he's also having a massive heart attack. Sam put the electronic thermometer probe under his armpit and its reading 106.4.

With his record blood pressure, massive heart attack, body temperature off the charts, there won't be a good outcome from this.

Eric and I each put IV's in. The emergency department appreciates the additional IV's on critical patients. His blood sugar is the only normal finding at 84.

I wasn't sure he'd make it to RGH before going into cardiac arrest. We transported with lights and siren and called ahead to declare a cardiac alert. This would give them heads up we have a potential serious cardiac emergency. He continued to mumble incoherently and continually fought against the belts and restraints. I gave him several doses of versed IV with almost no effect.

We arrived at RGH where he was quickly evaluated and less than ten minutes later went into cardiac arrest. The team worked aggressively for thirty-three minutes before discontinuing the efforts.

We never heard anything further as far as why the five days of meth use or anything else about him. The sad truth is there's no future with meth. It's a devastating drug that takes over virtually all control of a life, and for some that's the end.

It's finally the last day of the city's celebration and has been a busy week. Sandy organized a BBQ for the crews this afternoon and we're all looking forward to it. She said we'd have a special guest who was insistent on providing the hamburgers and an appreciation cake.

Tones interrupted this shadowy discussion and we walked through the pedestrian door leading to the truck bays.

"Medic 42, Rescue 41, respond code three for a child that has fallen through a plate glass window, severe bleeding, 14711 Meadow Brook... time out 1345 hours."

There are certain calls and words that heighten the sense of urgency, severe bleeding, plate glass, child involved; this dispatch had all of them.

As we turned on to Meadow Brook, we could see people about halfway down the block frantically waving and doing what looked like jumping jacks trying to get our attention. I felt and heard the engine rev as Rocky also saw them.

It's difficult to witness such intense fear and helplessness emanating from people on scene.

I opened the side door and quickly grabbed the main kit. We followed the group around the side of the house to the back yard.

The initial sight is worse than we'd imagined. A 12 year old girl was lying on the back porch in a massive pool of blood, all coming from the neck and lower legs. An adult male was cradling her and holding a large towel to the left side of her neck. A female has another towel and is frantically trying to stop blood flow from the legs. They are both crying with near panic.

We quickly learned the patient's name is Trina. The family was having a backyard picnic. Trina and two friends were horse playing and running through the house into the yard.

Somehow the sliding glass door was shut while they were in the house. She ran at full speed headed for the back yard, smashing through the glass and shattering it as if an explosion went off. She tried to get up and collapsed with blood spurting from her neck, instantly in a life and death struggle in the blink of an eye.

Trina is fully conscious and in a near "paralyzed" state. Her wide eyes followed our movements, her fear is palpable. She is ghostly pale. Her two friends are shaking nearly uncontrollably and tightly embraced a few feet away, sobbing.

Eric and Sam have large trauma dressings ready and prompted the man to move. As they removed the towel, blood spurted from the neck and shot out almost two feet. This laceration extended through a portion of the trachea, around the left side of the neck, and nearly slicing the left ear off.

Eric placed his dressing over the main part of the gaping wound. Sam placed hers over this and within seconds the bleeding stopped. There are bubbles coming from the opening in the front of the neck with each exhalation causing Trina to gag every few breaths.

It looked as if a cricothyrotomy had been created, albeit crudely.

My thoughts were, *"We have to secure this airway, and I think I can get an endotracheal tube through that opening."*

I looked at Trina and explained to her I was going to help her breathe and to please trust me. She nodded ever so slightly. This would be a very bold attempt but it would give us ultimate control of her airway.

I grabbed a 6.0 endotracheal tube and Eric was ready with the suction unit. Steve is standing by with additional trauma dressings and Sam is the extra pair of hands. We're ready.

Sam pulled the front bandage back and sure enough there are bubbles coming from the hole in the front of the neck. The damage is massive and extensive. I waited for Trina to inhale and gently placed the tube through the jagged opening and it slid into the trachea.

She gagged once then we immediately heard air coming out of the tube. We're in the right hole. Trina's now breathing through the tube in her neck. Steve then packed additional dressings around the neck and after assessing it, the bleeding is controlled.

Rocky took over for the female and secured pressure dressings to the leg lacerations. The one on the left leg is just above the knee and extends towards the middle of her leg. Its two inches wide and spread open deeply exposing fatty tissue and muscle. Bleeding from this wound is steady and dark purple. The laceration on the right leg is just below the groin. Its three inches wide and also gaping with exposed tissue and muscle. The bleeding here is minimal.

We placed Trina on the gurney and headed to the ambulance.

I had just seconds to quickly talk to the family and try to explain what we were doing and that we would be working very hard to keep her stabilized. They listened intently to my every word and had the most helpless and frightened looks.

We were on scene for seven minutes and now headed for the much-anticipated greeting at RGH by the trauma team.

Sam was physically holding the endotracheal tube and bandages around the neck in place to ensure they held. She's also focused on talking to Trina, almost as if they're best friends and narrating a story for her. Trina would move her eyes to Sam as if looking for encouragement. Sam would offer a smile and say, "I'm right here, sweetie, hold on."

Eric was able to place two IV's and we have IV fluids running wide open. I decided to give Trina the RSI drugs as the experience of having an endotracheal tube in your throat is frightening and uncomfortable.

Sam explained to Trina what was going to happen and would be with her throughout the transport. Trina blinked as she stared into Sam's eyes, and then quickly drifted off to sleep as drugs went through the IV line. Sam attached to the bag valve to the endotracheal tube and started giving Trina a breath every five seconds.

Trina's ghostly pale appearance is frightening. She has no color in her lips, small beads of sweat on her forehead and the skin is cool and clammy. She's in deep shock. As I looked at her innocent face I thought to myself, *"Hang on Trina, we got you!"*

After getting the LifePak 12 hooked up we were anxious to see the vitals. The blood pressure reading was low, as expected: 68/44; heart rate was high, as expected, at 144; the oxygen levels were at 90%.

We delivered Trina to the trauma team in Suite 12. Her stay didn't last long before heading to the O.R. After extensive repair to the arteries in the neck and throat and massive transfusions, we learned she was admitted to the trauma ICU in guarded condition.

Trina would make remarkable progress and was home five days after that fateful afternoon. She has no permanent internal damage. She has been referred to a plastic surgeon for her neck and leg wounds.

Back at the station, we had quite a bit of work to do getting the rigs back in shape. Before long it was time for the BBQ. Sandy announced over the intercom for the crews to please report to the training room. As we walked in we noticed a large banner with the words 'THANK YOU' and underneath it was Mr. Gustafson, our cardiac arrest patient from the diner. He was smiling and met with each of us, shaking our hands.

We wouldn't trade what we do with anyone!

CHAPTER 15

HIDDEN STORIES

The appeal to EMS has many facets. Seeing a patient survive their incident, getting a child back to their families, making a difference in people's lives...it's hard to pick just one aspect. Every day brings a new set of challenges. Keeping an open mind and creating good habits will pay off in dealing with challenging patients and scenarios that may not be what they seem.

During paramedic training one of the instructors dedicated an entire day to developing these traits. He told us one story about a crew that responded to a freeway rest area for a female that had reportedly been sexually assaulted and beaten quite severely.

The medics arrived and did a cursory assessment that was based more on the patient's account than on what they were actually dealing with. The patient stated that she had been raped and assaulted. She had multiple superficial cuts and swelling around the face and a strong aroma of alcohol. She admitted to having two mixed drinks but denied being under the influence. The medics acknowledged how pale she looked but attributed it to the alcohol. During the transport, her story changed several times but the medics again, thought it was secondary to alcohol. It was basically a *"ride to the hospital."*

When they arrived at the emergency department they transferred patient care and gave the nurse the report. They put the ambulance back in service and were about to leave when a security officer told them they were requested by the physician.

The doctor questioned them about the call and they gave the account of everything they found and did. He then asked if they knew about the GSW to the left lower abdomen or the fact that *"she"* was actually a *"he."* This left both medics speechless.

This had a powerful impact on me. How could they miss this?

He had another story of a crew that responded to a motor vehicle crash that involved a semi-tractor trailer that had rolled. The driver was treated by a bystander who claimed he was an Advanced First Aid provider.

He told the medic crew there was a small laceration to the back of the head and applied a dressing and wrapped it. He indicated it was a superficial wound and *"not that big a deal."*

The truck driver didn't recall the incident (big clue here) and didn't recall being helped by the first responder (another big clue). The medics thanked the first responder and transported the driver to the hospital. This was another ride without additional assessment.

At the hospital one of the first things they did was to remove the bandages and the nurse asked the medic in a whisper, "Did you guys happen to notice the brain matter coming from this open skull fracture?"

This was another powerful story that would have a great impact for me throughout my career. We all know how much trouble the word *"assume"* causes.

The days had gotten cooler, especially at night. The Emergency Support Shelters had an increase in attendance, people looking for respite on the cool nights. Only the hardy remained on the streets.

"Medic 42, Rescue 41, respond code one at the request of law enforcement for a male subject needing transport for detox. He's at the train station, behind the maintenance shop...time out 2053 hours."

The train station was a common hangout for transients and not uncommon to respond for an intoxicated person in need of assistance. These calls could present challenges as sometimes the patient could be difficult to assess secondary to alcohol levels and they were generally suspicious of police and EMS.

We arrived and one of the patrol officers met us. He explained they received a report from station personnel the patient had been lying motionless for the last couple hours. They were concerned he might be dead. He then stated when they first contacted the patient he grumbled at them and said something to the effect of "leave me alone".

They then found an empty half gallon bottle of wine and due to the limited interaction, made the decision he should be taken to RGH for evaluation. They were going to put him in the patrol car, but he wouldn't obey requests to get up and was quite heavily soiled with feces and urine.

After hearing this story, I said, "Okay...sounds like he belongs to us..."

I noticed the patient is breathing a little too fast; upwards of 30 plus per minute. He has a weak radial pulse at 120 per minute. Between the respiratory rate and pulse rate, we have more than an intoxicated patient here.

I put my hand on his shoulder and said, "Sir, can you hear me....hello, my name is Mark. I'm a paramedic; we're going to take you to the hospital."

No response.

I had Steve and Sam cutting clothing while Rocky was preparing the long spine board. We had no idea what happened prior to us getting here, so we're going with worst-case scenarios.

Sam got to the fourth level of clothing when she said, "Mark, we have blood coming from the lower right abdominal area."

Closer investigation revealed a stab wound from the mid-abdomen to the lower right rib margin and approximately six inches of eviscerated bowel protruding. (Evisceration is medical terminology referring to removal of bowel.) The outer clothing had no indication of the injury. It was only the last two layers of clothing that the blade had gone through. So after he was stabbed, he must have put on the light coat and then the heavier coat.

I called the officer over as Eric was putting a large dressing over the wound and said, "You guys have a pretty serious assault here...he has a major stab wound and is a sick guy right now."

"Did he say who did it?" The officer asked with interest.

"He doesn't respond to us; we're taking him to RGH for the trauma team," I said.

"Okay, we'll let the detectives know," as he grabbed his portable radio to alert the police dispatcher.

The patient is now secured to the spine board; we lifted him to the gurney and into the ambulance. Once en route we began to find out how critical he was. BP is 76/50, pulse rate is 126, and respiratory rate is 42 and shallow.

Eric put a 14 gauge IV in the right mid arm with normal saline running and called out, "Blood sugar is 146."

Besides the obvious evisceration, he has a collapse of the right lower lobe of the lung evidenced by decreased breath sounds on that side. It hadn't developed into a tension state and I am watching it closely.

Sam is at the head and applied an oxygen mask over his mouth and nose. With a sudden sense of urgency, she called out that we needed to "roll the patient."

He was starting to have dry heaves and as soon as we tilted the back board had two episodes of vomiting, both with copious amounts of bright red blood along with coagulated bloody clumps. This is a massive upper esophageal bleed that had nothing to do with the stabbing.

Sam suctioned out the remaining blood from the mouth and we rolled him back flat. The LifePak 12 is now showing a heart rate of 144 and BP of 70/44. He is bleeding to death.

I told Eric we will RSI him and he concurred. I drew up the drugs while Eric prepared for the procedure: the laryngoscope with curved blade is ready, suction ready, BVM ready--everyone is ready.

I pushed the drugs and Eric quickly intubated without difficulty. Sam was now in charge on the bag valve. She would alert us if there were any changes in lung compliance as this would indicate a tension pneumothorax.

I put a second IV in the left lower arm with another 14 gauge and another bag of normal saline.

We arrived at RGH and he spent fifteen minutes in Suite 12 before heading to the O.R. They repaired a lacerated liver, inserted a chest tube in the right side, and performed a bowel resection for the evisceration. He has an upper esophageal bleed secondary to his chronic alcoholism. He's a critical patient and will spend the next seven days in the ICU.

His alcohol level was .49 which would be considered lethal for almost anyone. There was no suspect information or arrest ever made for the assault. Life on the streets is tough. Drugs and alcohol can mask injuries and sometimes complicate them. Never get complacent!

Looking at the big picture is your only sure way of ensuring good patient care. It isn't too often the patient hands you a note that says, "Dear paramedic, this is exactly what happened or how many I took."

That isn't to say that we don't get plenty of "free medical advice" from some of the imbibed crowds.

We responded to a female who had fallen, hit her head and was unconscious for several minutes. She was highly intoxicated and complained of neck pain, along with the massive hematoma to the back of her head.

Her male companion challenged every question or interaction we had.

He tried to convince us he was medically trained by a Black Ops military group and could provide any care she needed. He also tried to convince her we only wanted to transport to "get her money."

We eventually transported and she was admitted to the trauma ICU with a subdural hematoma (bleeding in the brain) and could have died had she not come with us.

But then coming back to reality and tones...

"Medic 42, Rescue 41, respond code three for a male subject not breathing, possible overdose, 3434 Delaware Street...time out 2350 hours."

Traffic is heavy as it always seems to be at this time of night. There are more cars on the road now than during the day. This response should take three minutes but ended up closer to four.

Arriving on scene we find several police cars and a large party that's breaking up. A person walked close to the ambulance and yelled out, *"Better get your asses in there, the bro aint looking good..."*

Rocky grabbed the LifePak 12 and the suction unit, Sam grabbed the main kit, and Eric has the airway kit. Steve and I walked in; an officer met us and said, "Down the hall, guys, last door on the right, he looks pretty bad."

So far we are hearing the same theme: the patient isn't doing well.

The patient is a 16 year old boy lying in the bed and is having intermittent seizure activity. His face is almost blackish purple with bloody foam bubbling out of his mouth and rolling down his neck, creating a small pool next to his left ear. This is an anoxic nightmare. (Anoxic means a non-oxygen state.)

An officer points to a chewed up patch on the floor and exclaimed, "We found this fentanyl patch in his mouth...we got it out right before he started seizing."

Fentanyl patches are powerful narcotic pain relievers. They're reserved for severe pain cases and can be deadly if used in excess. Overdose of fentanyl depress the respiratory drive just as heroin does.

Eric and Sam immediately went the kid's head. Sam applied a jaw thrust maneuver as Eric has the suction on and working to clear the bloody secretions. Sam starts providing breaths with the BVM. We can see the chest rising and falling and within several breaths some of the color is returning to the face. The nail beds have a deep purple hue.

The pupils are constricted like two periods in a sentence. Rocky has the shirt cut off and starts to apply the LifePak 12 and I'm ready to place an IV in his left arm.

"Got that bag ready Steve?" I asked.

"Roger that," he said.

I got the IV in and Steve handed me the tubing which I secured with extra tape. We checked the sugar: 108, no problem there.

Eric said, "I'll just stay here while you push the narcan. Let's see if we can wake him up."

"Sounds like a plan," I said.

I slowly pushed the narcan and by the time it was in we saw no change. This caught everyone by surprise. We fully expected him to have some response. I got a second dose ready.

"Steve, check him everywhere, look for any other patches," I said.

Steve rolled the patient on his side and there are two patches on the lower back, one over each flank. He removed these and wiped the skin with the bed sheet.

"Check his legs too," I said.

After cutting the jeans off, he found one patch on each thigh. Those were removed and skin wiped clean.

His blood pressure is 60/34, heart rate 120 and zero respiratory effort. The oxygen sensor would not register due to the cold fingers.

"I'm going to go with one more narcan and if he doesn't wake up we are going to intubate," I said.

"That sounds good because we are still getting a lot of bloody foam here," Eric said.

As feared, there's no response to the second narcan. I switched places with Eric and got set up to intubate. As I introduced the laryngoscope blade down his throat, there's a near constant flow of blood-tinged foam coming from the lungs. After securing the airway we're now able to provide a higher concentration of oxygen.

We made one more careful check head to toe, ensuring we didn't miss any additional patches. He had the four patches on the skin and one in the mouth. The usual dosage is one patch which can provide up to seventy-two hours of sustained opioid pain control. Whether he was experimenting or suicidal, he would have died had he not been discovered.

We continued to ventilate and infused nearly a liter of fluid (The entire IV Bag). By the time we arrived at the hospital the BP was 100/76; the pulse was still around 100. The oxygen sensor was now reading at 88%.

In the E.D. the diagnoses was cerebral edema. This is swelling around the brain and can have devastating after effects. It's brought on by the anoxia. He's in critical condition and the next twenty-four hours would be crucial. We later learned his grandmother was using the patches for severe osteoarthritis and had forgotten she had them. In all there were ten missing; we accounted for five of them. We could only hope no one else from the party took the five unaccounted patches and used them in the same way our patient did.

Checking with Brenda the next shift we learned he woke up thirty-six hours after admission. He had no memory of the event. He was fortunate to not have permanent brain damage.

Our town has a factory that produces engines for small machinery. They have an on-site ERT (Emergency Response Team) and we occasionally provide basic training in first aid and evaluate their emergency medical equipment. The site has a very good safety record that would change today.

Just after lunch we were summoned to the truck bays by the familiar tones.

"Medic 42, Rescue 41, respond code three for a male subject with steam burns, ENG-CO Manufacturing, 800 Business Way Loop…time out 1330 hours."

Any type of burn can be catastrophic and have significant consequences. Steam burns were no different. Our primary considerations were ensuring the patient's airway remained patent, and controlling the pain. Both could be difficult when burns were involved.

It took five minutes to arrive at the main gate. We followed a security vehicle to the west side of the complex. We went into Building C and found a crowd of people near an emergency shower where the patient is standing under flowing water. He has his arms outstretched and is slowly rotating in a clockwise direction.

We were met by Pete who is the site Safety Superintendent and in charge of the site ERT. We have met Pete on several occasions, none involving anything this significant.

Pete looked at me nervously and said, "Hi Mark, your patient is Riley, he's 38, he was working next to a six inch steam line that burst and was caught pretty badly before we could get him out."

Riley was seriously injured by this event. Co-workers helped remove his clothes to the boxers prior to our arrival and then directed to the emergency shower.

He has large blisters around his forehead, eyes, cheeks and mouth. His lips are blistered and grossly swollen. His neck is red and blistered all across the front along with large pieces of skin hanging off. His entire chest, left arm and halfway down the left leg is blistered with large pieces of skin sloughing off. These are critical burns, third degree, and things are about to get worse.

Riley is making a frightening high pitched sound on inspiration which is indicative of stridor, an ominous sound reflective of significant swelling in the back of the throat. He then tries to speak and grunts out, "It's hard to breathe," with a horrified panicked look.

I looked at Eric and said, "You need to get me an IV in the right arm, now."

"Roger that," Eric said and placed the rubber tourniquet above the elbow on the right arm.

Steve has the gurney ready and Rocky has two large burn sheets. He placed one on the gurney and one over Riley as we sat him on the gurney. Pete is shuttling soaked towels to place over the most severe burned areas while we got our plan in motion.

Sam had an oxygen mask on Riley's mouth and nose as he is squeezing her left hand with his left hand. He's starting to shiver from not only the injury, but from being cold. When you lose this much skin, your ability to regulate your body temperature goes haywire.

There's no comparison for the pain and fear Riley is experiencing. I'm aware of each second ticking by and thinking about his airway closing off from swelling. Steve has the airway supplies out and RSI drugs drawn up; now we needed Eric to get the IV in.

Rocky got the LifePak 12 hooked up and called out the first numbers, "Heart rate 120, Sp02 94%, BP 154/96…"

"IV is in," Eric called out. He then hooked up the bag of normal saline and we were ready.

I nodded to Eric as I was in position at the top of the gurney. I leaned over to Riley's right ear and said, "I'm going to help you breathe my friend, and we're also going to make some of this pain go away…hang in there…"

Riley nodded slightly and blinked, then stared straight ahead, shivering. Eric pushed the drugs and the effects were quick, Riley was out. I had the top of the gurney slightly lowered and I positioned Riley's head into a sniffing position.

When I was going through paramedic school one of the instructors passed on a tip I would use today and be crucial for getting this airway secured on the first try.

He explained when you are facing a difficult or critical intubation, look at your patient's ears first. Do they align with the top of the shoulder?

If the ears are forward of the shoulder, place padding under the upper middle of the patient's back. If the ears are behind the shoulder, place the padding under the back of the neck. This would create the best alignment for viewing the vocal cords and opening to the trachea.

Riley's ears were slightly behind the shoulder. I placed a small towel under the back of his neck.

The opening to his mouth was less than half of normal from the swelling. His tongue was engorged; the soft tissue along both cheeks is swollen, everything is cherry red. I got to the back of the throat and found more redness and swelling. I reached down with my right hand and gently pressed on the front of the neck and moved it slightly to the right: THERE, the opening I was looking for, the vocal cords. It seemed like the opening was getting smaller as I looked at it.

I called to Sam, "Put your hand right here where mine is and hold this position...and hand me the 7.0 tube."

As I watched it go through the vocal cords into the trachea, the tissues immediately swelled around it. We had the airway and wouldn't get a second attempt. I held the tube as if Riley's life depended on it, and it did. After getting the tube secured, we're ready to go.

During the RSI procedure, there are several workers standing and watching this drama unfold. This was their co-worker and close friend. Never could they imagine the trauma that would visit them when they came on shift this morning.

Having Riley's airway secured took tremendous pressure off of us as this is his most immediate threat to life. If his airway had swollen shut, there is high probability he could have died. Trying to establish a surgical airway on a patient that has extensive airway burns is not something that is easily accomplished outside the emergency department or the O.R.

I now have to consider the amount of discomfort he's in. Even though he's unconscious, he's still in pain which is off the charts on a severity scale. As long as his blood pressure remains stable, I will administer as much morphine as he will tolerate.

We alerted RGH of Riley's status and they indicated they were ready for us in Suite 12. By the time we arrived we had given Riley 20 mg of morphine. They continued the morphine until he was admitted to the burn unit. We learned that Riley had over 50% third degree burns. He would be faced with many surgeries and tough days ahead.

Even though we would never see Riley again, the severity and intensity of his injuries would be something we would not forget soon.

There were always "lighter" moments around the station. Be it practical jokes or just sitting around talking. Early one evening Rachel was at the station visiting Rocky with Hank, Abby and Kelsey. They're the happiest dogs you would ever know. They make themselves right at home at the station and consider everyone part of their immediate family. All of the crews got along great with them and they were very therapeutic. If you were ever having a tough day or stressful calls, the "kids' knew how to help.

Hank is the consummate trouble maker. He's tall enough to *"counter surf"*; looking for anything that might be worth grabbing. On a previous visit we caught him with an entire loaf of wheat bread in his jaws, walking around the station with his head and tail up high while still sporting his ubiquitous ear-to-ear grin.

His latest trick is hiding shoes. We have just spent the last ten minutes looking for Sam's right boot. We found it in the day room, between two of the recliners.

Abby and Kelsey were rough housing when Kelsey suddenly stopped, sat down and looked up at the ceiling speaker. Seconds later the tones were going off.

"Medic 42, Rescue 41, respond code three for a traffic collision, 18th and Trenton Street…time out 1816 hours."

Traffic was light and this response would be less than four minutes. As we travelled down 18th, traffic is starting to back up as we got closer to Trenton Street.

Arriving on scene it looked like a vehicle ran the stop sign on Trenton Street and T-boned into a small compact vehicle travelling on 18th. The compact had at least eighteen inches of intrusion into the left rear door. There are two patrol cars on scene and the officers have started their preliminary investigation.

Our immediate concerns were how many patients did we have and was anyone sitting in that compact on the back left side.

One of the officers walked over to the ambulance and said, "Hi guys, everyone *seems* to be okay, we'd appreciate it if you could just check on the kid that's in that small car, his mom's with him now."

"No problem," I said and walked to the compact car where the mother was leaning in the broken window of the back door.

I caught a glimpse of the 8 year old sitting in the back seat and the hair on the back of my neck stood up…he has translucent candle wax looking lips, beads of sweat over his brow and forehead, rapid breathing and a scared look.

I immediately alerted Rocky to get things moving. He turned around to get the back board and gurney.

We would also need to get this back door open. Steve brought the rescue unit's large pry bar over and the door popped open easily.

I looked at the mother and said, "Hi there, my name is Mark, I'm a paramedic…who do we have here?"

She said, "This is Kenny...he says his wrist and stomach and chest are hurting."

"Hi Kenny...I'm Mark...we're going to take you to the hospital," I told him.

Kenny nodded ever so slightly. I reached to feel for a radial pulse and couldn't find one. This had every major red flag that could be flying.

Kenny was seat-belted during the collision. He has bruising over the left upper abdomen and chest. He also has an obvious fracture to the left arm just above the wrist. My working diagnosis is a ruptured spleen and fractured left wrist. The spleen has him on a clock he can't slow down and every minute is precious time we can't get back.

Kenny was easy to secure, as he's very small. Sam got into the car through the right rear door and held his neck to prevent any movement. Steve and Eric were able to slide the back board under him and he was out of the car in less than two minute. I estimated him to be 60 pounds or 30 kg. Once in the ambulance we quickly headed to RGH. We were on scene six minutes. Kenny was about twelve minutes into his nightmare.

Sam was next to Kenny's head and explaining what was going on. She applied an oxygen mask and was talking to him as I got ready to start the IV. Kenny is a very brave patient. He barely flinched with the 16 gauge going into his right mid arm. Eric had the left arm splinted and clothing cut off and LifePak 12 hooked up.

He then called out Kenny's latest numbers, "Heart rate is 138, BP is 64/36, and Sp02 is 91%."

Upon hearing these numbers, I decided to give Kenny a bolus of fluid through the IV for the low blood pressure. Based on his weight we would give him 600 cc which is a little over half the IV bag and will be in before we arrive at RGH.

On further reassessment, the bruising over the left upper abdomen and chest is becoming more pronounced. His breath sounds are remaining clear and equal. After the fluid bolus his heart rate came down to 124 and the blood pressure increased to 72/44. These were temporary improvements.

I conferred with Brenda by cell phone, she said the trauma team was assembled and an O.R. is available if needed. We would be there in two minutes.

We arrived and were directed into Suite 12. Kenny was the center of attention and getting plenty of it. Within minutes he would go to the O.R. for a splenic rupture. He spent just over an hour in the O.R. and had his spleen removed. He went to the pediatric ICU for the night. During the night he developed increasing shortness of breath and ended up with a tension pneumothorax and chest tube on the left side.

He spent the next two days in the pediatric ICU before being transferred to the pediatric floor and then five days later discharged home.

T-bone crashes with intrusion into the passenger areas are considered significant MOI (Mechanism of Injury) and can be devastating. The crashed vehicle offers many clues as to the potential injuries. This is why it is so important for us to take a good look at the vehicle before we leave the scene. The emergency department physician will also ask about the car based on this same theory. We are the eyes and ears of the physician outside the emergency department.

CHAPTER 16

SPEED

Over the years with all the motor vehicle crashes and collisions, speed has to rank up there near the top for contributing factors. As a teenager, there's something about getting that license and the inevitable temptation to go fast. From not being able to stop before a hazard, negotiate road conditions or the elements, it can all lead to devastating consequences.

Whenever we talk to young drivers or soon-to-be drivers, the focus has to include getting them to obey the speed limits and resist the urges and inevitable peer pressure to exceed them.

Saturday afternoon, Rocky and I, along with Steve, Eric and Sam and a few other station personnel had just finished a recertification class on Health Care Provider Level-CPR. Even though we use this skill in the course of our responses, we still need our certification cards updated every two years. I've been an instructor for the last few years and able to get everyone recertified. Things got a little carried away toward the end when Sam was finishing her final practical. The new standards included a catchy tune to help people stay in rhythm with completing compressions in an allotted time and the tune was from the Bee Gee's song 'Staying Alive.' Sam had the entire station singing for her as she kept perfect timing. It was a classic moment.

We started cleaning the mannequins when the tones broke the mood.

"Medic 42, Rescue 41, Engine 61, respond code three for a motor vehicle crash, car in to a tree, 1200 block of Montvale Road…time out 1408 hours."

We shared this stretch of road with District 6 for mutual aid response. Montvale Road was notorious for high speed crashes. It had long straight stretches and then deceiving curves. Today it would lay claim to another serious crash.

Dispatch had given us several updates from callers who were on scene and they were describing this as "a severe crash with people believed to be dead."

Even if it was only half as bad as they reported, it could be a serious scene.

Arriving we couldn't help but notice the hard skid marks that seemed to go on forever before leaving the road. Then, the scene revealed itself with a demolished car against a large tree that wasn't going to be moved by the small compact vehicle. The vehicle no longer resembled a car. It was more like a car you'd see in the movies that was crushed by the large compactors in the junk yards. The entire vehicle was no more than six feet long. The state patrol was estimating it leaving the road at 100 mph and just under that when it struck the tree.

The teenage female driver had somehow gotten out and was being attended to by bystanders. She's crying and has obvious small lacerations to the head and a fractured right lower leg. Sam and Eric began assessing her as I continued to the car. Rocky is pulling equipment from the ambulance and Steve is assessing the car for immediate hazards.

It's a frightening sight; I approached the passenger side of the car and see a hand protruding from the compacted and twisted wreckage. It's fractured near the wrist with a small bone protruding by a couple inches.

I touched the hand and was surprised to feel a radial pulse with a heart rate of 120. I leaned into the mangled mess and yelled, "Hello, I'm a paramedic, can you hear me?"

A soft female voice came from deep in the wreckage, "Help me... please...I can't move....please...."

I said, "Okay, listen to me, my name is Mark. I'm a paramedic and we're going to get you out of there. We won't leave you."

The voice responded with a feeble whimper.

I called for a second ambulance to transport the driver. We would obviously be here for a while with the trapped patient. The Engine 61 crew arrived and immediately set up two charged hose lines to protect the scene from any fire potential.

They immediately began the delicate task of cutting the car apart with the Jaws of Life. It was loud and the car would shudder as the twisted metal that entombed her was painstakingly peeled away; this patient is in a living nightmare.

This effort continued for fifteen minutes before we could see much more than the hand. I was finally able to see her frightened and bloodied face.

Her name is Kayla and she's 17. I did the best I could to explain everything we were doing and keep her focused and not panicking.

Rocky had the back of the ambulance set up with IV's, the LifePak 12--everything we would need for stabilizing Kayla once she was freed. Steve's working with the Engine 61 crew as they were taking turns running the heavy extrication tool. It was exhausting work. Each step had to be carefully evaluated, as we couldn't see how she was trapped and couldn't just blindly rip the car apart without potentially causing her more injuries.

After fifty-six minutes, we were able to extricate Kayla onto the spine board. She's a small girl, 5 feet tall and 100 pounds with short brown hair. She has a short sleeveless top on with jeans and her right tennis shoe is missing. Her clothes are bloodied and torn with serious injuries under them.

She has a gaping full thickness laceration across the forehead that extends through the right brow; the right eye is swollen shut with the orbit and nose fractured. She has at least three fractured ribs on the left side and possibly a flail chest. I can hear equal breath sounds. Her right wrist is fractured with bone protruding. There are several inches of eviscerated bowel protruding from a large puncture to the lower abdomen just right of the navel. There are bilateral femur fractures and bilateral lower leg fractures and several open lacerations on the legs that represent open fracture sites. Her color is pale with cool and clammy skin. These are the obvious injuries.

Once in the ambulance, Eric and Sam immediately went to work. We would have a nine minute transport to RGH. Sam put an oxygen mask over Kayla's mouth and nose while she dressed the forehead laceration and explaining things to Kayla. She seemed to be listening but had no strength to speak. Eric covered the abdominal evisceration with a saline soaked dressing.

I found a large enough vein on the left arm to get a 14 gauge into it. Eric secured the legs by splinting them against each other. I decided we would secure Kayla's airway with the RSI procedure.

Eric then had the LifePak 12 hooked up and called out our first numbers, "Heart rate 136, blood pressure 68/46, Sp02 88%," he said.

Eric was drawing the RSI medications up in syringes as I prepared for the intubation. Sam was ready with the suction as I nodded to Eric that we were ready. Kayla's eyes closed quickly as Eric pushed the drugs and she was off to sleep and paralyzed. I slid the laryngoscope blade down her throat and immediately found the epiglottis with a great view of the vocal cords.

"I think I can fit the 7.5 in there, hand me that one," I said to Sam without losing sight of the cords. It passed smoothly in to the trachea. After getting it secured, Sam took over with the bag valve.

Eric put a second IV in the right arm above the open wrist fracture as I called out our next vitals, "BP 66/46, heart rate 140, SpO2 will not read," I said.

We had done all we could; we needed Kayla to hang on for a few more minutes. Her color remains ghostly pale.

We arrived at RGH where Kayla spent eight minutes in Suite 12 and off to the O.R. The entire call was physically and emotionally draining. Steve wasn't too far behind us, when he stepped out of Rescue 41 he was covered in sweat and looked like he had run a marathon.

Back at the station we got an update from Brenda. Kayla had major injuries but would live. She has a stable C-3 neck fracture; her spleen removed and liver repaired. Her bladder and eviscerated section of bowel are repaired, both femurs with pins, both lower legs were pinned, a wrist with a pin, facial fractures and numerous lacerations sutured. She would spend at least the next month in the hospital, but as Brenda and I both agreed, she was alive.

Calls like these will challenge every part of the system, from getting the extrication safely completed to getting the right treatment at the right time. The human body is very fragile when you are dealing with speed and mass. Something has to give.

There had been a rash of convenience stores robberies committed in the area and this created an aggressive patrol effort in order to try to apprehend the suspects in these cases.

There were two individuals responsible and they used stolen motorcycles to conduct the robberies. Early one morning just after coming on shift,

Rocky and I were busy getting the ambulance ready for the day, when we were interrupted by the tones.

"Medic 42, Rescue 41, respond code three for a motorcycle crash, two suspects are down after a police chase...26th and Main Street...time out 0840 hours."

This call would assure a large police presence and we could also be dealing with potentially aggressive or combative patients. Hopefully the suspects would understand we were the ones that would be helping and be cooperative, but this was not always the case. Medics have been assaulted and even killed by suspects that have been cornered. We would take full precautions on this morning.

Within a couple blocks of the scene, dispatch updated us there's one confirmed DOA and one suspect with critical injuries. The seriousness of this response just escalated.

We arrived to a parking lot of patrol cars and unmarked police cars. Officers are creating a perimeter and lining the block with yellow police tape. Bystanders established a viewing line and this quickly turned in to a major scene.

There is a motorcycle sticking out of a hole in a brick wall on the side of a two story building. The hole had the outline of not only the motorcycle but a body as well. There are two individuals lying on the ground near this crash.

The first one is lying face up. He has massive open head trauma, his face is grotesquely sunken in; there's a pool of blood five feet in diameter surrounding the head. He has both femurs fractured with the right leg underneath him and the left alongside his chest.

He does not have any signs of life, no respiratory effort and no carotid pulse. He is DOA.

This individual was the driver of the motorcycle. During the high speed pursuit he lost control trying to make a turn he couldn't possibly have made at the estimated 90 mph. He drove head-on into the brick wall with no attempt to brake. He didn't have a helmet, even though it probably wouldn't have protected him at that speed.

His partner was riding behind him and is lying about ten feet away. On impact he was thrown backwards and hasn't moved since the crash. He's on his right side and having significant airway issues with prolonged grunting on exhalation along with obstructive snoring inspiration. It's a graphic presentation. He also has a large pool of blood surrounding his head. This is from a massive open injury to the back of his skull. He doesn't have a radial pulse in the left wrist.

All of our initial efforts will be focused on managing his airway and stopping bleeding from the head.

Rocky was preparing the long spine board. Eric and Sam were working on controlling bleeding and getting control of the jaw, which is in pieces making a seal with the BVM difficult.

Steve's cutting clothing away when I noticed him slide a small automatic pistol towards one of the officers. It was tucked in the left waistband. We have two officers with rifles standing near us in defensive positions.

I can hear the "clicking" sound of a camera but can't tell where it's coming from.

A quick listen to the chest with my stethoscope and I don't hear air on either side. I also find several rib fractures on the right. Both wrists are shattered and deformed; both lower legs are fractured with bones protruding.

I told Rocky to get me two of the "big needles" and he was gone in an instant. I informed Eric I would insert both needles as we were packaging him to the board, then to the back of the ambulance and secure the airway with RSI.

Eric nodded without looking up from the airway.

Rocky brought me three needles…two for the chest, and one to place as an IV while they were packaging him. I inserted the first 12 gauge-3 inch needle over the right chest and got immediate air followed by blood, and then the same result on the left.

I put the 14 gauge IV into the left middle arm while Steve and Eric were getting him secured to the backboard. This would prove to be crucial in getting the airway secured with the RSI procedure. Sam used tape to secure his lower legs to the spine board. The wrist fractures were stabilized at his side and held in place with the safety belts.

I looked at the closest officer and said, "Have dispatch alert RGH, we're going to be there in less than five," and then hopped into the back of the ambulance.

Our scene time was five minutes.

We also had an officer with us. He sat at the very back of the ambulance on the bench seat. He asked me on the way in, "Is this guy going to make it?"

I looked up and my facial expression must have said it all, because he shook his head side to side and then looked at the patient.

Sam hooked up the LifePak 12 and she called out some very poor numbers, "BP 60/36, heart rate 134, SpO2 84%," she said with a serious tone.

Eric had oxygen flowing by holding the mask over the patient's face and occasional suctioning as the blood would pool. I pushed the RSI drugs through our only IV and there was no return at this point, the patient was out. Now I have the difficult job of getting past the trauma of the upper airway and keeping a clear view.

Sam took over with the suction and followed my lead as I slowly slid the long curved blade into the back of the throat. There are large clots of blood and pieces of the jaw blocking my view. Sam would remove them with the suction as she could and then there it was…the epiglottis and vocal cords. I slid the endotracheal tube down the throat and watched it pass into the trachea.

After securing the tube, Eric took over with the bag valve and we were now just thirty seconds from RGH.

We arrived to a welcomed greeting by half of the trauma team and Dr. Swanson, who is the chief trauma surgeon for the hospital. Valiant and extraordinary efforts took place in Suite 12 but they couldn't get him stable enough to make it to the O.R.

Twenty-six minutes after arriving, the patient was declared dead. Life is so very precious, that's why we work so hard and do what we do. Both of these patient's fates were sealed when they ran from the police and hit the wall.

In EMS, calls obviously come at random and usually without any prior warning. After the catastrophic motorcycle crash last week things have been very minor in comparison.

It's Friday morning and we're ready for anything. Our first call is for a male having a seizure and found it to be more of a traumatic experience than it had to be, no thanks to his co-workers.

They were all in a meeting when the patient suddenly arched backwards with his eyes rolling back in their sockets, slid to the floor and began to display grand-mal seizure activity while foaming from the mouth and turning deep blue. This was a dramatic presentation to the unsuspecting group of professionals.

One of the co-workers yelled out, "We need to get something in his mouth before he swallows his tongue."

Of course this is a myth and you should never put anything in a seizing patient's mouth.

The only thing they could find was a large dry erase black magic marker. This didn't last long, as he chewed it up and got black ink all through his mouth, tongue, teeth, everywhere.

He then swallowed the cap to the marker and ended up with an obstructed airway we had to resolve.

When we got to the E.D. they just stared at us as if we did something dastardly to him. I walked by them shaking my head. Despite the co-workers' attempts to "knock him off," he survived the incident.

For this being Friday, the rest of the day continued with the atypical responses. I found myself half asleep on one of the recliners when the tones erased all thoughts of slumber.

"Medic 42, Rescue 41, Engine 61, respond code three for a vehicle into a house, 5420 Rudman Road…time out 2218 hours."

We've been to calls for crashes on Rudman Road before, none involving houses though. It's a 45 mph road and the houses were well off the lanes of travel. We shared a border along this road with District 6 and as usual always happy to work with them.

As we pulled up to the scene, there didn't seem to be any crash we could see. There's a man in a robe looking up at the second story of the house. It was then that we noticed the car.

A large sedan had been travelling at an estimated 75 plus mph when it failed to negotiate the curve in front of this home. It left the road and after hitting a small embankment, went airborne, crashing through a second story bedroom and landing squarely on top of the bed of a sleeping 13 year old girl.

The patient's mother is crying nearly uncontrollably and still reeling from the instant the car crashed through the house. The father explained how he and his wife were downstairs watching TV when they heard tires screeching and then the entire house shook like an earthquake hit and sounded like it exploded.

He explained, "I initially went outside and didn't see anything…I then see this guy climbing off this bumper sticking out of my house, falling to the ground and then running off…then another idiot right behind him…I screamed at them and ran for a few steps before realizing the car was in my daughter's room."

The car is completely inside the house; the bumper was near even with the exterior siding. The daughter, Erica, was asleep when the car landed on top of her, pinning her to the bed. This was also a water bed. The front and rear left tires are on the frame and the right tires are on the bed.

The Engine 61 crew arrived and quickly put up two ladders. We're able to see in the room from under the car and Erica is understandably petrified.

I couldn't see her in the bed but was able to talk to her. It was surreal looking into a second story bedroom with a car on top of the bed.

"Erica…can you hear me? My name is Mark, I'm a paramedic," I called out.

"Yes, I can hear you, there's a car on top of me," was her near panicked response.

"Okay, hang in there, we're going to get you out…do you hurt anywhere," I asked?

"My leg hurts, please hurry, I'm scared," she said excitedly.

"…anything else?" I asked.

"No, just that…how are you going to get me out of here?" She asked with great anticipation.

"Well we are working on that, don't move," I said.

Rocky yelled up to me they made their way into the bedroom from in the house. I came down off the ladder and went upstairs. The engine crew was behind me and Captain Neeves just stared as we walked in the room, "There's something you don't see every day," he said.

As we are surveying the room, we noticed a secondary problem: the bed was leaking and the car was listing more to the right. We weren't so sure she wasn't going to be crushed as the car sank into the bed.

Erica yelled out with innocence, "Do my parents know about this?"

I said, "Yes they do, and they're right here."

About then Erica's mother yelled out, "Baby, are you okay?"

Erica cried out, "Mom, there's a car in my bed."

Steve came up the stairs and said, "Hey Mark, the Engine crew thinks they can get her out through the front."

I told Erica we would start talking to her from the front of the house and she said, "Okay, please hurry."

We were able to ascertain from Erica that she didn't think her leg was broken, just sore. She managed to snake her way to the ladder and Brock, the Engine 61 fire fighter, carried her to the ground and to our gurney.

After a quick head-to-toe assessment, we found some wheel grease in her hair, a torn pair of pajama bottoms and a small laceration and abrasion to the right lower leg.

The transport was uneventful. In the emergency department Erica was somewhat of a celebrity. Several nurses came by and listened to her story.

Erica told them, "I thought I was having a bad dream and then I could smell the car and feel the heat coming from it…and then I realized…. there's a car on top of me and started screaming."

The two occupants that fled were later arrested. One of them sustained a compression fracture to his thoracic vertebrae and showed up at another hospital. His story to the nursing staff and doctor was suspiciously inconsistent and they had been alerted by police to be on the lookout for just such a person. He had a blood alcohol level of .24, and this was four hours after the incident. He claimed he was the passenger. When they caught up to the other guy, he said the same thing: "His friend was driving."

Captain Neeves said it best… "Definitely something you don't see every day, and hopefully never again."

Erica was discharged without further injuries.

It's Sunday morning and we are taking time for a station breakfast before working on special projects or maybe even a work out in the station gym. The Sunday newspaper is spread across the table and everyone is looking for "their" section when everything went by the wayside with our first call of the day and those familiar tones.

"Medic 42, Rescue 41, respond code three for a motor vehicle collision with possible entrapment, 1614 Hudson in front of Valley High School… time out 0845 hours."

Traffic was heavier than normal and we arrived on scene in just over four minutes.

This was a rear end collision and the rear vehicle took the brunt of the crash. A medium-sized sedan had run into the back of a stopped pickup truck. There were no skid marks. The sedan was bowed in the middle. The front end was smashed in an accordion fashion and shortened by at least two feet. There's a large puddle of green fluid leaking from the engine compartment and making a steady stream to the curbside.

The windshield has the outline of a face with embedded hair and blood and pushed out about twelve inches.

The elderly driver is staring ahead with a bewildered look and trying to talk but the words were slurred and mixed with blood. The steering wheel had been bent over the top of the column and the dash is broken in several places.

I reached in through the window to hold his head still as a precaution against aggravating a potential cervical vertebrae injury and at the same time said, "Hi there, my name is Mark. I'm a paramedic. I'm going to just kind of hold your head still. Try not to move."

This was greeted with an immediate denial of any type of problem and aggressive attempt to pull away. A heavy alcohol aroma emanated from the vehicle.

Steve and Eric were able to get the driver's door popped open quickly.

On the next attempt at holding the head still, I asked, "Sir, can you tell me your name?"

"It's Carter, if it's any of your business," was the sarcastic and angry response.

"Well, Mr. Carter, we really need to take you to RGH and get your face looked at," I said.

At that moment a police officer walked over and asked if there was a problem.

I said, "Well, we're concerned about his facial injuries and potential internal injuries; he's not being very cooperative right now."

The officer leaned in the vehicle and after a few seconds came back up and said, "He'll go with you."

Whatever he said, it worked. Along with the massive facial injuries a quick assessment showed he might have fractured ribs on the right side and a right wrist fracture. His pelvis was stable and was incontinent of urine. This was concerning, as it meant he may have been unconscious after the crash.

Sam got a cervical collar secured around Carter's neck, Eric had the back board ready, and we got him out of the vehicle and secured to the gurney.

Once into the back of the ambulance, we began to get a better idea of how serious Carter was. The frontal skull at the hairline had bits of bone and what looked like a depressed skull fracture. His right eye was swollen shut and the socket probably fractured.

The face had literally dozens of small lacerations along with bits of embedded glass and pieces of skin torn away. He has at least two ribs on the right that do not feel solid. He does have clear and equal breath sounds.

Eric is dressing the facial wounds. Sam was applying a cardboard splint to the right wrist. The LifePak 12 showed a regular rhythm with frequent extra beats which could be reflective of cardiac contusion, a bruise to the heart itself. His heart rate was 116, blood pressure 170/120 and SpO2 at 97%.

During the transport I placed two 14 gauge IV's in his left arm. We called for a trauma team and were told they would be ready.

Carter then decided he didn't want to be in the ambulance anymore and began fighting against the straps and swinging wildly at anything within reach. As we tried to keep him from moving he added screaming and cursing at all of us and was as strong as a bull. The concern is that if he has any type of cervical fracture he could end up paralyzed for the rest of his life.

Arriving at RGH, we had some fairly shocked looks upon wheeling Carter into Suite 12 as he was still swearing and fighting against the seat belts.

He ended up in the O.R. for repair of a skull fracture, a chest tube on the right side, a pinned right radial and ulnar wrist fracture. In addition to the surgical injuries he had a C-2, C-3 neck fractures that were stable and fortunately not made worse by the fighting episode. His right eye socket and nose are fractured and will end up with hours of facial suturing

Carter is 85 years old and had a blood alcohol level of .22, nearly three times the legal limit. We later heard that witnesses described him travelling at an estimated 40 plus mph and driving into the back of the stopped pickup truck with no hesitation.

The pickup truck suffered only a slightly bent bumper.

With a string of warm summer days, it was hard not to take advantage and fire up the BBQ. At the end of a three day weekend we made plans for an afternoon BBQ and having the crews and their families participate. We have a large area behind the station with a volleyball net set up and plenty of room for Hank, Abby and Kelsey.

Rachel said she mentions "going to see dad" or "the station" and they go nuts. As usual Hank does recon from the time he arrives to see what is within reach or worth getting into. We try to re-arrange things before he comes over but it's futility at best. He thinks it's a game we play and he wins every time.

We're getting ready to fire up the BBQ when tones took center stage.

"Medic 42, Rescue 41, respond code one to the field behind the County Land Fill, police on scene requesting a stand-by unit…time out 1350 hours."

We went en route and did not receive any further information. It was a mystery until we arrived.

A county deputy sergeant met us at the entrance to the Land Fill with a grim explanation.

"Hey guys…we had a couple of kids riding motorcycles and one of them found a leg…it had been severed at the mid-thigh…they soon found another one in the same shape and they look to be from the same person…we're looking around the area and would appreciate it if you guys could hang for a bit," he explained.

Wow. We had several railroad tracks very near here and there's a heavy transient population that hops the trains. We've had calls where the hop was unsuccessful and ended with horrific results.

We soon received a call from dispatch to respond to another entrance down the road where they found the patient with no legs. We had to hike off the road for about seventy-five yards. In a clearing we found a male patient, face down and evidence he'd been crawling before he stopped here.

He was obviously breathing, moaning and displayed non-purposeful movement. Both legs are missing from the mid-thigh with clumps of coagulated blood and dirt heavily impacted in both stumps. His shirt is tattered and torn, arms were bleeding superficially and his face is caked with dried mud and sand.

I started by putting a hand to his left shoulder and attempting a verbal response, "Hey buddy…can you open your eyes, my name is Mark…I'm a paramedic and we're going to help you…"

No response. He has a weak radial pulse at 120.

Eric and I cleaned as much of the debris away from the stumps as we could. We packed the ends of with large trauma dressings.

Rocky had the long spine board ready. Sam directed the roll by holding the head and neck in line and called out "one-two-three-roll."

He was on the back board and throughout the process gave no verbal response or grimace. We carried him back to the ambulance and are heading to RGH. We have both of the severed legs with us, wrapped in sterile burn sheets.

Eric cut all of the clothing off. The patient has abrasions over nearly every inch of skin.

"He had to have been crawling for a long time," I thought.

Sam's managing the airway. She provided oxygen by mask and called out, "Respirations at 12 and shallow."

Eric and I discussed using the RSI to secure the airway and determined the intubation would be moderately difficult. A small mouth opening along with almost no neck is two major strikes. We're confident we could ventilate him if needed, so we decided to proceed with the intubation. I got a couple of different blades and tube sizes ready.

We first needed an IV. I found one small vein on the left hand and managed to get an 18 gauge into it. I taped it securely, as usual you never want to lose a tough IV stick.

Eric then got the LifePak 12 attached and it showed a sinus tachycardia (fast heart rate) at 126. The blood pressure is 76/44, the Sp02 will not read. The glucose is 88.

Everyone is in place and I am ready for the RSI drugs to be pushed through the IV line.

Using my two right fingers I spread open the patient's mouth and inserted the long straight blade down his throat. The view is maybe half of what I am used to having. I can see the epiglottis and placed my right hand on the front of the neck and gently moved things around to where I had a better good view. The vocal cords suddenly came into view.

Without moving my eyes, I had Sam take over the neck pressure and then had another issue.

The mouth opening wasn't big enough to slide the tube in. I had Sam take her right hand, snake it under my left arm and using her right index finger, she pulled the side of the patient's mouth open, and this made the difference.

We call this the fish hook method. It creates a larger mouth opening. I slid the tube down the throat and watched it advance through the vocal cords. We got it. Now time to reassess. Pupils are equal and reactive. No trauma to the head that we could see. I can still hear clear and equal breath sounds. The heart rate is fast at 128.

There is a heavy alcohol aroma throughout the ambulance.

We estimated that with all of the abrasions and how dried the stumps were, he must have been run over by a train last night. He then crawled over half a mile from where the legs were found.

We arrived at RGH to a small army of assistance. The word of our transport had the trauma team at top readiness and they went into action immediately on our arrival. He was in the O.R. within twenty minutes of his arrival. The legs were not viable for reattachment. In addition to the amputations, he had a pelvic fracture. Beyond that, the abrasions were superficial.

His alcohol level was .27 and no telling how much it came down from since his last drink.

The patient's name is Jack. He is 47 years old. He's a veteran and has been a transient for several years. There were no reports from passing trains of seeing anyone on the tracks. There were nine trains that passed through the area that night.

Jack was eventually discharged to a Skilled Nursing Facility and Rehab Center and was fitted with prosthetics. We have not seen Jack since that day.

We got back to the station just before 1800. Most of the crews and families had gone home. Rachel and the kids were still there. When Rocky walked into the day room you would have thought he was gone for a year by the greeting he got from Hank, Abby and Kelsey. If you've never experienced this, your life is not complete.

CHAPTER 17

LOOKS LIKE A DUCK...

Over the years I've been heavily involved with teaching CPR and basic first aid classes to the lay public. These skills are very basic but important to employ prior to EMS arriving. One of the things I try to focus on is getting people to recognize an emergency and a big one people miss is the "denial" phase.

When someone is having those obvious signs like pressure in the chest, trouble breathing, sweating when everyone else isn't or pain that's radiating into the jaw, neck, arms or back, nausea...these are signs that would be hard to ignore.

However, it isn't uncommon for someone to rationalize with themselves that they can't be having anything serious and it only happens to other people.

This is called denial and it can be deadly. We have a saying in the pre-hospital arena when someone is having a potential cardiac emergency, *"time is muscle."*

This means the longer you wait after having these symptoms, the more potential damage that's occurring to the heart. This damaged muscle tissue cannot be replaced or re-grow.

We unfortunately see this play out sometimes and the tones would send us to a classic example.

"Medic 42, Rescue 41, respond code three for chest pain, 44 year old male, 107 Main Street, Suite 4, General Mortgage Company…time out 1054 hours."

Noon traffic was worse than usual for a Monday. It took four minutes to arrive. We had the "welcome party" on the curb waving and made sure we knew where to stop. A smartly dressed female and a male in a suit both walked over as we exited the ambulance.

"It's our boss, Mr. Delmar, he's having some pretty bad pain…he thinks it's something he ate," the female explained.

The male with her nodded his head affirmatively.

We followed them through the lobby and along cubicles of co-workers with worried looks and then into a large office

Mr. Delmar is sitting in a high back leather chair being attended to by a female who was standing next to him with her hand on his shoulder. His head was tipped back and a wet paper towel across his forehead.

Mr. Delmar is ghostly pale, sweating, subtly struggling for each breath and has an impending doom look we typically see with someone having a heart attack.

He's 44 years old and I estimate thirty pounds overweight.

"Mr. Delmar…my name is Mark, I'm a paramedic. Can you tell me what the main problem is right now?" I asked.

"Call me Gil…my chest is so tight, squeezing; it's hard to get a breath," he said.

'Okay Gil, we're going to do some things and see if we can get you feeling better…when did this start?" I asked.

"Well, I woke up with it at six, thought it'd go away. I can't stop sweating; the pain is in my jaw and arm. My wife thought it was something I ate last night," he replied.

Sam started Gil on oxygen by a mask, Eric was getting the IV started and Rocky got the LifePak 12 hooked up. He then handed me the 12 lead EKG print out.

Gil was having a heart attack, and probably has been throughout the morning. We followed our cardiac protocol and were about to give him an aspirin when the female next to him spoke up and said, "We've already done that…we gave him Ibuprofen."

We proceeded to give him one of our aspirins to chew up after a quick explanation that they were not the same.

Steve had the gurney in the office and ready to go and then whispered to me, "They said he's been like this all morning, nearly passed out a couple times, he's been eating antacid tablets since he got here…they also said he smokes and has high blood pressure."

I looked at Steve as we shared a *"This isn't looking good"* look.

Sam looked at the LifePak 12 and said, "Mark, his oxygen sensor isn't reading anymore, and his last BP was 80/40."

We quickly got Gil loaded on to the gurney and into the ambulance. We watched with great concern his color draining minute to minute. We were on scene less than eight minutes and now expediting the transport to RGH.

I started to question Gil about the discomfort when he went unresponsive with a blank stare and his left hand dropped over the side of the gurney.

He took a large gasp and rapidly went blue around the lips and face. A quick look at the monitor and Gil was in V-fib.

"Let's shock at 200 watts," I said to Eric.

"Roger that," was Eric's response and after the charge called out, "Clear," and delivered the energy.

Gil lurched at the shock and Sam began compressions. Eric began providing breaths with the BVM. He had good chest rise with each squeeze of the bag. After another two minutes of CPR, the rhythm check is still V-fib.

"Let's shock at 300 watts this time," I said.

After the charge I announced "clear" and pushed the discharge button only to receive part of the shock myself...I planted my knee against the gurney in order to steady myself and the energy travelled into my knee and halfway up my leg. It startled me more than it hurt and I instinctively jumped back and grabbed my leg.

Eric and Sam looked at me with their mouths agape. I looked at Eric and said, "Switch with Sam and take over on compressions; Sam, you got the airway."

"Are you okay?" Sam asked with serious concern.

I said, "Yeah I think so, it was just a little shock--probably won't try that a second time..."

I pushed epinephrine into the IV line and after two minutes of CPR checked the EKG. It was asystole, or flat line. Gil was slipping away.

I switched places with Sam in order to secure Gil's airway with intubation. As I placed the laryngoscope blade down his throat, I found it lined with a "chalky" green color and bits of un-chewed antacid tablets. The endotracheal tube was placed and secured.

We arrived at RGH and continued the efforts into the emergency department where Dr. Stein took over. After another twenty-eight minutes and no change in the rhythm he called the resuscitation efforts at 1142 hours.

Dr. Stein spoke with us after the conclusion of the resuscitation efforts.

"So what do you guys think we should do to get the public to recognize something like this and call before it is too late?" He asked.

I said, "Boy, that's a great question...he had just about every sign you could have...but only focused on the denial one."

Could this have had a better outcome if he received care earlier in the day? Who knows...it certainly couldn't have made things worse.

In EMS we are obviously aware of the need to maintain some degree of health and fitness. We see examples of neglected health regularly. Rocky and I, as well as Steve, Eric and Sam, get some daily workout at the station. We split our time between resistance training and cardio. Each day one of us would have a "theme for the day" and that would be our primary focus with the rest of the workout taking place around it.

Today was Sam's turn and she called "squats" and everyone made a sour face. We were saved from this punishment by the tones.

"Medic 42, Rescue 41, respond code three for a 48 year old male subject with dizzy spells, 1806 Glacier Street...The Athletes Health Club...time out 1600 hours."

We don't get many calls to a health club. Last summer we responded to a "crash and burn" incident involving a young female and a tread mill. She stumbled and it got ugly from there, the belt from the tread mill "sanded" her face for a few seconds. It didn't help the place was packed and she was quite humiliated.

Today's response took four minutes and we were met by one of the trainers.

"Hey guys…I have a guy that didn't want us to call you. He was on the treadmill and passed out. He came around pretty quick and said he was okay, just wanted to go home, we kind of didn't give him a choice about waiting for you guys," he said.

I said, "Well, that sounds good. We'll be glad to check him out."

When someone passes out, there are many possible reasons, the most serious being a heart-related problem. We were directed into the office and met Sean, our patient.

I said, "Nice to meet you Sean. My name is Mark, I'm a paramedic. What happened this afternoon?"

"It really wasn't any big deal…I was walking for about ten minutes and next thing I know I was waking up on the floor," he explained.

I said, "Okay, has anything like this ever happened before?"

We were not expecting the next response.

"Well, over the last month or so, I get this burning sensation after being on the treadmill for a few minutes. I think its heartburn; I can feel it in my jaw and lower back. Today was the first time I passed out after having it. Usually after I slow down or stop, it goes away in a few minutes" he admitted.

I said, "Sean is it okay if my partners hook you up to our equipment and we can check things out?"

"Sure, go ahead, I'm sure everything is fine," he said.

Eric had the LifePak 12 hooked up and got a 12 Lead. Sean is having irritability in the front part of the heart and warrants urgent evaluation by the cardiac team at RGH.

Sam called out the BP, "160/100."

I explained the need for us to transport him to RGH.

He said, "Well, if you think it's necessary, I could just drive myself up there."

"Well, that wouldn't be a good idea. You just passed out and until we get to the bottom of this, it would be the safest to stay with us," I said as we are all nodding affirmatively in unison.

"Okay, if you think so," was the slightly reluctant response.

Eric established an IV, we gave aspirin as directed by our cardiac protocol and transported. During the trip I asked Sean how he was feeling.

"Well, okay I guess, still having that burning sensation, it's a little hard to breathe and a little sick to my stomach--other than that, I feel fine," he said.

More of the *denial* thinking; the last thing a person wants to rationalize about is that they may be having a life-threatening experience. We gave a spray of nitro under the tongue which relieved the burning discomfort by the time we arrived at RGH.

As we were wheeling him into the E.D., Sean said, "I still don't think any of this is necessary."

We had called ahead and categorized Sean as a cardiac alert; he would get immediate attention in the emergency department. Sean ended up with emergency by-pass surgery and was described as a "walking time bomb" and "miraculous" he didn't drop dead either in the gym or while driving around town.

Over the last several days we had eight heroin overdoses in the county. Two of them died, as they were not discovered in time. In EMS we see an increase in the overdoses when a "new shipment" comes into town that is stronger than the users are accustomed to. Heroin users have big time denial about the addiction, even after they see us; they deny that their habit is a problem.

That afternoon we had been discussing the increases in heroin overdoses and the tones joined in on the conversation.

"Medic 42, Rescue 41, respond code three for a 21 year old male, not breathing, possible overdose, 318 Douglas St…time out 1550 hours."

This response would be quick, less than three minutes. Time would be critical if the patient was not breathing.

We received an update from dispatch, "Medic 42, Rescue 41, police on scene advising CPR in progress."

We arrived and found two patrol cars on scene, the front door open. We all grabbed a piece of equipment and made our way to the front door as one of the officers met us.

"Your patient's name's Dray, 21 years old, he's got a pulse now, still not breathing too good…the roommate called 9-1-1 after hearing him collapse in the bathroom…he said he thought he "*may*" have done some heroin," he explained with rhetoric tone.

Dray is lying face up near the bathroom on the floor. He's six feet tall and maybe 160 pounds. He's obviously missed his last several showers. He has IV track marks on both arms and along the right side of his neck along with scabs in various stages of healing on both arms and face.

His tee shirt has the logo, "C-O-P-S, *Watcha gonna do…*"

Steve and Sam started providing rescue breaths after determining Dray had a carotid pulse. I could see chest rise and fall with each breath they delivered. His purple face had shades of pink within a few breaths. Eric's looking for IV sites and asked Rocky to set up an IV bag as he tapped a vein a few times on the left arm.

I cut through the middle of his shirt and applied the EKG patches. His heart rate is fast at 100 per minute, blood pressure is 116/84, and his Sp02 is 92%. Eric got the IV established, which was a fantastic stick as there wasn't much to work with.

Rocky checked the sugar, "84," he called out.

There are two other officers with the roommate in the kitchen and we could hear them talking about heroin and "was there any more in the house" and that line of questioning.

Eric was about to administer the narcan and had everyone in position when we heard a commotion in the kitchen...now the roommate collapsed and stopped breathing.

I told Eric, "Go ahead and get this guy woke up...I'll go check him."

"Roger that," Eric said.

When I got to the roommate, I quickly adjusted his airway by bringing his jaw forward and calling out to him, "Wake up buddy, can you hear me?"

This drew a heavily sedated moan but nothing more. He'd take a breath about every eight seconds or so, which wasn't enough. He was quickly becoming purple throughout his face and lips.

I looked at Steve and said, "Let's get another unit here."

Steve was quickly on the radio to dispatch.

Eric pushed the narcan on Dray, after which he was awake, talking and cooperative.

Sam and Steve were now ventilating our second victim.

The officer told us this new patient's name is Kevin and is 24 years old. He's about five foot six, 140 pounds. He's also devoid of basic hygiene, has a shaved head with tattoos across his neck and large hooped earlobes.

His pupils are pinpoint and nearly non-existent. I can't see any IV sites on Kevin's arms but he does have a great external jugular vein on the left side of his neck. I put a 14 gauge into this vein and secured the IV line with a safety loop taped to the left shoulder.

Rocky called out the sugar on Kevin, "118," he said.

"Roger that," I acknowledged.

Joe and Brandon came walking through the door and Joe said, "Thanks for the invite, looks like a full house."

I nodded to Joe and said, "Good to see you guys. I think we'll give you Dray over there. Eric can update you…I still have some work to do for Kevin here."

Eric updated Joe on Dray as they were getting him ready for transport.

I was ready for the narcan on Kevin and we're all in position in case he decided to become aggressive after waking him up. The narcan went through the line and seconds later Kevin opened his eyes and suspiciously looked around.

"Are you with us?" I asked Kevin.

"What happened?" He asked with a bewildered fog.

"Well, it looks like you guys both overdosed," I said.

"Man, you can't pin that crap on me…I didn't even do any," he said.

"Well, then somehow it got in you and I still need to take you to Regional," I said with honesty.

It's nice having law enforcement on scene; you don't get too much arguing from anyone.

We arrived about ten minutes after Joe and Brandon. Joe had to give Dray additional narcan on the trip to RGH. By the end of the day, RGH had five more admissions to the emergency department with heroin overdoses.

CHAPTER 18

NOT AS EASY AS IT LOOKS

EMS has progressed over the years and it's pretty impressive the level of care that shows up at your door when you call 9-1-1. We're literally bringing the emergency department to your house or to your scene.

That being said, our help isn't always appreciated or necessarily wanted at that exact moment. Heroin addicts are seldom happy to wake up to a crowd of EMS and law enforcement people staring at them. A drunk who was just beat up isn't always the friendliest person as we are patching them up.

This is all part of excitement involved with EMS...you never know what that next call will be.

It had been a typical Saturday in the city, three calls so far: a 10 year old diabetic, a 94 year old with chest pain and a car crash with minor injuries which ended up being a non-transport. Tones set the direction for the rest of the afternoon.

"Medic 42, Rescue 41, respond code three for a male subject, possible low blood sugar, 811 Maplewood Drive...time out 1555 hours."

As we neared the scene, dispatch gave us an important update, "Medic 42, Rescue 41, the caller is reporting the patient may be violent, we will be sending law enforcement."

Steve and I both acknowledged the updated information.

We arrived at the residence and there's a young female, early 20's, standing at the end of the driveway. She came up to the ambulance as I was getting out.

I smiled and said, "Hi there…did you call?"

"Yeah, it's my boyfriend. He's a diabetic. I noticed he was acting odd over the last hour and then all of a sudden he started screaming and kind of freaked me out. I think he took his insulin and hasn't eaten anything…I'm really worried about him now," she said.

I said, "Well okay, we'll go check him out. What is his name?"

"His name is Charley…but you don't understand, he's massive--like 6 foot 4 and 260 pounds and he could hurt you guys. I promise he's the nicest guy," she explained, "But right now he isn't himself."

"You guys really need to be careful, and I don't want him to get hurt either. When he was in college this happened and he beat up five security guards," she said.

I didn't need to hear that last statement.

I asked, "Any weapons in the house, guns, baseball bats, bombs?"

"No, nothing like that," she said with a hint of a smile.

"And what is your name?" I asked.

"Melissa," she said.

"Well Melissa we'll figure it out and help him," I said.

A patrol car was pulling up and we filled the officer in on the situation. As we looked toward the house we could see Charley looking out the front window. He looked like a truck standing there.

There were six of us including the officer. We decided to call for another patrol car and officer before approaching the house.

During the "plan of action" meeting I emphasized, "Okay everyone, he isn't trying to hurt anyone, *at least intentionally*, let's make sure none of us end up on the wrong end of anything."

One of the officers asked, "Should we just taze him?"

I said, "Ahh…let's leave that as a last resort."

We approached the house as a small army. I knocked on the door and opened it slowly.

"Charley…can you hear me…my name is Mark, I'm a paramedic, and we want to check your sugar," I announced.

"I'm fine, get out of here, NOW," was the less than hospitable response.

"Charley, Melissa is worried about you and she wants us to check your blood sugar level," I said.

No response to that one. We walked in cautiously and found Charley leaning against the dining table and up close he looked even bigger than Melissa described.

"I told you I am fine; get out of my house NOW," he said with a bewildered stare.

At that point I thought I might try the sensible approach…I decided to walk toward him slowly and kind of politely tell him what we were going to do. This plan failed miserably as he lurched forward and grabbed me around the chest and down we went. It knocked the wind out of me and now Charley's on top of me with everyone trying to pull him off. Somehow we managed to roll over with Charley ending up on his stomach and in the next few seconds he was handcuffed. This was thirty-seconds of unplanned intensity I could have done without.

Sam cleaned a spot on Charley's finger and drew a drop of blood for the glucometer. She then announced, "Blood sugar says LO."

His glucose level is less than 20!

Now we had to get an IV started and Charley still wasn't completely out of fighting. I had to time the insertion with his movements and managed to get the IV in his right arm. We administered an amp of D50 IV, and within seconds he was relaxing and calmly said, "You can take these cuffs off me now, please."

I said, "Are you back with us now?"

"Yeah, if you could maybe tell me what the hell is going on?" He asked.

I gave him the short version and he apologized over and over and asked, "I didn't hurt anyone, did I?"

As we were taking the cuffs off I said, "No, you were just like a little puppy dog," which drew several puzzled looks.

Charley opted for not being transported. Melissa would be with him the rest of the day and was preparing him a peanut butter and cheese and banana sandwich with chocolate milk.

Melissa thanked us and we were happy it all ended well. It's amazing to witness how a patient can go from complete disorientation one second and completely back to normal the next.

When I was going through paramedic school one of the other students was telling us about a tragic diabetic call he had during one of his clinical rotations on the ambulance. They responded to a motor vehicle collision where a car was T-boned in an intersection. The car had gone through a red light and was broadsided by a large truck into the passenger door, instantly killing an 8 year old girl.

The girl's father, who was driving the passenger car, was found unconscious and the medics were thinking he might have a head injury. Turns out his blood sugar was low and after they started an IV and administered D50, he immediately awoke and first thing he said was, "Where's my daughter?"

Just prior to the crash he was aware that his sugar was low and dropping fast. He stopped at a convenience store and placed two candy bars on the counter, then abruptly turned around and walked out, leaving the candy bars and wallet on the counter. He got into the car and drove into the intersection.

Later that night, Rocky and I were dispatched to a call without Rescue 41. This didn't happen too often, generally only when the call sounded obvious that the two units wouldn't be needed.

"Medic 42, respond code one for a laceration, 1200 Division St...New Wave Club...time out 2301 hours."

Traffic was heavy at this time of night and Rocky and I would always wonder, *"Where are all these people going...is there a sale somewhere?"*

Rocky wanted to get on the loudspeaker and announce, "Everyone, go home, go to bed."

We arrived at the club and caught sight of a flashlight being flicked on and off. A police officer on scene was directing us to the side parking lot. As I got out of the ambulance he came over to me and said, "Hi guys, we got a subject here that pretty much got the crap beat out of him. He's inside with my partner, and he's pretty drunk too."

"Alright, we'll check him out," I said and Rocky and I walked through the door.

The patient is sitting on a chair and does look like he got the worst end of the confrontation. He's bleeding from a full thickness laceration to the right side of the head; the left eye is swollen shut and already has a deep blue color surrounding the eye socket. His upper lip is split open to the left nostril, two front teeth are knocked out and he's spitting blood.

We also notice he's been incontinent of urine which indicates he may have been unconscious at some point during the beating.

He said his name is Tick, 24 years old, and keeps repeating in a very slurred tone, "I'm fine, I don't need your Band-Aids."

I tried to explain, "Tick, my name is Mark, and I'm a paramedic. We need to take you to RGH and have them make sure you're going to be okay; we're concerned about some of your injuries."

Continuing in his slurred and defiant disposition, he said, "I told you…I aint going anywhere with you…I don't need your help."

This conversation wasn't going anywhere. I went to the officer and explained the predicament and he walked over and got face to face with Tick and said, "You're going with them…understand me?"

"Yes sir, officer sir," was Tick's overly sarcastic response followed by a mocking half-hearted salute.

Rocky did a great job with getting the head wound bandaged. We applied a cervical collar and secured him to the long spine board. For now, things *seemed* to be going a little better.

Once we started transporting, I did a reassessment and was about to get vital signs and for these few minutes Tick was actually being very cooperative.

I then asked an apparent explosive question, "Can you remember what happened?"

And with that he became enraged. He squinted with his right eye, growled, clenched his fists and started squirming, and like a magician in the blink of an eye wiggled free from the back board and ripped his cervical collar off and the fight was on.

This escalated to a violent knock-down, drag-out struggle between me trying not to get pummeled and Tick exploding with rage. We went from the bench seat to both of us getting wedged between the gurney and the bench seat as I am yelling out to Rocky, "Need some help back here…"

Rocky noticed the eruption and called for police backup and then gently stopped the vehicle, almost in the middle of the road. He had the overhead lights on and figured it would be easier to find us this way. He flew through the back doors and almost as quickly a police unit showed up and joined in. This was a terrible scenario. We had to be cautious not to cause any further injury, yet make sure we were not going to be injured. Within a few minutes things were back under control. Tick was once again on the spine board and now restrained with the seat belts tighter and soft restraints over the legs and arms.

Tick acted as if nothing happened and the rest of the transport was uneventful. In the E.D. we had Brenda and several other nurses listening to me narrate the "surprise fight" in the back of the medic unit. Shortly thereafter Dr. Stein called us over to the X-ray viewing screens and brought up Tick's neck films. He has a stable fracture of C-3. He also had an orbital and maxilla (upper palate) fracture. Tick was going to the O.R.

Had this been an unstable cervical neck fracture, Tick could have been paralyzed for life.

Paramedics face daily challenges with intoxicated patients and some are very difficult to reason with. But that's why we're here. If it was easy, everyone would want to do it.

Tick's surgery was successful and to date we have not met up with him again.

Eric took two weeks off to attend an EMS Conference in Las Vegas. He assured us the allure of sin city would not affect his dedication to bring back valuable knowledge and upcoming trends in EMS. This gave Dana an opportunity to work the open shifts. She finished her nursing degree and had been working part time in the pediatric ICU at RGH.

It was late Wednesday night and we only had a few calls for the shift. This meant we would be busy through the night. Whether you ran them during day or at night, we always seemed to get the quota of calls in for the shift.

Sure enough, the late night tones.

"Medic 42, Rescue 41, respond code three for a motorcyclist down... 1600 block of Fessler Road...time out 2345 hours."

Traffic was light and the roads were dry, temperature around 65 degrees. This response would take about nine minutes. I called dispatch and requested Mercy Flight be put on standby. We were advised they're on a mission and unavailable at this time.

We could see the overhead lights of the deputies' cars ahead of us at the approximate location reported. One of the deputies met us as we pulled up and walked over to my door.

"Hey guys...you got a patient that's hurt pretty badly. He don't look good...we had reports of a motorcyclist riding up and down this road at a high rate of speed…it's probably the guy we've been looking for," he explained.

"Alright thanks, we'll do the best we can," I said.

We had to walk about twenty-five yards off the road before seeing the motorcycle in a crumpled heap. He'd gone through a thick wooden fence before finally colliding with a large tree that might as well have been a solid brick wall.

The patient was another twenty feet away and lying on his back. He has a helmet on which was destroyed; split in half. We can hear him gurgling and it looked like he had gotten tangled in some type of rope during the crash.

Steve and Dana went right to working on his airway. The helmet was easily removed. There are massive facial injuries with bubbling coming from a gaping hole under the chin. It's difficult to gauge the severity of it in the dark with flashlights creating false illuminations. There's also a heavy alcohol aroma in the air.

Steve covered the penetrating trauma under the chin and was operating the suction as Dana was providing breaths with the bag valve mask.

As I looked closer I noticed the "rope" was actually several feet of bowel that had been eviscerated. It's still attached at the abdomen. Rocky finished cutting all of the clothing off. Sam's gathering the bowel segment and piling it on top of the abdomen. The gaping abdominal wound was above the umbilicus (belly button) and about five inches long and three inches wide. The bleeding from the site is minimal. We wouldn't replace the evisceration…it sat piled high on the abdomen. She then covered it with a large trauma dressing and taped it in place.

The left side of the chest was one large abrasion and I cannot hear lung sounds coming from that side. I can feel air under the skin throughout the left chest creating the "rice crispies" effect.

The left femur is horrendously fractured just above mid-shaft with at least four inches of sharp bone protruding. The leg is bent backwards underneath him with the foot is at his belt line. He has no radial pulse. The carotid pulse was counted at 130 and weak.

Steve looked up at me and said, "We can't keep the airway going like this…he needs a tube before we move him."

I nodded affirmatively and told him I would do a quick look. The large puncture wound beneath the chin could be a difficult injury to work around.

With Steve holding the patient's head in line I inserted the curved laryngoscope blade into the mouth. Each step of the intubation process required an intervention, suction of blood, manipulation, suction of more blood.

I finally had a good view of the vocal cords. Sam handed me the endotracheal tube and I felt a sense of relief on seeing it go through the tracheal opening. After quickly getting it secured, Dana is now ventilating with the bag valve.

We're now ready to get him secured to the spine board.

The left femur will have to be straightened and caution heeded with the several inches of bone precariously sticking up like a small spear. As Sam straightened the leg, the protruding bone spontaneously reduced itself beneath the skin with the familiar sound of bone ends grinding together.

Mercifully the patient is unresponsive to any of this.

We carried him to the road, where Rocky had the gurney ready, and then loaded into the ambulance and headed for RGH.

A quick reassessment of the airway showed no changes. The tube was in the right place and Dana said it was getting harder to squeeze the bag. This meant a tension pneumothorax; he could die from this alone at any second. I grabbed the 12 gauge 3-inch needle and inserted it in the left chest in between the second and third ribs, mid line with the clavicle. Even with the siren wailing we all heard the *"hiss"*, which was followed by bubbling blood.

"It's easier now, that did it," Dana said.

I asked Sam to get the LifePak 12 hooked up as I was searching for IV sites.

Sam nodded and then called out, "Heart rate 136, blood pressure 60/30, SpO2 84%," she said.

"Roger that," I said while tapping for a vein.

I found an IV site on the left mid-arm and put a 14 gauge in. I noticed another vein below this one and put a 16 gauge into that site. We now had two working IV's. It wasn't our fluids he needed…it was blood and a surgeon.

His color is terrible, pale, cool and clammy, he's in deep shock.

His right pupil is blown…the left is of normal size. There are facial fractures from the orbits, nasal structure and jaw. The penetrating chin wound has stopped bleeding. There's blood coming from both ears and bruising behind each ear. This is indicative of a skull fracture. The blood is still trickling from the chest needle.

I thought to myself, *"Is he going to die from the head injury or the chest injury and shock?"*

We were less than two minutes from RGH.

The back doors of the ambulance opened as we arrived with plenty of help to unload and heading to Suite 12.

I heard someone shout out, "Do we have a name?"

One of the admitting clerks had his wallet and said, "Terry...he's 26."

We just got him transferred to the Suite 12 gurney when a heart rate alarm starting chiming from the EKG monitor...

"He just coded," the charge nurse called out.

Dana was in position and jumped onto a small stool and started chest compressions. A surgeon made an incision to the left lateral chest and inserted a chest tube. It immediately filled with blood.

After twelve minutes they had Terry's heart beating again. It was now a mad dash to the O.R. where he spent the next eighty-five minutes with repairs to the aorta, bowel, liver and a small tear in the heart.

He was admitted to the trauma ICU. At 0420 the next morning he went into cardiac arrest again. This time he would not survive the resuscitative efforts.

Terry had a blood alcohol level of .32, four times the legal limit. They estimated he left the road on his "crotch rocket" doing in excess of 80 mph, crashing through the solid wooden fence and hitting the twenty-four inch round tree head on.

Those that can be saved are, those that can't aren't...the efforts are the same.

Our station was sponsoring an EMT class and there are twelve students in the program. Four of them were newer volunteers from our station. It was fun to be involved with the class and share tips and stories that they might rely on some day in their careers.

I will never forget my first days here and all the support and encouragement I had. I can see the same looks on their faces I had, seems like it was just yesterday.

They had come to the final few week of their program and were trying to get their mandatory ride time in on the ambulance. They had to log at least five calls where they participated in some form. For some of them it could be quite intimidating and of course we'd be supporting them throughout any task they were assigned.

One shift we had a student by the name of Thomas. He's a 22 year old college student and volunteer from a neighboring department. He's been responding to calls for a few months. He thinks he eventually wants to do EMS full time and become a paramedic.

Today he's scheduled to ride from 0800 till 2000 hours. Our first call was at 0830 hours for a traffic collision with resulting neck pain. Our patient was a 31 year old female who complained of pain to both sides of her neck after she was rear-ended while stopped at an intersection.

Thomas was heavily involved by holding cervical immobilization while we extricated her onto the long spine board. On the way to the hospital Thomas took blood pressures, assessed for injuries and did a really impressive job.

We got back to the station at 1030 hours and spent some time going over equipment in the back of the ambulance when the tones were calling.

"Medic 42, Rescue 41, respond code three for a gunshot victim, police are en route, 3452 Pelican Street…time out 1004 hours."

As we rolled out of the bay, Thomas said, "I haven't been on any shootings before."

I said, "Well, let's just see what we got. Stay close to me."

Thomas nodded with wide eyes.

Dispatch updated us as we were less than sixty seconds from the scene… "Medic 42 and Rescue 41, you are clear into the scene, law enforcement requesting to step it up."

"Received," came from both Steve and I.

We arrived on scene to a nice two-story home, perfect lawn. Across the street there were a couple of neighbors standing outside their homes with crossed arms and inquisitive stares. Walking into the house we're immediately met with the smell of gun smoke and hear commotion coming from the kitchen.

Walking around the corner was a terrifying sight.

The patient is sitting on the kitchen floor with his back against a cabinet. He's surrounded by a five foot circle of blood at least two inches deep. There are two officers frantically trying to stem the flow of blood from just below his left groin. They're using a kitchen towel over the wound and blood is spraying to the sides.

The patient's name is James. We quickly learned he's an off-duty police officer well known to both officers that are trying to save his life.

James returned from the police gun range and was sitting at the dining table cleaning his Glock 9mm police issued firearm. Somehow he discharged a round through his left femoral artery which instantly turned into a fight for his life.

He fell to the floor with excruciating pain and could feel the life ebbing out him with each heartbeat. He crawled to the phone and made a desperate and chilling call to 9-1-1.

Steve got James's pants cut off and the damage is horrific. The large wound looks like a small shovel dug a trough just below the left groin and there is no exit wound, the round is still in there somewhere.

The blood is relentless in its spurting flow. Dana placed the first trauma dressing and folded it in and around the center of the wound. Sam placed the second one over that and looked at Thomas with urgency said, "Put both of your hands over these dressings and hold them tight."

I looked at James as they were working and said, "Hey there James, my name is Mark, I'm a paramedic, we're going to take you to Regional," and gave him my best and most reassuring look.

James looked back at me and tried to offer a smile through his unmistaken look of fear.

I put a rubber tourniquet on his right upper arm in hopes a vein would pop up when we made it to the ambulance.

I then told Thomas, "You seem to have stopped the flow, and you're staying just like that until we get to the E.D."

Thomas nodded, still wide eyed.

We lifted James onto the gurney and were off to RGH in less than four minutes. Sam had an oxygen mask over James's mouth and nose. A vein popped up on the right arm and I was able to get a 16 gauge in as Dana had an IV bag set up. I taped it securely as we didn't need to lose any IV's we happened to get.

Sam hooked up the LifePak 12 and the initial rhythm was fast, as we anticipated: heart rate is 136…blood pressure is 72/44…Sp02 will not read because of the low blood flow.

James is critical. His problem is easy to figure out: he's bleeding to death. He is pale with cool and clammy skin; he's in classic hypovolemic shock, blood loss shock. He needs a surgeon and the O.R., and blood. Our job is to make that happen as quickly as possible.

I knelt next to James and with reassurance told him, "We got you stopped from going any deeper, Thomas is a brand new EMT. He's the star here today."

"Thank you Thomas," James said and weakly held his right hand in thumbs-up posture.

Thomas hadn't moved and was actually sitting on the gurney with James. This was Thomas's first gunshot call and he was the one responsible for saving the patient's life. We arrived at RGH and had four police officers escort us into the E.D.

Once in Suite 12, Thomas was relieved by one of the surgeons as he clamped the femoral artery and packed the opening. James had two units of blood started and was off to the O.R. in less than seven minutes.

We met with the officers after James was wheeled off.

Thomas was having trouble standing, his knee was stiff and hands were cramped and he was shaking. Two of the officers went to his side and supported him. The others patted him on the shoulder and offered heart-felt comments that literally overwhelmed Thomas.

There aren't any words for the intensity of that moment.

"Every call is a chance to make a difference in someone's life."

James was in the O.R. for ninety minutes. He was admitted to the trauma ICU where he would spend five days before being discharged to home. He would be off work for a little over a month and his recovery was no less than miraculous. The efforts of the entire team made the difference between life and death. And the biggest contributor was Thomas.

At the end of the shift, I spent some time with Thomas. I told him he had been given an incredible opportunity today. He was part of EMS at its finest…and he fit right in.

Thomas replied humbly, "If I ever had any doubts about wanting to do this full time, they were erased today."

We shook hands and Thomas headed home.

EPILOGUE

Being in EMS for the past 31 years has been an incredible privilege. I've had the opportunity to work among some of the most talented professionals the field has to offer. Not only have we made differences in people's lives, they've made differences in ours as well.

You can never see or learn it all. We'll always be students and the streets are the classrooms. The industry is evolving and improving every day. Some things will never change, and that's the desire to provide the highest level of competent care with the highest level of compassion.

I have shared these very personal stories for several reasons. First, people rarely get to look inside the exciting and chaotic world called EMS... this is a chance to ride with the crew as they see it, day in and day out. Second, to show some of the challenges we face and how we overcome odds that are sometimes overwhelmingly against us. And finally, this may encourage First Responders or EMTs to take that next step, to advance their training and ultimately become paramedics.

The men and women of the EMS, Fire, 9-1-1 Dispatch, Police and all other branches that serve the public go to work each and every day. Chances are good the average person will never meet one of us. If they do, they can be assured that they're getting the best--an individual who has a dedication to reach levels we did not think possible.

It's gratifying and humbling when a citizen off the street sees us, maybe in a restaurant, maybe at the bank, maybe in the hospital, and they take the time to stop and say, "Hey, thanks for being out there. We really appreciate you guys," or "Hey, you guys saved my mom or dad or brother or friend."

As successful as the EMS system is, it's only as strong as the first person on the scene. It starts with recognizing an emergency exists, and placing that lifesaving call to 9-1-1. Then, providing basic initial care until the medic unit arrives can sometimes be that crucial link in making the difference between life and death. Can providing care for a few minutes before EMS arrives really make a difference? Ask some of the people in this book.

There are teams all over the world that are made up of people like me and Joe and Rocky and Brandon and Steve and Eric and Sam and Dana and Thomas. Whatever time of day, whatever day of the week, we'll come and help you. We have the enthusiasm, the dedication and the competence to bring the emergency department to your door.

All of these stories are based on actual calls that I have responded to over the years. The names and some of the events have been altered to protect the confidentiality of not only the patients but the families and friends of the patients.

What's the fastest way to become part of this team? Stop by your local station. They're more than happy to talk to you. You've taken your first step. See you on the streets…

GLOSSARY

<u>A</u>

AED-This is the Automated External Defibrillator. It's an automated device capable of analyzing the EKG rhythm during cardiac arrest and delivering a shock if needed. It's designed to be used without any prior training as the voice prompts from the machine walk you through each step. The four critical steps of using an AED are: **1**-Turn it on, **2**-Apply the chest pads, **3**-Allow it to analyze the rhythm and **4**-Press the shock button when prompted. These machines are located in many public places: airports, airplanes, casinos, malls. The device is only used during cardiac arrest. If you find someone in a public place having chest pain, ensure 9-1-1 is contacted and immediately call for an AED.

Acetaminophen suppository-A medication we use to treat a high fever in a pediatric aged patient. This is a semi-solid "rocket shaped" preparation that's inserted into the rectum. Fever can be the cause of seizures in small children and infants. These little preparations are also known as "rectal rockets."

Amitriptyline-This is an anti-depressant medication. Overdose can cause major cardiac abnormalities, dangerously low blood pressure and if untreated, death. There is no antidote.

Amp-This refers to a pre-filled syringe of medication. We might say, "Let's give an amp of narcan."

Anaphylactic shock-This is an exaggerated response to an allergic reaction. Common allergies include bee stings, peanuts, shell fish and some medications. During anaphylactic shock the blood pressure drops, the smaller airways in the lungs constrict and swelling can occur in the throat and the airways can close off. Any person suspected of having an allergic reaction needs immediate evaluation by EMS. People who have had severe reactions will carry an epi pen or auto-injector. You can help a person having an emergency with their auto-injector but **NEVER** use it on them if they are unconscious.

Anoxia-This is medical terminology that means without oxygen. An=without, oxia=oxygen.

AOB-This is a slang term we use that means, "Alcohol on Board." When we are talking to the doctor or nurse, or police officer, we will say, "He also has AOB," and this will catch the patient off guard as they look at us suspiciously wondering what we just said.

Appears-This is a word that should never be in your EMS chart. It means "you don't know." Write what you see.

Aspiration-This is any foreign substance that is inhaled into the lungs. It can be liquid or solid. This includes vomiting, drowning, food, etc. This is one of the reasons we will RSI a patient that is unconscious and at risk for aspiration. Once they are intubated, their airway and lungs are protected from this potentiality.

Aspirin-This is part of the pre-hospital care guidelines to administer aspirin to a patient with a suspected heart attack. It can be dangerous to administer and should **NOT** be given unless directed by a physician. We have specific questions we ask before administering it and there are contraindications in some cases. It does not "thin" the blood like people think; it delays the clotting process to buy the patient time to get to the cath lab.

Asystole-This is flatline, a "straight line" on the EKG screen, no electrical activity in the heart. We **DO NOT** shock this rhythm despite them shocking it on TV and miraculously getting the heart started again. We have treated cardiac arrests where families got upset that we didn't "shock" their loved one and complained because, "They do it on TV and it saves them."

B

Bag Valve Mask-Used for delivering breaths to a person not breathing or needing assisted breathing. It consists of a self-inflating "football" shaped rubber bag with a mask which fits over the mouth and nose. It can be used by one or two persons. The optimal use is by two people, one will squeeze the bag while the other will hold the mask over the face making an adequate seal. Once a patient is intubated, the mask is no longer needed. The bag valve will then be attached to the endotracheal tube and deliver breaths straight into the lungs.

Benadryl-A medication we use during an allergic reaction in combination with epinephrine and solu-medrol. Benadryl relieves the itching and hives. Hives are red blots all over the chest, back and arms. The medical word for hives is *urticaria* and itching is *pruritus*. Benadryl is also known as diphenhydramine.

Blown pupil-This is unequal pupils; one is of normal size while the other is dilated or large. The patient is generally **NOT** conscious with this presentation. It is associated with serious rising intracranial pressure. There's usually some significant MOI involved like a recent head injury or some major insult to the brain. "Blown pupil" is the slang term.

BVM-This is the abbreviation for "bag valve mask."

C

Cardiac Alert-This is something we will advise the receiving hospital of. It's a cardiac patient that fits the criteria for immediate evaluation on arrival to the emergency department and could be a candidate for the catheterization lab or clot busting medication to resolve the blocked coronary arteries. The pre-hospital mantra for this is, "Time is muscle."

Cardiac contusion-Usually results from blunt force trauma to the chest. Symptoms can mimic those of a heart attack with irregular beats and rhythms and severe contusions can reduce the pumping ability of the heart and result in shock. Motor vehicle crashes and collisions are major causes. A properly worn seat belt and airbags can reduce this risk to almost negligible. It's one of the reasons we not only inspect the chest but also the steering wheel after a major motor vehicle crash. If we see a picture of your steering wheel in the form of a bruise on your chest, it gets our attention.

CCU-This is the Coronary Care Unit. When you have a cardiac emergency you will end up here after being stabilized in the emergency department or the cath lab or maybe even the O.R. You can be monitored very carefully here. After you are stabilized from here, they will transfer you to a medical floor before being discharged home.

Cerebral edema-This is an accumulation of fluid surrounding the brain. The brain doesn't have much room for swelling. As this happens, we see a change in the mentation and maybe a "blown pupil." Cerebral=brain, edema=fluid

Circumoral cyanosis-This is medical terminology that means blueness around the lips from lack of oxygen. We see it in asthmatics, emphysema and in trauma with pneumothorax and any condition that makes the person hypoxic. Circum=around, Oral=mouth, Cyan=blue, Osis=condition.

Clavicle-This is the collar bone. This bone is a reference point for inserting the "big needle" during a tension pneumothorax. The "big needle" is inserted between the second and third ribs, and "mid-line" with the clavicle.

Clinically Dead-You're clinically dead the second your pulse stops. Without treatment and restoration of a heartbeat, you will become biologically dead after several minutes. Clinical death requires immediate CPR. The local newspaper did an article about us one day and got this terminology mixed up. The headline for the article read, "Paramedics Revive Biologically Dead Man."

Coded-This term is used to indicate a patient has just gone into cardiac arrest. Someone that is monitoring a patient and the EKG would shout out, "He just coded" and this will bring the resuscitation team. At that point the patient is clinically dead.

Combo-pads-Rectangular pads with strong adhesive backing to stick firmly to the patient's chest used to monitor the EKG rhythm and deliver a shock during cardiac arrest. There are small wires from each pad with an attachment that plugs into the Life Pak 12. One pad is placed on the upper chest above the right nipple and the other on the lower chest below the left nipple. On patients who have a thick "carpet" or "rug" of chest hair, we use a disposable razor to "trim" the area to ensure the pad makes good contact with the skin and that we reduce the risk of fire.

Cricothyrotomy Kit-This is a kit used to make a surgical opening at the cricothyroid membrane in the neck. It creates a temporary airway during a traumatic or catastrophic medical emergency where an airway cannot be obtained by, head-tilt chin lift, jaw thrust, BVM or intubation. It's also one of the five "Extreme Event Items."

Crow's foot laceration-This is a laceration that resembles a "crow's foot." It is usually above the eye and "full thickness" meaning it is fairly deep. If you ever see one, you'll look at it and think, "That looks like a crow's foot!" After it is sutured the patient does fine.

CT scan-This is Computed Tomography. It is a sectional view of the body part or area that is being evaluated. It is useful for assessing head injuries and not used in the pre-hospital arena, yet.

Cyanosis-This is medical terminology that refers to bluish skin color from lack of oxygen. Cyan=blue, osis=condition. This person will get supplemental oxygen by face mask and if it doesn't increase their oxygen levels or improve the skin color, we will perform the RSI procedure on them.

D

D50- This is a medication we give someone with a low blood sugar that is either unconscious or too obtunded to take in food or sugar orally, or by mouth. It's a concentrated bolus of sugar water that is administered through the IV line. It rapidly raises the blood sugar levels and wakes them immediately from insulin shock. It's important they eat something afterwards as the bolus will not stay in the system for very long.

Dextrose 50%-This is "D50."

Diaphoretic-This is the medical term for sweating or sweat or moist skin. A patient with chest pain suggestive of cardiac origin can be diaphoretic. Diabetics in insulin shock have diaphoresis to the extreme and are literally "soaked" as if they went swimming with their clothes on. Diaphoresis is also a subtle sign associated with myocardial infarction or heart attack, don't ignore this!

DOA-Dead on Arrival-not something you want written on your medical record.

E

Ecchymosis-This is bluish discoloration to the skin, a bruise.

Electronic thermometer-This is a small hand held device that is battery powered. It accurately measures the body temperature in several different areas. Orally is under the tongue, axillary is under the armpit and rectally is "down there." There are two different probes used depending on the body part being measured. For under the tongue and armpit, the "blue" probe is used. For a rectal temperature, the "red" probe is used. If you're at your doctor's office having your temperature taken electronically make sure you have the "blue" probe if it's going in your mouth. Remember the handy mnemonic "red=rectal."

Emesis-This is medical terminology that means vomiting. This is another symptom a patient can experience during a heart attack. Sometimes nausea is a complaint people may not associate with a heart attack. If in doubt, get help.

Endotracheal tube-This is a long plastic tube inserted orally (into the mouth) and into the trachea during the intubation process. The portion sticking out of the mouth will be attached to the bag valve in order for breaths to be given. This is the ultimate protection of an airway that a patient cannot protect themselves. These are people that are unconscious, severe trauma, facial burns etc.

Epidural bleed-This is bleeding in a layer of the brain. It is a collection of blood just under the skull. Epi=on top of, dura=the outer layer of the brain. This person may have a decrease in their mentation or be unconscious. This also qualifies as a TBI (traumatic brain injury).

Epiglottis-This is the flap in the back of the throat that sits above the tracheal opening. Not the little "punching bag" that's visible with the mouth open, which is the uvula. The epiglottis is further down and a landmark during the intubation process. Once we see this, we know the tracheal opening us just beneath it.

Epinephrine-This is a medication used during cardiac arrest to stimulate activity and for anaphylactic shock. In cardiac arrest it's given intravenously or IV. For anaphylactic shock it's given as an injection in the upper arm. People with severe allergies and at risk for anaphylactic shock will carry an epi pen and inject this into their lateral thigh and through clothing during an emergency. A bystander can assist this person but should **NEVER** administer it without their consent.

ERT-This is the Emergency Response Team. It's a team of first responders at an industrial site or factory setting that can rapidly respond to any type of emergency and provide care prior to EMS arriving. It is comprised of employees that take on this additional responsibility. It's generally a voluntary position.

Esophagus-This is the long tube that goes from the back of the throat to the stomach. When you swallow food, you hope this is the tube it goes down. It's located behind the trachea.

Esophageal bleeding-This is bleeding from ruptured areas in the esophagus and can be catastrophic. Causes include severe alcoholism and chronic gastric disorders. The bleeding will be bright red blood and can include large coagulated clumps.

ETA-This is the Estimated Time of Arrival.

ETOH-This is the abbreviation for ethanol, a substance found in alcohol. It's also an acronym we use to talk about a patient that's clearly intoxicated. Some of us in EMS will refer to it along the lines of, "Extremely Trashed or Hammered" which pretty much sums up the patients we use it for.

Etomidate-This is a medication we use during the RSI procedure. It induces anesthesia or deep sleep and is a powerful amnesiac mercifully giving the person going through the procedure the benefit of not recalling the trauma of going through it.

Evisceration-This is a protruding section of bowel from the abdomen. It is very graphic.

Extreme Event Items-These are the 5 items that are used during "Extreme Events" and warrant everyone on the crew knowing their location and complete understanding on using them. They consist of: **1**-The "big needle",12 gauge-3inch catheter used for tension pneumothorax, **2**-The OB kit, **3**-The Burn Sheets, **4**-The Cricothyrotomy Kit and **5**-The 10x30 inch Trauma Dressings.

F

Fentanyl patch-This is a powerful narcotic pain reliever. It's an opiate derivative. It is applied to the skin and the medication is slowly absorbed trans-dermally. One patch can be worn for up to 72 hours and provide sustained released opioid pain control. Overdose can depress the respiratory drive and the person can die if they are not helped. The patches must be handled carefully as the medication is absorbed through the skin.

Fish Hook Method-This is a trick to gain an advantage during the intubation process on someone with a small mouth opening. An assistant will use one finger, generally the right index finger and pull the right cheek out to the side and thereby increasing the size of the opening to the mouth allowing more room to insert the endotracheal tube. The assistant has to work in conjunction with the person performing the intubation and not just pull blindly.

Flail Chest-Three or more adjacent ribs fractured in two or more place. This is major injury considering the amount of force required to generate this much damage.

G

Glucometer-Small hand held device used for measuring blood glucose levels in the blood. Normal readings are 80-120 mg/dl. We have two ways to illicit the blood sample needed for the measurement. One is use blood from the IV needle after the IV is established. The other is to use a small lancet and prick a finger drawing a small amount of blood. If this method is used we will use the lateral (side) portion of the finger as opposed to the pad (front). The lateral side of the finger is less painful.

Grand-mal seizure-This is violent uncoordinated muscle contractions secondary to brain activity. There are many reasons for the seizure including epilepsy, low blood sugar, low oxygen levels, high fever, head injuries, tumors and sometimes no cause found. It's important to protect the person having the seizure from harm; placing something soft under their head to prevent them from banging their head against a hard surface can prevent a secondary head injury. **DO NOT** physically restrain them as this can cause injury. **DO NOT** put anything in their mouth during the seizure. Once the seizure has stopped check to make sure they are breathing, ensure 9-1-1 has been called.

GSW-Gun Shot Wound.

H

HBD-Has Been Drinking. This is an acronym we use to discretely describe a patient that has obviously been drinking and denies it. We may pass on this suspicion to the nurse or doctor or officer and say, "He's also HBD" and the patient doesn't know what you just said, but looks at you suspiciously anyway.

Head Tilt/Chin lift-A method used to open or maintain a patient's airway if no cervical spine injury is suspected. One hand is placed on the forehead while applying backwards pressure and the fingers of the other hand are placed under the chin and gently lifting at the same time. It's important not to exaggerate the maneuver.

Heroin-This is an illegal narcotic and highly addictive. It's an opiate derivative. Overdose suppresses the receptor sites in the body that measure rising carbon dioxide levels and you just fail to breathe. If the person isn't discovered within a couple minutes cardiac arrest ensues and they die. The drug can be injected, snorted and smoked. We see increases in overdoses when a new shipment of the drug comes to town in a stronger concentration than users are accustomed to.

Hematoma-This is a collection of blood under the skin making a bluish discoloration, a bruise. In EMS slang it is also called a "hema-tomatoe."

Humerus-This is the upper arm bone and one of two "long" bones in the human skeleton. The other "long" bone is the femur. Both of these bones require great force to fracture.

Hypoxia-This is medical terminology meaning low oxygen state. The patient may have secondary cyanosis along with it. Hypo=low, oxia=oxygen.

I

ICU-This is the Intensive Care Unit. After you are stabilized in either the emergency department or after the operating room, you are sent to the ICU where you get more intensive monitoring and care. After you are stabilized in the ICU, you are transferred to a medical floor before being discharged home.

IM / Intramuscular-This is a shot like you would get at the doctor's office or clinic. IM stands for intramuscular. It's generally given in the upper arm. It's not a quick way to get a drug into the system, IV is the quickest. When we give something in the IM route, we can only hope it gets into the system quickly.

Insulin-This is a medication taken by diabetics with a non-functioning pancreas and the inability to produce insulin. Insulin is needed to control blood sugar levels. Taken regularly with a proper diet, blood sugar levels stay in check. If a diabetic uses insulin and fails to eat, the sugar will drop and they can become unconscious and this is known as insulin shock.

Insulin Shock-This is too much insulin. The patient will have an altered mentation and can "go downhill" very quickly. The lay public will sometimes call this a "diabetic coma" which is actually the opposite, extremely high blood sugar. For the insulin shock, we need to get an IV started on them and administer D50 which wakes them rapidly. They will then need to eat a carbohydrate to sustain the sugar levels.

Intubation-This is a procedure that secures the airway with an endotracheal tube. Any patient that cannot actively control their own airway is at risk for aspiration and hypoxia. It is considered the "gold standard" for protecting the airway.

IO-This is an acronym for intraosseous. It is a way to establish IV access in a patient where there are no veins visible or in very small children where veins are very small. It involves using a short bone marrow needle that is placed in the lower leg bone and into the center of the cavernous network of blood vessels. Fluids are absorbed into the circulation at the same rate as if it were in a vein.

IV-This mean intravenously, into the vein. We place plastic IV catheters into the veins to administer fluids and/or medications. The largest IV catheter we can place in a vein is a 14 gauge. A small IV would be a 20 gauge. The smaller the number, the larger the catheter is. In trauma, we use the larger catheters.

J

Jaw thrust-Method used to open an airway with suspected cervical spine injury. The patient that needs this will make snoring sounds indicating the tongue is creating a partial obstruction of the airway. The jaw thrust brings the tongue forward and relieves this condition. It's easiest to perform this maneuver from the top of the patient's head, using both hands along the jaw line and with the index fingers used to gently displace the jaw in a forward motion. If someone is snoring and keeping the household awake, this maneuver will work, unfortunately you won't get any sleep, but you won't have to listen to "that noise" any longer.

K

KISS Theory-Keep It Simple Stupid. Don't complicate things, they aren't that hard.

Krebs cycle-This is an incredibly complicated explanation of how the body produces energy at the cellular level and aerobic metabolism. It is part of the physiology in paramedic school and very few medics walk away unscathed from being exposed to it.

L

Laryngoscope blade-This is a long stainless steel instrument with a light on the end that is attached to the laryngoscope handle. It's used during the intubation process. There are two basic designs, a straight blade and curved blade. Other names for the blades are, Miller (straight blade) and Macintosh (curved). Most paramedics have their own preference on which blade they will start with. You should be proficient with using both blades.

Laryngoscope handle-The laryngoscope blade is attached to the laryngoscope handle. The handle is stainless steel and contains two 'C' cell batteries.

Level One Trauma Center-This is a hospital capable of delivering the highest level of care, 24/7 and 365 days a year.

M

ME-This is the abbreviation for the Medical Examiner or coroner.

Methamphetamine-An illegal street drug classified as a stimulant. It is manufactured illegally in meth labs in homes, cars under extremely dangerous conditions and is highly addictive. It can have adverse effects to the heart, brain and cause death. The user will have dilated pupils (large), sweaty, and "tweaks", unable to remain still, smacking the lips and can stay awake for days.

MICP-This is an acronym for Mobile Intensive Care Paramedic, as in Mark Mosier or Joey Capthorn.

MICU-This is an acronym for Mobile Intensive Care Unit, the ambulance.

MOI-This is the Mechanism of Injury. We make a point to examine the car after a motor vehicle crash and this can give important clues as to type of injuries there may be. If it was a fall, how far did they fall? If they were stabbed, how big was they knife?

Morphine-This is a potent medication and powerful narcotic pain reliever. It's an opiate derivative. We administer it intravenously-IV. It has the potential to interfere with level of consciousness, lower blood pressure and can depress the respiratory drive.

MVC-This is a Motor Vehicle Crash or Collision. Years and years ago it was known as a Motor Vehicle Accident or MVA. The "accident" part was changed to crash or collision. To this day, people still refer to it as "accident."

Myocardial Infarction-This is medical terminology for heart attack. Myo=muscle, Cardial=heart, Infarction=dying or death. Remember the mantra, "Time is muscle." This means no delays for getting a patient into the E.D. The longer you delay, the greater and potentially more damage that occurs.

N

Narcan-This is a medication that is a narcotic antagonist which means it reverses narcotic overdose or influence. It stops the narcotic to influence on receptor sites that are responsible for adequate breathing.

Nitroglycerine tablets / spray-This is a medication used for chest pain suggestive of cardiac origin. The pain is caused by lack of oxygen to the cardiac tissues secondary to narrowing of the arteries or blockage. Nitro is a vasodilator meaning it will increase the size of the arteries and allow more blood flow and oxygen to the tissues. It can secondarily lower blood pressure and we use it with great caution during a suspected myocardial infarction. There are two preparations we can use, spray form and small white tablet form. Both are administered beneath the tongue.

Normal Saline-This is an IV solution that's infused into the vein through the IV catheter. It's used for fluid replacement which can temporarily raise blood pressure during blood loss. It doesn't have the oxygen carrying capability that blood does; we also have to be very careful not to overload the system.

O

OD-This is the abbreviation for Overdose.

Oxygen tank-A small portable tank used to provide supplemental oxygen to a patient with difficulty breathing or in shock. Lack of oxygen can cause cardiac and brain cells to die. When we're in a patient's home we need to ensure these small bottles are not left in a standing position. If the patient is lying on the floor and the bottle gets knocked over and hits them in the face, it's not going to be a good rest of the day for the patient or the crew.

Osteoarthritis-This is a degenerative joint disease. It can be extremely painful and difficult to control. Extreme cases can benefit from fentanyl patches.

P

PALS-Pediatric Advanced Life Support-This is one of the certifications we need to maintain in order to work as a paramedic. It's good for 2 years and then the class needs to be updated.

Periorbital ecchymosis-This is medical terminology for a black eye, shiner.

PHTLS-Pre-Hospital Trauma Life Support-This is one of the certifications we need to carry in order to work as a paramedic. It is good for between 2-4 years and then the class needs to be updated.

Pinpoint pupils-This is the hallmark sign of narcotic influence. The pupils are extremely small; they resemble two periods in a sentence. This is something the patient has no control over. When someone has tiny pupils and everyone else in the room has normal pupils, it is a "billboard" advertising what they have been doing. The droopy eye lids don't make their case any stronger.

Postictal phase-This is the phase that follows a grand-mal seizure. The patient may have mild disorientation to extreme combativeness. It can last from a couple minutes to several hours.

Pulmonary Contusion-This is a bruise lung tissue and collapse of the small air sacs in the lungs secondary to blunt force trauma to the chest. A major cause is motor vehicle crashes and collisions. Air exchange may be compromised leading to hypoxia. The patient will have trouble breathing and maybe cyanosis.

R

Radial Pulse-Found on the thumb side of the wrist. If this pulse can be felt, the blood pressure is at least 80-90 for the top number. This means the patient is getting oxygenation to the brain and other vital organs. It is a great guide to quickly tell how bad your patient is when you first arrive.

Retrograde amnesia-This is short term memory loss. It can result from trauma such as a concussion or event that deprived the brain of oxygen. It can occur after a concussion; the patient will not recall the event or have repetitive questioning.

RGH-Regional General Hospital-This is a Level One facility and capable of handling any type of emergency. There is no higher level of care facility.

Rhabdomyolysis-A condition in which skeletal muscle breaks down into myoglobin which is toxic to the kidneys and can result in kidney failure and death. Causes can include electrocution and crush injuries

Rice Crispies-This is air present in the subcutaneous layers of the skin. This is just below the level of the outer skin. In this case it is referring to the skin over the chest. It can also be felt just under the skin in the neck or back. It has a characteristic "crackling feeling" when palpated thus the slang term of "rice crispies." The actual term is subcutaneous emphysema. Subcutaneous referring to just under the skin and emphysema referring to trapped air.

RSI-Rapid Sequence Intubation-An elective procedure to put a patient to sleep and paralyze them in order to place an endotracheal tube into the trachea and take over the breathing process or protect the airway of severely injured person. RSI is only used for patient's that have a respiratory drive. We generally have three reasons to consider this procedure: **1**-Unable to maintain an open airway, maybe severe trauma, **2**-Unable to maintain a good oxygenation level, low Sp02 values, like maybe asthmatic or drowning, **3**-The anticipated clinical course of the patient, like a severely injured person that might go straight to surgery.

S

Shock-This is inadequate perfusion to the tissues/cells resulting in vital organs shutting down or dying, heart, brain, kidneys. The 5 types of shock include: **1**- Hypovolemic-blood or fluid loss, **2**-Cardiogenic-pump failure, **3**-Anaphylactic-allergic reaction, **4**-Septic-massive infection, **5**-Spinal-Interruption of the spinal cord. People also confuse shock and anxiety. Anxiety is being upset after you wreck your car. At car crash scenes someone might say, "That guys in shock" and we notice he's smoking a cigarette and talking on a cell phone to his insurance agent. You don't die from having anxiety. You die from untreated shock.

Sinus rhythm-This is a normal rhythm on the EKG screen with a heart rate between 60-100 beats per minute.

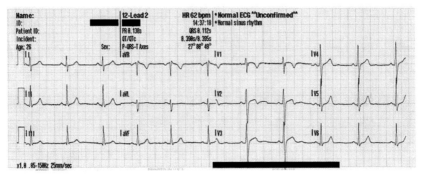

This is what a 12 lead print out looks like. This one is of a "Normal Sinus Rhythm." All of the tracings are of the same activity; we're seeing 12 different "views" of the heart from different angles. If you're having a heart attack, we'll see it here "live."

Sinus tachycardia-This is a rhythm that is over 100 beats a minute. It is by definition an abnormal rate so we need to figure out why it is going so fast. One serious reason could be blood loss. One not so serious reason could be fear. We better be able to figure out which one it is. Sometimes it is both of them.

Solu-Medrol-This is a medication used to reduce swelling and anti-inflammatory reactions during anaphylactic shock.

Sp02 Monitor-Measures the amount of oxygen saturation of hemoglobin. Hemoglobin is a protein molecule found in red blood cells and responsible for carrying oxygen molecules to the tissues. The Sp02 clip fits over the end of the finger and has an infrared light that measures the percentage of hemoglobin molecules that are saturated with oxygen molecules and displays the number in percentage values. We want the percentage to be over 94%. As a patient's saturation declines such as during the

RSI procedure, we need to ventilate them in order to re-saturate the hemoglobin molecules.

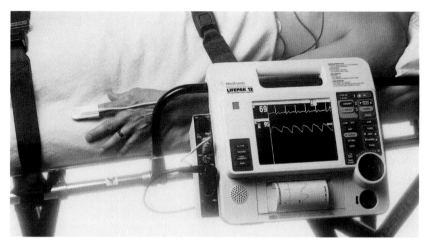

On the left hand we see the Sp02 probe and this read out is also on the front of the LifePak 12 screen.   We can see the current reading is 95%.

Stent-This is a small mesh device that is placed in your blocked coronary artery and in the cath lab. It can allow for blood flow to be restored to the heart and thus preventing permanent damage to the heart. The key is time. Our mantra in the pre-hospital arena when you're having chest pain is, "Time is muscle."

Stridor-This is extreme narrowing of the airway in the back of the throat. It's a high pitched sound similar to a deflating balloon as it is stretched restricting the air flow. It's a dangerous presentation and associated with inhalation burns and anaphylactic shock.

Subcutaneous Emphysema-This is "rice crispies."

Subdural Hematoma-This is bleeding in the brain, a collection of blood beneath the dura level of the brain. It's a very small area right above the actual brain tissue. It qualifies as a TBI (traumatic brain injury).

Succinylcholine-This is medication used during the RSI procedure. It's a short acting (up to eight minutes) muscle paralyzing drug that renders the gag reflex ineffective. When the gag reflex is stimulated, it can raise the blood pressure precipitously causing significant injury to the brain. The medication is also known as "Sux."

Sucking chest wound-This is an opening in the chest cavity usually from a penetrating source, stab wound, gunshot wound, and impalement. If the wound is larger than the tracheal opening, air will rush in during inhalation compromising the uninjured lung and interfering with the oxygenation process. The wound may have bubbling during the breathing phase.

Sux-See Succinylcholine

T

Tachypnea-This is medical terminology and means fast breathing. Tachy=fast, pnea=breathing.

TBI-Traumatic Brain Injury-This is broad diagnosis of a probable brain injury until it can be defined by CT scan.

Track marks-These are small needle marks from repeated injections along the vein tracks in the arms, hands, neck and feet. This is evidence of IV drug use that includes heroin, methamphetamine and cocaine. Sometimes the user will wear long sleeve clothing whenever in public to hide the marks.

Truck bays-This is where we park the apparatus, the ambulance, the rescue, the fire engine.

12 Lead EKG-A diagnostic assessment of the heart conducted when someone is having pain suggestive of cardiac origin. We place six electrodes on the chest, one on each arm and one on each leg which gives us a view of the entire heart and can see the heart attack happening in real time. Even though we only place 10 electrodes on the patient, the Life Pak 12 will add a "virtual interpretation" of two additional leads thus making it a 12 lead. We will call the hospital and declare a "Cardiac Alert" if we find obvious problems.

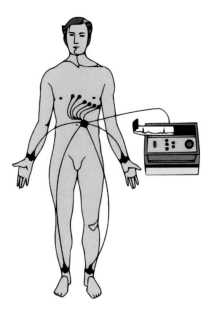

Two beers-This is pretty much the standard answer for the question of, "How much have you had to drink today?" It's usually a patient from an assault or motor vehicle crash. They are also always "The victim" and "Didn't do anything" to be in the position they are in. Generally multiplying this answer by five is a more accurate assessment.

V

Versed-This is powerful muscle relaxant used for sedative purposes. It is given both IV and as an intra-muscular (IM) injection.

V-fib-This is chaotic activity of the heart that does not produce a pulse, cardiac arrest. The patient requires CPR and defibrillation. The shock does not "jump start" the heart as people think. It does the opposite of this; it stops all activity and then hopefully allows the heart to restart on its own by its internal pacemaker.

Vocal cords-This is the opening to the trachea and lungs. During the intubation process, as the laryngoscope is advanced down the throat, the first structure to be found is the epiglottis. Below this is the vocal cords and target for placing the endotracheal tube. The tube is inserted through this opening about 1-2 inches.

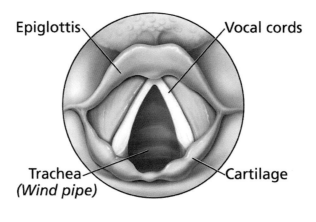

National Cancer Institute

W

Watt Seconds-A measurement of energy delivered during defibrillation. With cardiac arrest in adults we start with 200 watt seconds on the first shock, 300 watt seconds for the second and 360 for the third and subsequent shocks. The patient "jumps" with these shocks as the muscles contract. The only rhythm we shock is ventricular fibrillation. We do not shock asystole which is flat line. We may shorten the terminology by saying, "Let's shock at 200 watts."

X

X-ray-A radiologic assessment of bone and can be diagnostic for fractures.